SPANISH FASCISM IN THE FRANCO ERA

SPANISH FASCISM IN THE FRANCO ERA

Falange Española de las Jons, 1936–76

Sheelagh M. Ellwood

Visiting Fellow, Centre for Contemporary Spanish Studies
Queen Mary College, London

St. Martin's Press   New York

First published in the United States of America in 1987

Printed in Hong Kong

ISBN 0-312-00540-7

Library of Congress Cataloging in Publication Data
Ellwood, Sheelagh M., 1949–
Spanish fascism in the Franco era.
Bibliography: p.
Includes index.
1. Falange Española de las Juntas Ofensivas
Nacional—Sindicalistas—History. 2. Fascism—
Spain—History—20th century. 3. Francoism—.
4. Spain—Politics and government—1931–1939.
5. Spain—Politics and government—1939–1975.
I. Title.
JN8395. F26E45   1987   320.5'33'0946   86–29665
ISBN 0-312-00540-7

For Janet P. Ellwood, My Mother, *in memoriam*

Contents

Introduction:
The Historiographical
Recovery of Francoism

Until recently, analysts of 20th-century Spain, both inside and outside the Iberain Peninsula, seem to have shown a marked preference for studying in depth the left of the political spectrum. The right, by contrast, has usually received only cursory or generalised attention.

There are, of course, some very valid reasons for this imbalance. In the first place, while the regime headed by General Franco was still in force, access to vital primary sources was frequently denied to would-be researchers. All too often, the barriers surrounding crucial institutional archives could only be surmounted by resorting to the arbitrary but inevitable use of a well-placed *enchufe* (contact). Anyone outside the regime was unlikely to have, or to be able to make, the relevant *enchufes*. Those inside the system, precisely because they were part of it, had no desire to use their privileged position to reveal its inner workings. They were the guardians of its, and their own, secrets.

In the second place, even if it were easy, it is not pleasant to delve into the entrails of a dictatorship whose creation and maintenance were based, in large measure, on repression and injustice. Anyone with a minimal democratic sensitivity is naturally repelled.

Yet, while both these factors help to explain why the Francoist right has received relatively little critical attention from historians of contemporary Spain, neither justifies the lack. Important though it undoubtedly is to know and understand the nature and development of the remnants and heirs of the socio-political forces which were decimated by the Spanish Civil War (1936–39), it is equally necessary to analyse the composition, behaviour and interrelations of the so-called victors. Otherwise, it is impossible even to begin to understand the persistently manichean, profoundly anarchic, always contradictory society that Spain was throughout the regime which arose in and from those three years of conflict. In undertaking a study of one of the components of the Franco regime – *Falange Española* (Spanish Phalanx) – I have tried to go some way towards redressing the balance; to contribute to what Professor Gabriel Jackson has called the historiographical recovery of Francoism.[1]

My Spanish connection dates from 1970 when, as a student of the Latin American area in the Sociology Department of the University of Essex, I spent five months in Madrid to improve my grasp of the Spanish language. It was not until 1973, however, that the general interest in Spanish history which had been awakened in me by repeated visits to the country began to clarify as a particular interest in the creation and nature of the Franco regime, then still in power. The seed of curiosity with regard to the *Falange* was finally implanted shortly before I graduated from Essex and for that I should like to thank D. Joaquin Romero Maura (then Director of the Iberian Centre at St. Anthony's College, Oxford), whose suggestion that I consider undertaking a study of *Falange Española* undoubtedly and without exaggeration changed my life. The final result of that suggestion – the present volume – reflects not only forty years of the history of Spain but also thirteen of my own.

In those thirteen years, eleven of which have been spent as a resident of Madrid, my view of the country, its people and their history has changed many times; my knowledge and, I hope, my understanding, of them have broadened and deepened. No merit is due to me for that. The many Spaniards from all walks of life with whom I have come into contact over the years have, through their conversation and their attitude towards my work, afforded me insights into the complexities of their country which, as an outsider, would otherwise have escaped me. Some have become close friends; others were ships that pass in the night. All, including the few who expressed hostility to the foreigner who wanted to poke around in Spanish affairs, have contributed in no small measure to my desire and determination to live and work here.

It might be expected that the Falangists themselves would be among the group who were unwilling to allow me to enquire into their past. It is true that I made little headway in my attempts to gain access to the archives of such Falangist institutions as the Party Secretariat, the National Militias or the Syndical Organisation. Of the contacts made requesting personal interviews, however, almost all received a positive response. A good deal of patience and more or less persuasion were required, certainly, but I was eventually able to carry out some thirty interviews, most of which were revealing and enriching. I should like to express here my thanks to all those Falangists who were kind enough to devote some of their time to answering my questions.

My deepest debt in gratitude is undoubtedly owed to Professor Paul Preston, Director of the Centre for Contemporary Spanish Studies at Queen Mary College, London, and supervisor of the doctoral thesis on which the present volume is based. Since 1974, when I first discussed with him the subject of the *Falange* his support, help and friendship have been an unfailing vote of confidence which I greatly appreciate. As an expatriate, I should also like to thank him and his wife, Gabrielle, for their kindness in offering me their house as a home from home when I am in London.

There are, of course, a number of people who do not seem to 'fit' in any of the above paragraphs and who, nevertheless, have, provided over the years those apparently minor kinds of support without which one's life and work would probably be more difficult and certainly more arid. My father has bailed me out on many occasions, with everything from HM Inspector of Taxes to degree certificates urgently required in Spain. My brother, Dr David Ellwood, has given me many insights into the comparisons which may and may not be drawn between contemporary Italy and Spain. Gonzalo Pontón has shown a friendly concern for my welfare which goes well beyond the bounds of his publisher's professional obligation. On his periodic visits to Madrid, Paul Heywood's company and conversation have been a pleasant interruption to the daily round. From Sandra Lotti, Laura Lisci, María Izquierdo and Sheena Ellwood, I have received the solidarity of other, single, working women and the warmth of their good-humoured friendship. The Alfaya family have, likewise, been more than generous with their friendship and hospitality. And Golo has alternately driven me mad and kept me sane.

It goes without saying that, whilst I am grateful to all these people for their help, I do not in any way hold them responsible for the shortcomings of this book.

Madrid

Notes

1 On the occasion of the presentation of his book, *La República española y la Guerra Civil, 1931–1939* (Barcelona: Editorial Critica, 1976).

Part I
Falange Created

1 The Antecedents, 1931–36

Until the political watershed marked by the military rising of 18 July 1936, the history of the Spanish fascist party, *Falange Española*, founded in 1933, is that of a party incapable of achieving, on its own merits alone, a position of influence in the country's power structures. Indeed, in the course of those three years, the party's very existence was placed in jeopardy on several occasions on account of its inability to attract a following. It was not seen by contemporary observers as a political innovation, nor as a serious competitor in the political field. Rather, it was considered as one more in a series of thereto unsuccessful attempts to launch a movement which was violently opposed to Marxism, liberalism and parliamentary democracy based on universal suffrage, and in favour of a socio-political and economic system organised on nationalist, authoritarian and corporativist lines.[1] The Falangist attempt ultimately turned out to be the longest lasting. Up to 1936, however, it seemed that *Falange Española* was destined to suffer the same failure as its predecessors. Its nature and development were very similar to theirs, consisting as it did of a succession of alliances and splits between small, economically insecure groups of parallel, when not identical, socio-political origins, values, ideology and practice.

The ideological currents inspiring *Falange Española* dated from 19th-century Spain and combined with those produced in 20th-century Europe.[2] Spain, however, had remained largely isolated from the social, political and economic upheaval which had shaken the rest of Europe in the first two decades of the 20th century and which had provided the breeding ground of fascism. Falangism, although akin to and influenced by Italian fascism and German national-socialism, was a peculiarly Spanish phenomenon, produced by the particular configuration of historical and political circumstances of contemporary Spain. Of these, the one which acted most directly as a personal and political catalyst for the creation of *Falange Española* was the fall, in January 1930 and after seven years in power, of the Dictator, General Miguel Primo de Rivera y Orbaneja.

On 2 May 1930, José Antonio Primo de Rivera, eldest son of the deposed Dictator, was appointed Vice-Secretary of the *Unión Monárquica Nacional* (National Monarchical Union), founded in April of that year. He spent the Spring canvassing throughout Spain for the organisation, led by well-known conservatives and partisans of General Primo de Rivera such as Ramiro de Maeztu, José Calvo Sotelo and Count Guadalhorce. The foundational manifesto gives an indication of the kind of ideas that Primo de Rivera espoused in 1930:

> What we advocate is not a new dictaroship, but the legal modifica- tions which, without reducing the functions of the *Cortes* and the King, will promote the strengthening of the executive power.[3]

Similarly, Primo de Rivera's own definition of the aims of the *Unión Monárquica* reveals what were his political values in 1930 and gives a foretaste of what was later to be the credo of *Falange*:

1. Indestructible national unity.
2. Supremacy of the interests of Spain over and above all party political interests.
3. Exaltation of national sentiment as a basic principle of our politics.
4. Reconquest of the economic independence of Spain.
5. Establishment of a civil discipline which is conscious, severe and of a high patriotic spirit.
6. Existence of an Army and a Navy capable of maintaining at all times the prestige of Spain.[4]

In the Autumn of 1930, the *Unión Monárquica* provided Primo de Rivera with his first important public political appearance, at a meeting in Bilbao on 6 October 1930. Although, in a reference to Primo de Rivera's speech at the meeting, a Falangist author assures his readers that 'it is unlikely that (Primo de Rivera's) discourse had a reactionary intention', he also admits that 'it had – because of the personal circumstances of the orator and the political circumstances of the moment – a rightest nuance'.[5]

It certainly had the latter and it is difficult to accept Ximénez de Sandoval's opinion that it did not also have the former. The defence made by Primo de Rivera in Bilbao of religion, discipline, tradition, nation, the family and the Armed Forces was common to all contemporary Right wing parties. Primo inveighed against the Repub- lican form of State:

> There are only two courses open in these transcendental moments: revolution or counter-revolution. Either our traditional order or the

triumph of Moscow . . . and Moscow will triumph if the revolution truimphs. It will not be a revolution against the Monarchy, but complete subversion of the social order. The conservative Republic is but a step (in that direction).[6]

He warned, too, against the enemy within:

The enemy is in the Universities. In our Universities, not controlled, but monopolised, by the State and in which, nevertheless, the most active and dangerous adversaries of all that is fundamental for the State have their nest.

Your sons will indeed find wise and venerable teachers, but they will also pass through the hands of a series of madmen ("*extravagantes*") who will teach them to lose respect for you, for religion, for the Fatherland, for the Army, for national honour. . . . And when the State returns your son to you, if God has not protected him well, it will return him to you unbelieving, irreverent, de-classed, cowardly, the enemy of all that you respect most and who knows if not also – for even of that he will have heard with a willing ear – given over to the most shameful vices.[7]

The socio-political atmosphere, however, was not favourable for attempts to launch parties which defended fallen or falling figures and the *Unión Monárquica*, like other similar groups, was unable to continue for lack of suport.[8] Primo de Rivera remained on the sidelines of active politics for almost a year after the failure of the National Monarchical Union. Once the Republic had been declared in 1931, however, he again pledged his support for the Right when he stood as a candidate in the Madrid by-election to the *Cortes* in October of that year. A contemporary journalist, Juan Aparicio, recalls that Primo de Rivera stood 'with a group of his friends, not politicians, former partisans of his father. . .'.[9] Primo stood as an independent candidate, but the 'group of friends' referred to by Aparicio were former members of the rightist organisation formed in support of General Primo de Rivera in 1924, the *Unión Patriótica* (Patriotic Union) and Primo's 1931 campaign was based explicitly on the defence of his father's memory. It was not successful, however, and the seat was won by the liberal art historian, critic and padagogue, Manuel Bartolomé de Cossío.

1931 had already seen the birth of two groups which were later to be intimately connected with José Antonio Primo de Rivera.

During the interim dictatorship of General Dámaso Berenguer (January 1930–February 1931), a handful of young intellectuals who, in the words of one of them, had 'recently reached national responsibility',[10] established a small discussion group in the centre of Madrid. Amongst them were journalists, university teachers, diplomats, writers and civil servants. The latter included Ramiro Ledesma Ramos, a severe-looking young man who earned his living as a post-office clerk, but whose real vocation was philosophy and politics, for both of which he possessed considerable intellectual and practical capacities.[11]

In February 1931, the group issued a 'Political Manifesto: the Conquest of the State', described in 1935 by Ledesma Ramos as the first attempt to raise 'a national and social flag'.[12] The manifesto was followed by a newspaper, also entitled *La Conquista del Estado* (*The Conquest of the State*). In spite of the rabidly revolutionary tone of the paper and the professed left-wing sympathies of its contributors,[13] Ledesma and his companions evidently had no qualms about seeking economic support amongst the representatives of the most conservative of the capitalist classes. Until it ceased publication, in October 1931, *La Conquista del Estado* was partly financed by Alphonsine monarchists and by certain Bilbao business men. One of the former, Pedro Sainz Rodríguez, recounts in his memoirs how the group of which he was a member, *Acción Española*, gave Ledesma Ramos 'assistance for his organisation and a motor cycle he needed for his propaganda trips'.[14] In return for this generosity, Ledesma 'undertook not to offer hostility to the Monarchy nor to oppose a possible restoration'.[15]

José Antonio Primo de Rivera had no direct contact with *La Conquista del Estado*, but was certainly informed of its ideas and development. One of the future founders of *Falange Española* was, however, a member of the *Conquista* group: Julio Ruiz de Alda, a popular hero of the time on account of his having participated in the first transatlantic crossing by air, from Spain to Argentina, in July 1926. By 1931, Ruiz de Alda had 'conceived the idea of forming a National Movement of a totalitarian and deeply popular nature' and, 'together with men who were later to join the ranks of Falange', had begun to sound out the representatives of the different right wing political groups. Among these were Ledesma and the *Conquista del Estado* people, whom Ruiz de Alda visited in mid-May 1931, 'demonstrating and even signing his support for the political line of the paper'.[16]

Ledesma and his followers needed more than verbal expressions of support to ensure their political survival, however and, in October 1931, announced that *La Conquista* would join forces with a similar organisation operating in North Castile, the *Juntas Castellanas de Actuación Hispánica*, JCAH (Castillian Committees for Hispanic Action). The new organisation would be known as the *Juntas de Ofensiva Nacional Sindicalista*, JONS (Committees for National Syndicalist Offensive).

The leader of the *Juntas Castellanas* Onésimo Redondo, was similar in social, intellectual and professional background to Ledesma.[17] According to *Conquista* secretary, Juan Aparicio, the fusion of the two groups represented 'a very generous intellectual effort. We wanted to join together the two ends of the Spanish rainbow. . . . We wanted to unite the anarchists with the Carlists'.[18] Whilst Ledesma shared with the anarchists a belief in the use of 'direct action' to achieve political aims and Redondo's strong Catholic strain could also be found in Carlism, it cannot be said that either the *Conquista* group or the *Juntas Castellanas* were representative of these two ideologies. They represented other political currents, perhaps equally extreme, but nontheless distinct: fascism and Catholic nationalism. The real reason for the amalgamation was more mundane. Both groups were small and in an economically precarious state. Given that they coincided on the majority of ideological points, the way to maximise their possibilities of survival as the organised and public expression of that ideology was to join forces.[19]

The hopes of growth with which the new group was created in the Autumn of 1931 were not fulfilled, however, and 1932 was a year of virtual inactivity for the JONS. In an atmosphere of increasing mutual antagonism between moderate Republican governments and their opponents to Right and Left, Ledesma (effectively the leader of the JONS, despite the formal existence of a three-man control committee) tended further towards an overtly fascist position, in an attempt to capitalise on the growing discontent among the conservative middle classes.[20] As yet, however, those same classes were repelled rather than attracted by the revolutionary content of Ledesma's ideas.[21]

With a membership consisting mainly of middle class students and service employees in the towns and labourers and small farmers in the country, the organisation was of national scope, but its presence was, in fact, mainly concentrated in Galicia, Valencia, Valladolid and Madrid. In 1932, the violent, anti-democratic, anti-Marxist nationalism advocated by what, to most Spaniards, must have seemed a tiny group of fanatics, did not appeal to the conservative classes who were later to look to armed intervention for solutions to what they termed 'the nation's problems'. Certainly, there was misgiving and indignation, carefully and relentlessly manipulated by Right wing newspapers like the Catholic *el Debate* or the Carlist *el Siglo Futuro*, whose readers were appalled at the legislative steps taken to reform the Army and to reduce the power of the Catholic Church and the property-owning classes. Certainly, too, the machinations of the Monarchists – both Alphonsines and Carlists – had not ceased since the declaration of the Second Republic on 14 April 1931.[22] As yet, however, as the abortion of the coup attempted in August 1932 by General Sanjurjo showed, violent solutions to the 'problem' of a Republic governed by liberal and Left wing politicians were not viable.[23]

The year 1933, however, was one of important changes. In Europe, the year opened with Adolf Hitler's assumption of the German Chancellorship on 30 January. In Spanish political spheres, 1933 saw the collapse of the Socialist-Left Republican alliance and a closing of the ranks on the right. In March, a number of conservative groups joined together to form the *Confederación Española de Derechas Autónomas*, CEDA (Spanish Confederation of Autonomous Right-wing Groups). The CEDA's reluctance explicitly to state its loyalty to the Republic and the approval of anti-Marxism in Europe expressed by its leader, José María Gil Robles, were a clear indication that, beneath the so-called 'moderate' Right's apparent desire to participate in the Republic, lay anti-democratic sentiments more in line with contemporary European fascims.[24]

The extra-Parliamentary Right in spain also prepared to take maximum advantage of the changing political atmosphere.[25] From a meeting between Primo de Rivera and Ledesma Ramos in early 1933 came the decision to launch a newspaper entitled *El Fascio*. The Editor was to be Manuel Delgado Barreto, Editor of the conservative daily *La Nación* and founder of a satirical weekly (*Gracia y Justicia*) financed by a Catholic publishing concern, the 'Editorial Católica'.[26] The first, and only, issue of *El Fascio* was published on 16 March 1933 and was immediately confiscated by the Police. The group involved in the stillborn project consequently split up, although this did not mean the end of attempts to launch fascism in Spain. The intitiative in these efforts was now taken by Primo de Rivera.

With the help of half a dozen supporters, he organised a nationalist group with socialist overtones, the *Movimento Español Sindicalista*, MES (Spanish Syndicalist Movement), which had a tiny following in

Madrid and some of the provinces.[27] This attempt to mobilise nationalist, anti-Marxist feeling was no more successful than that to put *El Fascio* into circulation. In the case of the MES, however, the stumbling-block was not governmental prohibition, but simply lack of interest on the part of putative recruits. It may seem paradoxical that, in a national and international political context increasingly favourable to the Right, the MES could not get off the ground. The problem, however, was precisely that there were already many Right-wing parties, all contending for the same political clientele. An embryonic and extremist group like the MES could not compete with the nation-wide organisation, established sources of finance and apparently 'safely' conservative politics of the CEDA, the Carlist *Comunión Tradicionalista* or the Alphonsine *Renovación Española*. Moreover, whilst the socialistic nuance of the group's title was sufficient to frighten off possible middle class interest, it was not enought to attract mass support away from socialist, communist and anarchist organisations.

Undaunted by the poor response to the MES, in the Autumn of 1933, Primo de Rivera made yet another attempt to find a niche in national poliotics. On 29 October, he chaired a public 'event of national affirmation' (*un acto de afirmación nacional*), held in a Madrid theatre. This was followed, on 2 November, by a private, organisational meeting at which the movement launched on 29 October, conceived as an 'efficient and authoritarian instrument at the service of that . . . irrevocable unity called the Fatherland',[28] was formally christened with the name *Falange Española*.[29]

The *Falange's* credo, expressed in doctrinal documents like the 'Nine Programmatic Points', published in late November 1933, or the party newspaper, *FE*, which appeared in December, was a curious mixture of archaism, classical Spanish conservatism and populist socialism. In addition to a nostalgic view of Spain's history, which identified the age of Spain's greatness as the 15th century, the heyday of Castillian centralism, the Falangist ideology contained three further essential elements: anti-separatism, imperialism and Catholicism. An authoritarian concept of discipline and hierarchy was translated into belief in a functional and élitist notion of social organisation; whilst an unstinted admiration for military values was the basis for reliance on the Armed Forces as the supreme political arbitrators. Finally, there were vague promises to 'redeem' the working and peasant classes and an explicit commitment to the use of violence, if necessary, to achieve the party's aims.

Ramón Serrano Suñer, a close friend of Primo de Rivera and, in 1933, a member of the *Unión de Derechas* (Right-wing Union), writes that Primo created *Falange* 'under pressure from those who wished to create in Spain a transcription of the Italian Fascist Movement'.[30] This was, indeed, the turn that the organisation was soon openly to take. At the moment of its conception, however, in the light of the *El Fascio* failure and perhaps, too, looking at the difficulties being experienced by the JONS, the promotors of *Falange Española* were careful to avoid giving the impression that what was being launched was 'a transcription of the Italian Fascist movement'.[31]

In the short time available between the creation of the *Falange* and the general elections held on 19 November 1933, the party was not in a position to organise its own campaign. Nevertheless, the decision to launch the party precisely at that moment took full advantage of the electoral atmosphere, in which political interest was greater than at other times. The inclusion of Primo de Rivera as an 'independent' in the *Unión de Derechas* list for Cadiz gave him a timely and useful platform for the kind of non-policy which *Falange* claimed to embody.[32] Primo openly admitted that he did not believe in and even despised the parliamentary system for which he stood as a candidate.[33] Nevertheless, he did not reject the seat which 'the lottery of 19 November 1933' gave him, for it afforded him two important advantages.[34] In the first place, *Cortes* membership gave him 'parliamentary immunity' and, in the second, 'the use of the *Cortes* for ideological propaganda, with its natural echo in the Press'.[35]

In the final months of 1933, the founders of *Falange Española* devoted themselves to promoting their party. In spite of the personal and social attraction of Primo de Rivera, and in spite of his having been elected to the *Cortes*, neither supporters nor finance were forthcoming in sufficiently large quantities. The electoral victory of the 'moderate' Right had temporarily quelled the anxieties of the conservative upper and middle classes and the attraction of radical ideologies consequently diminished. By the end of the year, *Falange's* situation was critical. The total lack of funds reduced propaganda and proselytism virtually to nothing and made even the maintenance of the party's headquarters problematic.

Primo de Rivera's erstwhile colleague in the *El Fascio* venture, Ramiro Ledesma, and the JONS, were in similarly straitened circumstances by the end of 1933. The unconcealed violence of the JONS' theory and practice was counterproductive with respect to recruiting members and financial support, for, as we have noted earlier, it repelled the monied classes whilst, at the same time, it provoked governmental repression.[36] Moreover, the creation of the *Falange*, though scarcely an overwhelming success, had nevertheless curtailed the JONS' possibilities of growth and recruitment had begun to fall off. The nationalist, anti-Marxist appeal of the two organisations was fundamentally similar, but *Falange* was less crude in its style and *modus operandi*, less overtly in favour of contemporary European fascist movements and led by a man personally and socially more attractive than the leaders of the JONS.

Falange was far from firmly established, however, and the JONS had things to offer which Primo de Rivera's party needed: a minimal degree of implantation outside Madrid and, especially, in the rural areas; organisational experience; more clearly defined ideas on political praxis; and an already familiar set of symbols, lexicon, propagandistic channels and so on. In the Spring and Summer of 1933, Ledesma and Primo had discussed but failed to agree upon possible collaboration between their respective groups. By the end of the year, however, it was in the interests of both to reconsider joining forces and after 'discussions lasting several weeks', it was decided, on 13 February 1934, to fuse the two organisations as *Falange Española de las JONS*. The leadership was to be shared by an 'Executive Committee' composed of Primo de Rivera, Ledesma Ramos and Ruiz de Alda.[37]

Throughout the Spring and Summer of 1934, FE de las JONS concentrated on strengthening its position, alternating its tactics between public meetings, the distribution of propaganda and armed clashes with members of the Socialist party.[38] The Falangist Press frequently expressed its scorn for the constituted Government as amateurish and ineffectual. However, *Falange* was, first and foremost, the bastion of anti-Marxism and when it came to a choice between inefficient conservatism and Left-wing revolution, *Falange* naturally defended the former. Although Primo and Ledesma were agreed on the necessity to crush the forces of the Left, tension between them made its first appearance in early 1934, on the question of tactics. Ledesma criticised Primo's policy of holding meetings in small, rural villages, maintaining that the party should enter into 'revolutionary rivalry with the subversive organisations' where these were strongest – the capital and the largest cities.[39] For Ledesma believed that it was in these places that the Socialists were preparing a *coup* and that the main priority of the party must therefore be the preparation of the counter-offensive.

Primo de Rivera, however, maintained that FE de las JONS must recruit support in the rural areas, where the essence of the pure, 'true' Spain was to be found. His poetic manner of expressing this populist tendency was, in fact, based on two purely practical considerations. In the first place, the competition from other political organisations was weaker in the rural areas than in the urban centres. In the second, Spain was then an essentially agrarian society and economy and it was logical that Primo should aim his reactionary appeal at the most conservative elements of that society, since it was there that such an appeal was most likely to arouse sympathy. In the villages of Castile, *Falange Española de las JONS* was not looking so much for the spiritual heritage of the 'Spain of the Catholic Monarchs' as for the physical and moral support of the small farmers and the financial backing of the landowners.

In the increasingly rarified political atmosphere of 1934, the anti-Republican Right felt compelled to try to close ranks to meet an open clash between Left and Right which they believed and hoped was imminent.[40] Primo de Rivera had never broken off the relations he had maintained with the Alphonsine Monarchists prior to the foundation of *Falange* and had even allowed them a certain degree of influence in the structuring of his party.[41] Now, in the Summer of 1934, an agreement was signed between the leader of the Monarchist group *Renovación Española*, Antonio Goicoechea, and Primo de Rivera as 'President of the leadership of *Falange Española de las JONS*'. The pact stated that the two groups coincided in their basic social and political viewpoints and that both were against 'Marxist sectarianism'.[42] The Falangist assault commandos were to be expanded to form militias which would be stimulated to the maximum, so that they might 'be able to take the place – with respect to Marxist power and violence – of the functions of the State'.[43]

In addition to signing his consent to *Falange's* acting as Goicoechea's shock troops, Primo de Rivera also agreed that his party's propaganda would not attack *Renovación*, and that *Falange* would not stand in the way of the realisation of the Monarchist ideology.[44] In return, and in order to make effective the desire for the 'maximum growth of the combative militias', Goicoechea undertook to assist *Falange* economically as far as the funds he administered permitted.[45]

As in the case of the agreement signed with the JONS in February 1934, the pact signed with the Alphonsine Monarchists in August demonstrated Primo de Rivera's willingness to salvage the physical and political existence of his party at the expense of its independence and ideological purity. However, whereas the amalgamation with the

JONS had represented joining forces with a group whose ideological characteristics were essentially similar to those of *Falange*, even if its social and political origins were not, the agreement with *Renovación Española* represented subjugation to a movement commited to aims quite different to those of FE de las JONS. Goicoechea and Primo de Rivera could easily coincide as far as anti-Marxism, anti-republicanism, patriotism and religion were concerned. Even the problem of economic organisation was capable of solutions acceptable to both parties, since the 'anti-Marxist workers' trade union organisation' proposed by *Renovación* was compatible with the national syndicalism of the *Falange*. The restoration of the Monarchy, however, was clearly not compatible with the national syndicalist State as this was conceived of by Ledesma Ramos. Yet Primo de Rivera had committed FE de las JONS to supporting precisely that objective, in return for a monthly subsidy. He had, in effect, sold out to the patron offering greatest possibilities of survival.

By the Autumn of 1934, an internal split was imminent in FE de las JONS, over the question of the form of the party. Ledesma was intent on creating a mass organisation, capable of channelling the anti-bourgeois and patriotic energies of 'people of all kinds'.[46] Primo de Rivera, by contrast, aimed at making the movement selective, based on strict principles of hierarchy and discipline, in which a hard core of activists would act as the mailed fist of a small, 'poetic' élite. Against a background of increasing social and political tension throughout the country, FE de las JONS held a meeting of its National Council in the first week of October 1934, to discuss the question of the structure and leadership of the party, for some of the party's leading figures were of the opinion that the three-man control committee had, by then, outlived its usefulness.[47] What was to be decided at the Council meeting was whether authority and responsibility at national level should be assumed by one man or by a collegiate body. When this was put to the vote, sixteen votes were cast in favour of collegiate leadership and seventeen in favour of a single leader. Thereupon, the delegates acclaimed Primo de Rivera as National Chief.[48] His personal, political and tactical victory over Ledesma was now almost complete.

Primo de Rivera was assisted in the execution of his internal *coup* by the sense of urgency generated by the contemporary political situation in Spain. The *Falange* Council meeting coincided with the formation of a government headed by the leader of the Radical Party, Alejandro Lerroux and which included three members of the CEDA and two of the conservative *Bloque Agraria* (Agrarian Bloc). The more radical sectors of the Left had warned on more than one occasion that they would not tolerate the inclusion of the CEDA in any government. Consequently, in the first half of October, Madrid, Cataluña and, especially, the mining area of Asturias were the scene of the strikes, demonstrations and violent clashes subsequently known as the 'October revolution'.[49] The rising was immediately and brutally repressed by Police and Army detachments. In some places, they were assisted by *Falange* militants, who thus revealed the truly reactionary nature of their loyalties.[50] In spite of the *Falange's* professed aversion to the Right-wing Government and, in particular, to the CEDA, orders were immediately issued which showed the party's willingness to assume the role of instrument of that Government, especially in its repressive aspects:

> When the crisis arose . . . the Organisations were given orders to be on the alert and to support the Armed Forces in the repression of the movement . . . *Falange* ordered its Front Line to be prepared first thing on the following day (i.e. 5 October) in case it were necessary to take up arms.[51]

Primo de Rivera went in person to the Ministry of the Interior, to 'offer the *Falange* to the Government as an instrument of struggle and combat against reds and separatists'.[52] On 7 October, the *Falange* organised an anti-Marxist, anti-separatist demonstration which marched, with Primo de Rivera at its head, to the Ministry of the Interior in the centre of Madrid. There, the Falangist chief delivered a speech in which he urged the Government to take action against separatism (he was referring to the rising in Cataluña) and pledged the support of his followers in the enterprise.[53]

The 'October revolution' was not the first occasion on which Primo de Rivera had offered the services of the *Falange* for purposes of repression. In September 1934, he wrote to the GOC of the Balearic Isles, Major General Francisco Franco Bahamonde, offering him the support of *Falange* activists to put a stop to what he considered was governmental irresponsibility with respect to 'rampant social indiscipline' and Communist subversion, 'planned according to the Trotskyist school'.[54] Although he received no reply from Franco, Primo made a further attempt to rouse the sympathies of the Army in November 1934. This time, he directed an open letter to an unnamed military man ('Everyman' of the Armed Forces) in which he invited

the unidentified soldier to 'accompany (him) . . . in a silent medita-
tion' on the 'pressing anguish of Spain'.[55] Like the one written in
September, the tone of this letter was alarmist and tendentious,
prediciting disaster at the hands of a Government considered incapable of containing the Marxist 'threat' and suggesting that the 'true'
duty of the Army officers was to assist, or at least not impede, 'the
national movement . . . in its assault on power'.[56]

Primo de Rivera's approaches to the Army, like the pact with
Renovación Española in August of that same year, were motivated by
the *Falange's* continued failure to attract more than a minority
following. The attempt to bolster the party externally was accompanied by measures to consolidate it internally, such as the establishment of its organisational and executive structures and the elaboration
of a document which synthesised the party's aims and beliefs in '27
Programmatic Points'.[57] Whilst these initiatives did little to increase
the party's appeal to politically conscious Spaniards, they did provoke
the breaking of the internal crisis which had been brewing for several
months.

By the end of 1934, Ledesma Ramos considered that the *Falange*
had no future as it stood and that a change of tactics was necessary to
save his national-syndicalist ideas from extinction. Disagreeing with
the élitist notions imposed by Primo de Rivera, in January 1935,
Ledesma secretly proposed to leave FE de las JONS to form a separate
party with a group of former JONSists. His intentions, however, were
discovered and his comrades persuaded to abandon the idea.[58]
Nevertheless, Ledesma sent a Press release to *la Nación*, announcing his
separation from FE de las JONS. Instead of publishing the note, the
Editor of the paper (Manuel Delgado Barreto, erstwhile member of
the *El Fascio* staff) informed Primo de Rivera of Ledesma's move.
Primo thereupon forestalled the publication of Ledesma's note with
one of his own announcing the expulsion of Ledesma Ramos from the
party. Only a handful of JONSists followed Ledesma out of *Falange*,
convinced as everyone appears to have been that Primo's personal
charisma was a more valuable political asset than Ledesma's ideological radicalism.

With Primo de Rivera's single-handed control of *Falange* unequivocally established, the party resumed its constant search for external
support. Falangists have always denied that their party had any
connection with German or Italian totalitarian movements, quoting
invariably the refusal of Primo de Rivera to attend an international
Fascist gathering held at Montreux in 1934. Their insistence on this

point has been supported by those historians who have underestimated the extent of the *Falange's* links with Hitler and Mussolini.[59] More recent research, however, shows clearly that during the twelve months preceding the outbreak of the civil war in July 1936, the National Chief of F. E. de las JONS maintained regular contact with high-ranking members of both the fascist and the national-socialist parties.[60]

Of the two, the Italians undoubtedly showed most interest in cultivating relations with their Spanish comrades. Between June 1935 and May/June 1936, the Italian Embassy in Paris was the channel for sending a substantial monthly stipend to José Antonio Primo de Rivera.[61] It is not known why the money was sent via Paris and not, for example, through the Italian Embassy in Madrid, but it is likely that Primo de Rivera collected the payments in person. His personal means and situation made periodic visits to France entirely feasible and Italian sources suggest that such visits were indeed made. On 16 October 1935, the Italian Press Attaché in Paris informed the Press and Propaganda Office in Rome: 'Primo de Rivera has not appeared yet'. A month later, he repeated:

> Primo de Rivera's two remittances are still pending: one for the letter he replied to and one for the letter . . . of 1 October 1935, asking why the recipient has not come. I have written to him, as agreed, asking him to come and see me, so that we can clear up this account.[62]

In early 1935, Italian (and German) machinery was offered for the launching of a Falangist newspaper in Madrid. 'The Italian offer', writes García Venero, 'was the equivalent of a concession without monetary obligations and would not engender any political undertakings'.[63] García Venero does not tell us whether or not the offer was accepted, but the first issue of *Arriba* appeared on 21 March 1935. In its pages, support was frequently expressed for the Italian cause, in particular for Mussolini's aspirations in Abyssinia. A graphic report on the 'social state of Abyssinia' in the edition of 14 November 1935, for example, was unequivocally in favour of Italian imperialist activities in that country.[64]

In May 1935, Primo de Rivera made a trip to Italy, during which he visited 'the Eternal City, some fascist organisations and the "Committee for the Universality of Rome"'.[65] A month later, the Italian subsidy to *Falange* began. Soon afterwards, FE de las JONS opened a branch in Italy. In August 1935, Primo de Rivera visited Italy again and authorised the creation of *Falange* in Milan.[66]

Clearly, then, there were multiple contacts between Mussolini's Fascists and Primo de Rivera's Falangists at least from May 1935 onwards. Falangist leader Manuel Hedilla's affirmation that the Italians were trying to 'convert the *Falange* into a political bridgehead' was probably true,[67] but it is no less true that, far from being an unconscious party to the operation, as Hedilla implies, *Falange* had once more mortgaged its independence as a means to ensuring its survival.[68] The relevant documents from the German Foreign Ministry show that Falangist denials of all relations between *Falange* and Nazi Germany are equally unfounded.

In January 1934, the German Ambassador in Spain, Welczeck, suggested to his superiors in Germany that Primo de Rivera and others be invited to Berlin at the end of the month, to attend the commemoration of Hitler's rise to power a year earlier. For Primo, wrote the Ambassador, was 'extraordinarily interested in the new Germany and, especially, in the organisation of the S.A. and the S.S.'.[69] The visit did not, in fact, take place, since no celebrations were organised, but Primo de Rivera maintained contact with Welczeck and a further invitation was proposed by the latter for the 1 May parade in Berlin. Since neither the German Foreign Ministry nor that for Propaganda wished to assume responsibility for the invitation, this was issued through the Nazi party.[70]

Whilst these negotiationm were in progress, the German authorities were approached by a supposed emissary of Primo de Rivera, Elsa Paege, with a view to obtaining financial support for FE de las JONS.[71] Welczeck was apparently unaware of her activities and found it difficult to believe that Primo had authorised her to act on his behalf. The *Wilhelmstrasse* officials were equally wary of her person and her proposals and toyed with the idea of again postponing, or even of cancelling, Primo de Rivera's visit. Welczeck considered, however, that this could not be done without giving offence and Primo duly travelled to Germany at the end of April 1934.

In Berlin, Primo de Rivera had an interview with Hitler. The question of financial support, however, does not seem to have arisen and the visit was used, rather, to examine the organisational methods of the Nazi party. At any event, it appears that, in contrast to their Italian comrades, the German authorities were not convinced that there were benefits to be derived from financing the *Falange*. In a note written in November 1934, the official in charge of the Spanish and Portuguese section at the *Wilhelmstrasse* commented,

> With the sum requested (by Elsa Paege), it cannot be expected to exercise any important influence on the internal Spanish political revolution. If such development leads to a Right-wing Government, relations between Spain and Germany will come of their own accord and need not be preceded by such "gratuities" . . . the Ministry of Propaganda is of the same negative opinion.[72]

After the 1934 'October revolution' and, particularly, after a large Falangist gathering on 19 May 1935, at which Primo de Rivera delivered a speech on 'the Spanish revolution',[73] foreign interest in FE de las JONS increased somewhat, but not to the extent of making an anti-Republican rising organised by the *Falange* a viable proposition. In June 1935, the same month that the *Falange's* Italian subsidy began, the party's *Junta Política* held a meeting at which the possibility of effecting a *coup* was discussed. Primo de Rivera reported that there existed the possibility of obtaining arms, technical assistance and the leadership of an Army General. The plan came to nothing, however, in view of the lack of support from Falangists and military men and because Army Chief of Staff, General Francisco Franco, was not in favour of the idea.[74] When the *Cortes* were dissolved on 7 January 1936 and general elections called for 16 February, *Falange* was still the minority group it had been at its foundation two years earlier.

Throughout 1935, the parties of both Left and Right had been negotiating the formation of internal alliances. With the political arena increasingly dominated by this question, the isolation of *Falange Española* reduced even further its already slim chances of electoral success. The Falangists were fully aware of their weakness and had attempted to remedy it even before President Alcalá Zamora dissolved the *Cortes* in January 1936. At a meeting of the party's National Council held in November 1935, *Falange* leaders discussed and approved the 'circumstantial necessity of forming a National Front' with the parties of the Right.[75] Their call for unity aroused little response. This was scarcely surprising, since one of the Right's leading figures, José Calvo Sotelo, had been refused membership of *Falange* and another, José María Gil Robles, had been constantly vilified in the pages of *Arriba* throughout 1935. Nevertheless, when, in December 1935, Gil Robles also proposed publicly the formation of a 'National

Counter-revolutionary Front', with the participation of FE de las JONS, the Falangists, indignant at what they considered the usurpation of their initiative, chose to insist on a strict interpretation of Point 27 of their doctrinal code, which stated, 'We shall pact very little . . .'. They refused to participate in any alliance unless the prestige and autonomy of their party were previously guaranteed. No agreement was reached.

Once the *Cortes* had been dissolved and with electoral considerations uppermost in all minds, the pace of efforts to conclude alliances quickened. On the Left, socialists, communists and left Republicans signed the pact creating the Popular Front on 15 January 1936. On the Right, *Arriba* announced on 9 January the creation of the Falangist National Front and its proposal to present candidates in Madrid and eighteen provinces. The possibility of admitting other parties to the Front was not yet closed, but no applications were received and, on 14 January, Primo de Rivera visited Gil Robles in an eleventh hour effort to reach agreement on an alliance.[76] The attempt was in vain and, on 27 January, instructions were issued ordering Falangists to abstain from voting in those districts where no Falangist candidate was standing.

The last-ditch attempt to ensure even minimal electoral success had failed completely. The note published on 11 February, stating that '*Falange Española* (had) not concluded an electoral pact of any kind in any province of Spain . . .' and that there had even existed, in the parties of the Right, 'the categorical instruction to exclude (the *Falange*),'[77] was no more than a face-saving way of admitting the FE de las JONS had no option but to accept its political isolation. *Falange's* failure to obtain a single seat in the 16 February poll fully confirmed that situation.

There was no place on the contemporary political stage for parties of the character, ideology and practice of *Falange*, JONS, *Juntas Castellanas* or *Movimiento Español Sindicalista*. In the first place, the parliamentary democratic system still served the purposes of the ruling classes for the control of social, economic and political power. Consequently, up to the electoral victory obtained by the Popular Front on 16 February 1936, they did not feel it necessary to resort to the anti-democratic methods proposed by FE de las JONS.[78] Secondly, in spite of *Falange's* professed rejection of parliamentary democracy, the electoral space it nevertheless aspired to cover was already occupied by parties of longer standing. Conservative voters preferred the parties of the traditional right – the *CEDA*, *Renovación Española* or the Carlist *Comunión Tradicionalista*. For their part, working class voters were more impressed by the repressive attitude adopted by the *Falange* in October 1934 than they were by its national-syndicalist promises.

The electoral *débâcle* suffered by *Falange* in February 1936 left it only two possibilities of survival: the conclusion of a fresh life-saving alliance, or the collapse of the system it rejected and which had clearly rejected it. The events of the period from February 1936 to April 1939 were to provided both opportunities.

Notes

1. The political organisations of the Right received *Falange Española* as a fellow-traveller and as an expression of solidarity with the ideals they themsleves upheld; see, e.g. *Acción Española*, 1 Nov. 1933 and *Informaciones*, 30 Oct. 1933. The Left considered the group's efforts destined *a priori* to failure and, in any case, not a threat to their own existence; see, e.g. *El Socialista*, 31 Oct. 1933. Cf., Blinkhorn, M., *Carlism and Crisis in Spain, 1931–1939* (Cambridge University Press, 1975) pp. 114, 167.
2. For the ideological and philosophical background of *Falange Española*, see e.g.: Mainer, J. C., *Falange y Literatura* (Barcelona: Editorial Labor, 1971) pp. 16–27; Jiménez Campo, J., *El fascismo en la crisis de la II República* (Madrid: Centro de Investigaciones Sociológicas, 1979) pp. 43–110; Brocá S., *Falange y filosofía* (Salou: Editorial Universitaria Europea, 1976) pp. 47–79 and 123–228; Galkin, A., *Fascismo, Nazismo, Falangismo* (Buenos Aires: Editorial Cartago, 1975) *passim*.
3. Quoted in Morodo, R., *Acción Española: orígenes ideológicos del franquismo* (Madrid: Tucar Ediciones, 1980) p. 88.
4. Quoted in Gibello, A., *José Antonio, apuntes para una biografía polémica* (Madrid: Doncel, 1974) p. 79.
5. Ximénez de Sandoval, F., *Biografía apasionada*, private ed. (Madrid, 1972) pp. 62–3.
6. Gibello, A., op. cit., p. 80.
7. Ibid., p. 81. This is an eloquent example of the concept of the relationship between father and son which permeated Primo de Rivera's ideology throughout his political career. See also, e.g. 'La hora de los enanos' (1931); 'Por una sagrada memoria. ¡Hay que oír a los acusados!' in *ABC* (Madrid, 29 Nov. 1931); 'Los intelectuales y la dictadura', prologue to *La Dictadura de Primo de Rivera juzgada en el extraniero*; 'Informe de J.A. Primo de Rivera en la defensa du su padre' (1931), all reproduced in Primo de Rivera, J. A., *Obras completas* (Madrid: Ediciones de la Vicesecretaría de Educación Popular de FET y de las JONS, 1945) pp. 685–721.
8. Such groups as *Reacción Nobiliaria*, *Acción Monárquica* or the *Partido Socialista Monárquico de Alfonso XIII* were as unsuccessful as the *Unión Monárquica Nacional*; Morodo, R. op. cit., pp. 88–9.

9. Juan Aparicio López interviewed in Madrid, 24 June 1977.
10. Ledesma Ramos, R. *¿Fascismo en España?* (hereafter *¿Fascismo?*) (Barcelona: Ariel, 1968) p. 78 (first published in 1935 under the pseudonym of 'Roberto Lanzas').
11. For details of the personal, political and academic life of Ledesma Ramos, see e.g.: Sánchez Diana, J. M., *Ramiro Ledesma Ramos, biografía política* (Madrid: Editora Nacional, 1975); Borrás, T., *Ramiro Ledesma Ramos*, (Madrid: Editora Nacional 1971); Moreno, M., *El nacionalsindicalismo de Ramiro Ledesma Ramos'* (Madrid: Delegación Nacional de Organizaciones del Movimiento, 1963); Montero Díaz, S., 'La evolución intelectual de Ramiro Ledesma Ramos in Ledesma Ramos, R., *Escritos filosóficos*, Sucesora de Minuesa de los Ríos (Madrid, 1941); Aguado, E., *Ramiro Ledesma, fundador de las JONS* (Madrid: Ediciones de la Vicesecretaría de Educación Popular, 1941).
12. Ledesma Ramos, *¿Fascismo?*, p. 77.
13. Ernesto Giménez Caballero, one of the founder members of the group around Ledesma, stated in an interview with the present writer in June 1977, 'In *La Conquista*, we were all Leftists . . .'.
14. Sainz Rodríguez, P., *Testimonio y Recuerdos* (Barcelona: Editorial Planeta, 1978) p. 220.
15. Ibid., p. 220.
16. Ruiz de Alda, P. Prologue to Ruiz de Aldo, J. *Obra completa* (Ediciones F.E., 1939) pp. 26–7.
17. Onésimo Redondo was born in 1905 in a village in the province of Valladolid. He was educated by Jesuit priests, through whom he subsequently obtained the post of Spanish Assistant at the Catholic University of Mannheim. On his return to Spain, he worked as a Civil Servant in a Treasury Department office in Valladolid. He also acted as Secretary to an organisation of Castillian sugar-beet producers.
18. Juan Aparicio López, interviewed, 24 June 1977.
19. See Ledesma Ramos, *¿Fascismo?*, p. 99. The *Conquista group* viewed with scorn what they considered the excessive Jesuit leanings of the JCAH, but 'allowed' their entry because it was necessary to increase the size of the organisation.
20. Ibid., 'The spirit of the JONS', wrote Ledesma, 'contained certain concessions to what might be called the spirit of the Right and, partly in order to defeat Marxism, sought the necessary support in its ranks.'
21. On 2 Apr. 1932, he delivered a lecture in the Madrid *Ateneo*, entitled 'Fascism versus Marxism', which he was unable to finish on account of the uproar caused by the indignant opponents of his views.
22. Cf. Blinkhorn, M. op. cit., pp. 41–111.
23. Redondo, evidently implicated in the coup, took refuge in Portugal. Ledesma, also suspected of being involved, was detained in Madrid for three weeks. José Antonio Primo de Rivera was arrested in San Sebastian, although no charges were brought. See Ximénez de Sandoval, F. op. cit., pp. 78–9; Borás, T., op cit., p. 328; Cardona, G., Abella, A. and Mateo, E., 'La Sanjurjada' in *Historia 16*, no. 76 (Aug. 1982) pp. 43–67.
24. Cf. Preston, P., *The Coming of the Spanish Civil War* (London: Methuen, 1983), p. 43.

25. Ledesma Ramos, R., *¿Fascismo?*, p. 104.
26. Ximénez de Sandoval, op. cit., p. 81; Garcia Venero, M., *La historia de la Unificación Falange y Requeté en 1937* (hereafter, *HU*), Distribuciones Madrileñas (Madrid 1970) pp. 16–17; Bravo, F., *Historia de la Falange Española de las JONS* (hereafter, *HFE*) (Madrid: Ediciones F.E., 1940) p. 12; Ledesma Ramos, *¿Fascismo?*, pp. 106–7.
27. García Venero, *HU*, p. 18; Pavón Pereyra, E., *De la vida de José Antonio* (Madrid: Ediciones FC, 1947 (?)), p. 51; Velarde Fuertes, J., *El nacionalsindicalismo 40 años después* (Madrid: Editora Nacional, 1972) p. 78.
28. From the speech made by Primo de Rivera on 29 Oct. 1933, reproduced in *Obras completas*, p. 22.
29. For how the title *Falange Española* was chosen, see Sánchez Diana, op. cit., p. 187 and Montes, E. in Sánchez Mazas, R., *Fundación, hermandad y destino* (Madrid: Ediciones de Movimiento, 1957) p. XV. For the creation of the *Falange*, see also Gibson, I., *En busca de José Antonio* (Barcelona: Planeta, 1980) pp. 64–70.
30. Serrano Suñer, R., *Memorias* (Barcelona: Planeta, 1977) p. 473.
31. With regard to Primo's reluctance to associate with fascist enterprises at this time, cf. Southworth, H.R., *Antifalange; estudio crítico de 'La Falange en la Guerra de España' de M. García Venero* (hereafter *Antifalange*) (Paris: Ruedo Ibérico, 1967) p. 75, n.8.
32. '*Falange Española* is not a rightist movement, nor is it a leftist movement, nor is it a centrist movement', wrote Rafael Sánchez Mazas in *FE*, no. 1 (7 Dec. 1933). In the edition of 18 Jan. 1934, the same writer commented, 'we are at the same distance from Largo Caballero as we are from Gil Robles'. In the Nov. 1933 elections, Primo de Rivera declined the offer of a place on the CEDA list for Madrid.
33. See, e.g. 'The wingless victory' in *FE*, no. 1 (7 Dec. 1933).
34. Primo de Rivera, 'The Wingless Victory', loc. cit., Primo's candidacy benefited from the fact that his family was well known in western Anadulcía. The Right also took advantage of the anti-Republican backlash and the mass absention of Anarchist voters following the Casas Viejas tragedy in Jan. 1933, in which several peasants were killed in a confrontation with Assault and Civil Guards. The incident seriously damaged the liberal image of the Republic.
35. García Venero, M., *HU*, p. 20.
36. Between 19 and 22 July 1933, and as a result of rumours of a conspiracy between the Anarchist *Federacion Anarquista Ibérica* (FAI), JONS and members of other Right-wing groups, some 3000 people were arrested throughout the country, including Ledesma Ramos, Juan Aparicio and a number of other *JONSistas*.
37. García Venero, HU, pp. 25–7; Sánchez Diana, op. cit., p. 188; Ledesma Ramos, in the JONS magazine, *JONS*, Feb. 1934.
38. The death of numerous Falangists and two attempts on Primo's life in the first half of 1934 led to the formation, in June 1934, of Falange's 'Front Line' assault comandos. Jiménez Campo, J., *El fascismo en la crisis de la II República* (Madrid: Centro de Investigaciones Sociológicas, 1979). pp. 263–78; Bravo, *HFE*, pp. 40–53; *FE*, 1/2/34, 1/3/34, 26/4/34.

39. Ledesma Ramos, ¿Fascismo?, p. 167.
40. Ledesma Ramos, ¿Fascismo?, p. 165; Sainz Rodríguez, P. interviewed in Madrid, 21 Feb. 1986. Cf. Gil Pecharromán, J., 'El Bloque Nacional' in La Guerra Civil Española, vol. 3 (June 1986) Historia 16, Madrid.
41. Sainz Rodríguez, P., op. cit., pp. 220–1.
42. Ibid., p. 375, Cf. Gil Robles, J. M., No fue posible la paz (Barcelona: Ediciones Ariel, 1968) p. 442
43. Sainz Rodríguez, op. cit., p. 376; Gil Robles, op. cit., p. 443.
44. Sainz Rodríguez, op. cit., p. 376; Gil Robles, op. cit., p. 443.
45. Ibid., Cf. Gil Pecharromán, loc. cit., who suggests that, in fact, Goicoechea did not fulfil the economic side of the bargain.
46. Ledesma Ramos, ¿Fascismo?, p. 176.
47. Ibid, p. 186; García Venero, HU, p. 34; Bravo, HFE, p. 61.
48. Falangist Jesus Suevos, interviewed in Madrid (22 Nov. 1977); García Venero, HU, p. 37; Bravo, HFE, pp. 62–6.
49. For the 'October Revolution', see e.g. Jackson, op. cit., pp. 148–68; Preston, op. cit., pp. 127–32 and refs; Shubert A., 'The epic failure: the Asturian revolution of October 1934' in Preston, P. (ed.) Revolution and War in Spain, 1931–1939 (London: Methuen, 1984) and Hacia la revolución (Barcelona: Critica, 1984) pp. 206–14.
50. Cadenas Vicent, V., Actas del último Consejo Nacional de FE de las JONS (hereafter, Actas) (Madrid, 1975), p. 9; Alcazar de Velasco, A., Los 7 días de Salamanca (hereafter, SDS), G. del Toro (Madrid, 1976) p. 34. Cadenas participated with the León Falange and Alcazar de Velasco was decorated with the Falange's highest award for bravery for his part in the repression of the rising in Asturias.
51. Bravo, HFE, pp. 60, 63.
52. Ibid, p. 63.
53. Ibid, p. 72 Bravo's affirmation that Primo 'would not have pacted officially' with the Government on this occasion is strangely in contradiction with his own account of the preceding ten pages.
54. Alcazar de Velasco, A. Serrano Suñer en la Falange (Madrid: Ediciones Patria, 1941) pp. 145–9; Primo de Rivera, J.A., Obras Completas, pp. 623–6. The letter scarcely corroborates S. G. Payne's assertion that 'José Antonio had flatly stated his opposition to consorting with the military, saying that the Generals could never be trusted' (Payne, S. G., Falange, a History of Spanish Fascism (Stanford University Press, 1961) p. 68.
55. 'Carta a un militar español', reproduced in Primo de Rivera, Obras Completas, pp. 645–53. The 1945 edn. dates the letter as writen at some time in 1935, however the content of the text suggests that the date given in the 1952 edn – Nov. 1934 – is the correct one.
56. Ibid.
57. Ledesma Ramos, ¿Fascismo?, p. 197; Bravo, HFE, p. 76; Southworth, H.R., op. cit., pp. 80–1. The Falangists could not know it in 1934, but this, their political charter, was to become the formal ideological basis of the Francoist State from 1937 onwards.
58. Bravo, HFE, pp. 84–5; García Venero, HU, p. 39; JONSist Ricardo Nieto Serrano, interviewed in Madrid on 15 Mar. 1977.

59. E.g. Payne, op. cit., p. 77; Cierva, R. de la, *Historia de la Guerra Civil Española. Antecedentes, Monarquía y República, 1898–1936*, Editorial San Martin (Madrid, 1969) p. 559 and *Historia Ilustrada de la Guerra Civil Española* (Barcelona: Ediciones Danae, 1970), p. 221; García Venero, *HU* p. 34.

60. Particularly revealing is the research done by Angel Viñas among the documentary material captured by the Allies in Italy in 1943, the results of which are detailed in *La Alemania nazi y el 18 de julio* (Madrid: Alianza Editorial, 1974) and 'Berlin: salvad a José Antonio' in *Historia 16*, nos 1 & 2 (May & June 1976). See also, Coverdale, J., *Italian Intervention in the Spanish Civil War* (Princeton University Press. pp. 57–8; and Gallo, M., *Spain under Franco* (London: Allen & Unwin, 1973) pp. 48–9.

61. Up to February 1936, the subsidy was 50 000 lire per month (some £12 000 in 1982), but was reduced to half that amount from Mar. 1936 onwards).

62. Viñas, A., *La Alemania nazi y el 18 de julio*, p. 153.

63. García Venero, *HU*, p. 34.

64. See also the editions of 31 Oct. and 7 Nov. 1935.

65. Ximénez de Sandoval, op. cit., p. 89. *Arriba*, 25 Apr. 1935 also refers to Primo's inability to attend a meeting that month on account of his being in Italy.

66. Southworth, *Antifalange*, p. 153; Gallo, op. cit., p. 149.

67. In García Venero, M., *Falange en la Guerra de España. La Unificación y Hedilla* (hereafter, *FGE*), Ruedo Ibérico (Paris, 1967) p. 323.

68. By the end of 1934, the headquarters of Falange were without light or heating for lack of funds to pay the outstanding account; Ledesma Ramos, *¿Fascismo?*, pp. 167–8 and 199–200.

69. Quoted in Viñas, *La Alemania nazi y el 18 de julio*, p. 155.

70. Ibid., p. 157.

71. Ibid. During the Spanish Civil War, Elsa Paege was a close friend of the German Ambassador, von Faupel, and his wife and acted as a contact between Falangists and Nazis.

72. Ibid., p. 158. Paege had requested one million Deutschmark.

73. Primo de Rivera, *Obras completas*, pp. 73–87; *Arriba*, 23 May 1935.

74. Payne, op. cit., p. 87; García Venero, *HU*, p. 55; Ximénez de Sandoval, op. cit., p. 132. A second insurrectionary plot was evidently attempted in Dec. 1935: Montes Agudo, G., *Pepe Sainz, una vida en la Falange* (Ediciones Pallas de Horta, 1939 (?) pp. 61–62; Southworth, *Antifalange*, pp. 89–94.

75. Bravo, *HFE*, p. 114; *Arriba*, 21 Nov. 1935.

76. Ximénez de Sandoval, op. cit., p. 114; Gil Robles, op. cit., pp. 444–5; *Informaciones* (Madrid, 15 Jan. 1936). See also, Arrarás, J., *Historia de la II República española*, vol. IV (Madrid: Editora Nacional, 1968) pp. 39–43.

77. *Arriba*, 13 Feb. 1936.

78. Until then, the Right was confident that it could win the elections. According to Santiago Carrillo, then leader of the Socialist Youth movement, until very late on 16 Feb., the Left thought it was going to lose (interview by S. Ellwood in *La Guerra Civil Española*, no. 2, Historia 16 (Madrid, May 1986).

2 Falange and the Civil War, 1936-39

Paradoxical though it may seem, the victory of the Popular Front was readily capable of translation into a victory also for a *Falange* struggling to save itself from extinction, for it supported the Falangist contention that the parliamentary democratic system was incapable of resisting the imminent 'invasion of the barbarians'.[1] In this view, the electoral result was simply the first step towards a complete communist take-over in Spain. The classes which had not previously been convinced by the Falange's arguments might now be more favourably disposed towards supporting a non-democratic response to the 'problem' of the Popular Front majority. In effect, their loss of faith in the ability of the 'moderate' Right to defend their interests was reflected in a sudden and massive increase in applications to join *Falange*.[2] Among certain sectors of the Armed Forces, the 16 February result provoked an intensification of the plans for sedition already in existence since 1935 and, indeed, since the declaration of the Republic in 1931.[3]

The wind at last seemed to be blowing in favour of *Falange*. With its political rivals discredited by their electoral defeat and with concrete plans taking shape to reverse the triumph of the Popular Front by force, the *Falange* now sought to ally itself with the conspirators, in the hope of achieving by illegal means the 'conquest of the State' it had been unable to achieve democratically. This was not to say, however, that *Falange* could immediately realise its anti-democratic aspirations. In the first place, its activities were curtailed by Government measures such as the closure of its centres and the suspension, on 5 March 1936, of *Arriba*. In the second, in spite of his repeated overtures to the Armed Forces, Primo de Rivera was not invited to participate in the meetings of the military conspirators, although each party was informed of the proposals of the other.[4]

The Falangist conviction that drastic measures were called for was confirmed and increased by the arrest, on 14 March 1936, of Primo de Rivera, the *Junta Politica* and various provincial leaders. It was decided that the moment had arrived 'to forge a conspiracy of wide scope, an ample popular insurrectional movement . . . to save society

and the Fatherland'.[5] On the day of his arrest, from the cells of Police
Headquarter in Madrid, Primo de Rivera issued a manifesto in which
he called for the cooperation of 'students, intellectuals, workers,
soldiers, Spaniards . . .' in a 'dangerous and delightful enterprise of
reconquest'.[6] However, whilst the *Falange* was anxious to forge an
alliance with the Armed Forces to carry out this operation, it was also
concerned not to cede all the initiative to them. Aware of the political
risk entailed if the 'enterprise of reconquest' were orchestrated and
spearheaded by forces outside their own ranks, *Falange* leaders
instructed militants to offer 'complete and loyal aid in the tasks
assigned by the military leaders for the assistance of the Armed
Forces', but to act under the orders of their own party leaders and 'with
absolute independence of the rest of the civilian forces which may be
used for these services'.[7]

On 4 May 1936, Primo de Rivera issued yet another appeal to the
Armed Forces. His 'Letter to the Military Men of Spain' sought, as had
the previous letters of September and November 1934, to stir up the
anti-Republican feelings of certain sectors of the Army, with the by
now familiar demagogy against the components of the Popular Front:

> Their watchwords come from outside, from Moscow. You have
> heard their cries in the streets, 'Long live Russia!' and 'Russia, yes,
> Spain no!' The character of the approaching movement is radically
> anti-Spanish. It is the enemy of the Fatherland. It despises honour, it
> encourages the collective prostitution of young working women in
> country sprees where all kinds of shamelessness are cultivated. . . .
> It undermines the family, substituted in Russia by free love, by
> collective canteens, by facilities for divorce and abortion (have you
> not heard Spanish girls recently, shouting 'Children, yes, Husbands,
> no!'?)[8]

This diatribe, entitled 'The invasion of the barbarians', was followed
by a eulogistic reference to the Army as the 'safeguard of what is
permanent' and a call to launch 'the great task of national
reconstruction'.[9] As in his previous letters, Primo de Rivera intimated
that the latter would be a joint effort by the *Falange* and the Armed
Forces. Recognising that 'without your strength, soldiers, it will be
titanically difficult for us to triumph in the struggle', he wrote of Army
and Falange as persecuted by the same enemy, united in present
adversity and destined to remain united in the fulfilment of their future
aims:

You – tempered in the religion of service and sacrifice – and we, who have voluntarily imposed on our lives an ascetic and military sense, will teach everyone how to bear the sacrifice with a happy face.[10]

Falangists and others have frequently pointed to the circular issued by Primo de Rivera on 24 June 1936, to Territorial and Provincial Chiefs of the party, as 'proof' that he did not wholeheartedly support the conspiracy which led to the rising of 18 July 1936. It is true that, in the said circular, the Falangist National Chief stated that

The political projects of the military . . . are not ususally accompanied by success . . .the participation of *Falange* in one of those premature and naïve projects would constitute a grave responsibility and would involve its total disappearance, even in the event of victory.[11]

It is important to note, however, that, in the same document, Primo makes a significant exception in his negative opinion of the 'political projects of the military': 'except, naturally, those which are elaborated by a highly prepared minority which exists in the Army'.[12] It was not that Primo wanted to keep the *Falange* out of a rising, but that he wanted to make sure his party cooperated in the right one, that is to say, in the one staged by 'the highly prepared minority' and, therefore with greatest chances of success. Far from rejecting the conspiracy, he was concerned to avoid the abortion of the plans he knew to be in an advanced state of preparation by a precipitate action, perhaps on the part of over-eager Falangists. Thus, the orders given in the 24 June circular were designed to ensure maximum control over the Falangist forces in their dealings with the military, but not to prohibit nor prevent *Falange's* participation in the 'possible immediate rising against the present Government'.[13]

When the rising came, in mid-July 1936, the difficulties occasioned for *Falange* by the repressive measures taken by the Government in the Spring were exacerbated by the arrest of more of its leaders and sympathisers. This did not, however, constitute an obstacle to immediate action for, by then, militants had, on several occasions, received instructions to place themselves at the disposal of the local leaders of the *coup*. Even if they had not been given explicit orders to do so, they would undoubtedly have volunteered to assist the rebels, for identification with military values and with the anti-Republican cause was of the essence of Falangism. For that reason, the party had, for the last two and a half years, been urging armed intervention in national politics.

The arrest of Primo de Rivera in March 1936 proved ultimately to be a permanent loss for the *Falange*. Partly on account of the party's dependence on its National Chief, partly because of the context of war, in his absence FE de las JONS became progresively more subjugated to the dictates of the military command.[14] In the first weeks of the conflict, however, political questions, however important, were overshadowed by military considerations, as the failure of the *coup* in the main centres of political and economic power turned what might otherwise have been a rapid, 19th century style *pronunciamiento* into a full-scale war of unforeseeable duration and consequences. By 25 July, several thousand Falangists had volunteered for service under rebel officers. One such volunteer, Falangist Patricio González de Canales, recalled the situation in the Summer of 1936:

> In the beginning, we did not think about a National Command, because the problem of manning kilometres and kilometres of the battle front weighed us down. It was an immediate question of life or death. That is, we devoted ourselves to the war without thinking of anything else.[15]

By the beginning of the Autumn of 1936, the volunteers had been organised into disciplined fighting units, participating on all battle fronts alongside other volunteer forces and regular Army battalions.[16] The Falangist leadership was evidently in agreement with the party's subordination to the military command. In September, a letter was sent to the General in Chief of the Army of the North, which stated that it was the *Falange's* desire, 'subject at all times, to the orders of the Military leadership and the demands of the campaign', that all Falangist units should be trained to ensure their 'combative efficiency'.[17] A week later, a further communication indicated that

> our Militia units shall, at all times, and as determined by the military authority, be instructed by military officers, who will command them when they are sent to the front.[18]

Military historian and Army officer Rafael Casas de la Vega indicates the crucial importance to the war effort of the volunteer forces:

> At all times, the flanks and the rearguard, as well as vital supply and evacuation lines, were assured, whatever the outcome of the operations.[19]

The participation of the Falangist militias, in proportion to other volunteer forces and to the Nationalist Armies in their entirety, in October 1936, is summarised in Table 2.1 below. A summary of the proportional participation of the Falangist militias over the course of the war is given in Table 2.2.

Table 2.1   Falangist participation, October 1936

	Total Troops	Total Militias	Falangist Volunteers	FE as % of Militias	% Total Troops Militias	Falange
South	29 505	9 490	5 410	54	32	18
Aragon	31 100	9 777	6 481	66	31	21
Centre	44 604	11 704	10 264	88	26	23
North	46 485	30 177	10 254	34	65	22
Galicia/Asturias	36 887	4 100	3 140	76	11	8.5
Total	188 581	65 248	35 549	54	35	19

Source: Casas de la Vega, R., *Las Milìcias nacionales en la guerra de España* (Madrid: Editora Nacional, 1974).

Table 2.2   Proportional participation FE militias, July 1936–January 1939

Militias	July 1936	Oct. 1936	%	Apr. 1937	%	Jan. 1939	%
FE	n/a	36 809	56%	37 080	56%	72 608	75%
Requeté	n/a	22 107	34%	21 720	33%	23 768	25%
Others	n/a	6 192	10%	7 200	11%	–	
Total	35 000	65 108	100%	66 000	100%	96 376	100%
Total Armed Forces		188 581				553 000	

Source: Casas de la Vega, R., *op. cit.,* see Table 2.1

Whilst the majority of the volunteers were used at the front, a certain number, which varied from region to region, were employed in the rearguard. Although some analysts are of the opinion that the military authorities were more responsible than FE de las JONS for the repression of adversaries in occupied territory,[20] it is known for certain that Falangists participated in executions, policing and prison duties as part of the so-called 'cleansing' of the rebel rearguard.[21] Party Secretary Raimundo Fernández Cuesta admitted in a recent interview that the Falangists 'did the dirty work, like carrying out executions'.[22]

It is considerably more difficult to make a quantitative assessment of the non-military aspects of the Falangist contribution to the anti-Republican war effort. Indeed, the divisions between 'military' and 'civilian' were blurred on the one hand, by the very para-military nature of the *Falange* and, on the other, by the fact that this was a *civil* war, which mobilised the entire population in a huge military operation. Nevertheless, there is ample evidence that FE de las JONS played an active part in a variety of ways, which may be summarised, broadly, as falling into three categories: social work, Press and propaganda and political organisation. As with respect to *Falange's* military and para-military activities, the party's alleged reluctance to take part in the rising is not sustained by the reality of its participation in these areas.

In October 1936, on the initiative of Mercedes Sanz Bachiller,[23] Falangist women created *Auxilio de Invierno* (Winter Aid) in Vallado-lid, in response to the hardships caused to the civilian population by the military hostilities. Founded as a centre for children, by October 1937 it had 711 branches throughout the area controlled by the insurgent forces and had changed its name to *Auxilio Social* (Social Aid). By the following year, some 1250 centres provided canteens, maternity and child care and clothing for the destitute. In addition, *Auxilio Social* provided volunteer labour for munitions factories, front-line laundries and military hospitals. By the end of the war, it had opened almost 3000 centres all over Spain and was a vital source of food and shelter for those left hungry and homeless by the conflict.[24] Whilst the aid provided by *Auxilio Social* was undoubtedly very necessary, it was a bitter irony that it should be given by an organisation which was an integral part of the forces responsible for the devastation and bloodshed which had occasioned the necessity.

When the prestigious philosopher Miguel de Unamo said, in Salamanca,[25] that Franco's armies might conquer but would never convince, he was, in fact, identifying one of the most fundamental differences between the two forces in conflict. Whereas the defenders of the legally constituted regime believed the legitimacy of political power to be derived from the ability of its holders to convince the electorate of the validity of their ideological arguments, the insurgents believed that the exercise of power could be legitimated simply by demonstrating superior physical strength. The anti-Republicans' lack of concern for mass persuasion was reflected in their scarce production of press and propaganda materials, in stark contrast to the enormous quantity and wide variety of the Republican production.[26] The mass media which do not exist in the rebel zone were almost exclusively controlled by *Falange*. At the beginning of the conflict, the party used them not only to extol the values defended by the anti-Republican forces, but also to promote the notion that the national-syndicalist revolution could be carried out simultaneously with the war. The latter was, in this view, the first step in the realisation of the former. As time went by, however, the objectives of the party as a distinct political entity were progressively fused with and subordinate to those of the military campaign. By the end of the war, the Falangist-controlled media were not at the service of any revolution, but at that of the establishment and maintenance of the conservative, authoritarian, Francoist State.

The Falangists were responsible for the creation of 'an aesthetic style, through posters, newspaper illustrations, magazines, calendars, uniforms, the stage management of ceremonies and film production',[27] but it was the Press which constituted the most important facet of the rebel propaganda machine. This was virtually monopolised by the *Falange*. Of the national dailies in circulation in July 1936, only the Monarchist *ABC* and the Falangist *Arriba* continued to be published thereafter in what came to be referred to as the 'National' zone.[28] In addition to *Arriba España*, the *Falange* also had some forty provincial dailies and periodicals, as well as its theoretical organ *FE*; a cultural magazine, *Vértice*; a children's paper, *Flechas*; and a 'national-syndicalist graphical weekly', *Fotos*, which began publication in February 1937.[29]

Falange had begun the war with an organised Press and propaganda department, which was immediately able to take charge of coordinating and promoting Press activities in the rebel zone. In November 1938, the department's *jefatura nacional* issued orders that, henceforth, all 'articles, posters and handbills (should) be issued by the National Headquarters of Press and Propaganda'.[30] The National Chief of Press and Propaganda, Vicente Cadenas, had, by February 1937, drawn up a far-reaching project for the organisation of the mass media in the New State. This was to include a Press Agency, a National Publisher, and Schools of Journalism and Political Studies.[31] For a time, the military leaders allowed the Falangist Press and propaganda department to function with a considerable degree of autonomy (although, given the general State of War in force, its activities were, of course, subject to military censorship). This is explained partly by their preoccupation with the strictly military aspects of the conflict; partly by the lack of an alternative body to take charge of Press and propaganda; and partly because *Falange's* basic commitment to the war made it unlikely that the party would use its mass media for anything other than the good of the common cause.

The confidence that this implied in *Falange's* unanimity was not, however, entirely well placed. Whilst the Falangist rank and file contributed actively to the war as militiamen, nurses, gaolers, journalists, artists, drivers or policemen, the party leaders not imprisoned in Republican territory took advantage of the general social and political upheaval to try to further their particular political ends. Throughout August and September 1936, Provincial Chiefs in Castile and Andalusia jockeyed for positions with respect to the national leadership of the party and exerted their local authority as though the war were the opportunity they had been waiting for to eliminate not only Republican adversaries, but also rivals within their own ranks. The death of the former *Juntas Castellanas* leader, Onésimo Redondo, was a case in point.[32]

As yet, the leaders of the rising paid little attention to *Falange's* internal wranglings and maintained towards the party the same ambiguous attitude they had shown it before the war. When, on 25 July 1936, the *Junta de Defensa Nacional* (National Defence Committee) was set up as the body responsible for the political coordination of the rising, *Falange* was not represented on it. Nor, indeed, was any other political party, for the military men considered the war an essentially military matter, in which civilian participation was, at best, of secondary importance. On the other hand, the insurgent generals could not dispense with the military and para-military assistance of such groups as the *Falange*. Thus, when proposals began to be made for attempting to rescue José Antonio Primo de Rivera, it would not have been politic to oppose them.[33]

In September 1936, Franco placed one million pesetas at the disposal of a rescue expedition organised by the Chief of the Falangist militias, Agustín Aznar.[34] The transport of the Falangists was undertaken by ships of the German fleet in the Mediterranean. The plan met with the opposition of the German Consul in Cartagena, Völkers. He refused to authorise the disembarkation in Alicante of two Falangists, Aznar and Rafael Alzaga, in possession of false German passports, which he promptly withdrew. Aznar was eventually landed alone, but failed to accomplish his mission.[35]

A second attempt was made at the beginning of October 1936, again approved by Franco, again with the collaboration of von Knobloch and the German fleet and again with the opposition of Völkers, who was anxious to avoid compromising the German Government, which still maintained diplomatic relations with that of the Spanish Republic. Again, the attempt was unsuccessful.[36]

It was unlikely that any of the attempts would prosper for, apart from the opposition which the Republicans would naturally offer to the escape of so important a prisoner, unbeknown to von Knobloch and the Falangists, Franco was also against the operation, at least from mid-October onwards. Franco had been proclaimed Supreme Commander (*Generalísimo*) of the Armed Forces and Head of State on 1 October 1936. There was therefore no place in the rebel zone for the division of authority which the presence of a prestigious political leader would have supposed.

On 19 and 21 October, Lieutenant Walter Warlimont, in charge of coordinating German military activities in Spain, sent telegrams to the Commander in Chief of the German naval units in Spain, Rear Admiral Carls, indicating Franco's instructions with respect to the rescue operation. The *Generalísimo* wanted it to be carried out with a minimum amount of ransom money, without the participation of von Knobloch, with maximum precautions as to the identity of the prisoner and, in the event of securing Primo's release, with his immediate isolation, on the grounds that there were doubts as to his sanity.[37] Franco had evidently reversed his approval of the rescue, but preferred that the brake should appear to be applied by the German High Command. The support of the *Falange* was necessary to the rebel cause and Franco could not risk either partial loss of its control by the liberation of Primo de Rivera, or, much less, its complete loss by the revelation that he himself was responsible for the suspension of the rescue operation.[38] Primo de Rivera was tried in Alicante and executed on 20 November 1936. His death was not officially made known in what, by then, was referred to as the 'national' zone until a year later.[39]

Although the death of José Antonio Primo de Rivera left the *Falange* definitively without the all-important figure of its first National Chief, the party had already taken steps to remedy what was then expected to be a temporary situation of lack of effective leadership. In September 1936, while Aznar launched the first bid to free Primo de Rivera and the advance of Franco's troops towards Madrid proceeded apace, the National Council of Falange met in Valladolid.[40] From that meeting came the creation of a Provisional Command Committee (*Junta de Mando Provisional*), consisting of seven members, one of whom would be its President. The Provincial Chief of Burgos and León, Manuel Hedilla Larrey, was nominated

President, with the general approval of the rest of the Councillors.

Hedilla was a working-class man who had never held a political post of national scope and had no particular distinction within the *Falange*. Yet he was elected President of the governing body of the party, in temporary substitution of Primo de Rivera and in preference, for example, to the only member of the *Junta Política* then present in the rebel zone, José Sainz Nothnagel. The opinions expressed on this point by Falangists interviewed are illustrative of the party's repeated tendency to place personal and immediate convenience before long-term or ideological considerations:

> The personality of Hedilla was politically more convenient than, for example, that of Sainz, because of his humble status. Not that Pepe Sainz was any *señorito*, but the image of Hedilla had more force and greater attraction for a proletarian mass than that of Sainz.[41]

> Hedilla was elected as a person of little intelligence, to take the place of José Antonio until he came so that if, for any reason, he didn't come, it wouldn't be difficult to remove Hedilla.[42]

In spite of the general consensus whereby Hedilla was theoretically recognised as the head of the Provisional Command Committee, the indications as to how the arrangement worked in practice are contradictory. Hedilla clearly considered himself as holding a position which gave him the power to give and sign orders.[43] The Committee had been created, however, as a compromise solution to a circumstantial problem and Hedilla's colleagues equally clearly considered his authority to be merely nominal:

> We all felt ourselves backed by and in possession of our own authority, because it came from José Antonio. Within the *Junta de Mando*, even though there was a President, whom the members themselves had designated, his authority existed because they had seen fit to give it to him, whilst they, designated as they were by José Antonio, were as much members of the *Junta* as he was. . . . There was not, strictly speaking, any serious hierachical subordination.[44]

> In reality, Hedilla did not and could not represent the head of the *Falange*. He didn't have the personality to occupy that post. . . . There were people like Raimundo Fernández Cuesta, José Antonio ór Julio Ruiz de Alda who were unquestionable in the *Falange*, because they were far above Hedilla's provincial level.[45]

In any case, with normality disrupted by the war, the local, provincial and territorial party chiefs in fact exercised more authority in the areas under their control than was possible for Hedilla from an ambiguous position in an unorthodox entity in which, moreover, he could not count on the unconditional support of the other members.

If Hedilla's relations with his Falangist comrades appear to have been somewhat strained, his *rapport* with General Franco was good in 1936 and early 1937. In September 1936, Franco's military GHQ (the *Cuartel General del Generalísimo*) was transferred from Burgos to Salamanca. In early October, the Falangist Command Committee also moved to Salamanca, in spite of the fact that the insurgents' political organism, the *Junta Técnica*,[46] remained in Burgos. Hedilla clearly knew where real power was located. Faithful to the Falangist tradition, in Salamanca he cultivated cordial relations with Franco. The *Generalísimo* and Hedilla evidently talked on several occasions about 'the war, collective effort and, sometimes, political questions . . .' and Franco once asked the *Falange* leader, 'What do you think of the Monarchy, Hedilla?'[47]

Such gestures of *camaraderie* notwithstanding, the *Cuartel General* had the upper hand in the relationship. A request made by Hedilla in September 1936 to transfer Falangist militias from León to Burgos for training purposes was refused.[48] Similarly, when Hedilla suggested that contacts be made to secure the safe passage of his family from Republican to rebel territory via an exchange of prisoners, the *Cuartel General* replied that the exchange of Hedilla's family was not of sufficient strategic interest.[49]

To a certian extent, the relationship between Hedilla and Franco was symbiotic, Hedilla, lacking the unconditional support of most of the other *Falange* leaders, needed the security of the *Generalísimo's* backing. Franco, for his part, as long as he was not himself the leader of the *Falange*, needed the cooperation of Hedilla as the chief – however nominal – of the principal political and para-military force in the 'national' zone. Franco, however, controlled the force of arms and, therefore, had the power to turn relationship into one of domination. In the final weeks of 1936 and, increasingly, in the Spring of 1937, this was precisely the direction that the relationship began to take.

The *Falange's* independent military potential had been partially undermined when the replacement of troops began in August 1936. Volunteers already at the front were instructed to remain with their respective militia units, but those in the rearguard were to join the regular Army units to which they were assigned. This meant that the number, size and composition of specifically Falangist units (*banderas*) could not increase thereafter, since the Falangists were dispersed throughout the Armed Forces. The *Falange's* potential capacity to back up political activities with independent military action was thereby controlled and reduced. In November 1936, as we have noted, the *Falange's* political prospects were left in a state of suspension by the death of Primo de Rivera. One month later, the *Cuartel General* took a step which at once consolidated and extended its strictly, military power and divested FE de las JONS of an important part of its remaining independent political potential. On 20 December, Franco decreed that, henceforth, all voluntary militias would come under the sole command and discipline of the regular Army. Units at the front would be responsible to the corresponding military authority, whilst those in the rearguard would be subject to the same disciplinary norms as the Civil Guard.[50]

What was happening was what Primo de Rivera had foreseen in the Spring: *Falange* was being taken over by the Army. He had been aware of, and had accepted, that risk. In so doing, however, as subsequent events showed, he fatally overestimated the rising's possibilities of immediate success and also, what was worse, the degree to which the insurgents would be prepared to concede, or even share, political power thereafter.

The political dimension of the operation of absorption came to the fore in the first half of 1937 but can be traced back to the Autumn of 1936, when the idea of forming a Francoist party was mooted by the *Generalísimo's* brother, Nicolás. Such a party, it was suggested, would provide all those fighting for the 'national' cause with a channel to express their 'unconditional support for Franco'.[51] There were, however a number of factors which advised against such a move. Firstly, the officers who had elected Franco as Head of State and of the Armed Forces might oppose the creation of a Francoist party, for while they considered the war a common *professional* venture, they did not all hold the same *political* views. Secondly, it would be necessary to resolve the question of coexistence with the Carlist *Comunión Tradicionalista* and the *Falange*. If the conclusion of political negotiations was a complex task in peacetime, how much more difficult would it be in the rarified atmosphere of a civil war. Thirdly, and perhaps most important, Franco was reluctant to repeat the unsuccessful experience of the dictator General Primo de Rivera with his party created from power, the *Unión Patriótica*.[52]

Yet Franco did not entirely reject the idea. In September 1936, the preamble to the Decree appointing him as head of State had argued that 'All kinds of reasons indicate the advisability of concentrating in a single power all those powers which are to lead to the final victory and to the establishment, consolidation and development of the new State.'[53] Even after this Decree, the nexus between military and political power was still weak, limited as it was to the coincidence of the two in Franco's person and the application of a general State of War. Francoist power was based almost exclusively on the prowess of the rebel armies and on repression, whilst the political power represented by the *Falange*, the *Comunión Tradicionalista* and the old parliamentary Right enjoyed a certain independence. The problem was how to eliminate the potential political competition of the parties without alienating their military and para-military support.

The *Generalisimo's* solution was a variation on his brother's theme: a system which would erase the discord of political competition by eliminating the existing parties and replacing them with a single organisation, of which he would be the head. It cannot be stated with certainty exactly when Franco arrived at this conclusion, but he is said to have studied and made notes on the *Falange* and on the *Comunión Tradicionalista* in the latter months of 1936, reflecting that it would be easy and convenient to unite them.[54]

His attention to the matter was perhaps stimulated by the contemporary progress of the war. By mid-Autumn 1936, the fall of Madrid and, consequently, the end of the war, were considered by many to be imminent. In November, with Franco's troops not 10 kilometres from the centre of the capital on its western flank, Falangist Felipe Ximénez de Sandoval was commissioned by Franco and Hedilla to produce a project for a single party system.[55] Contrary to all expectation, Madrid resisted and Franco was, for the moment, deprived of the opportunity to implement Ximénez de Sandoval's scheme, but the idea was not abandoned. In December, it was taken up by the Carlist *Pensamiento Navarro*, in an article entitled 'An idea: *requeté* and *fascio*'. This prompted a reply from Manuel Hedilla, in which he discussed the possible points of agreement and disagreement, political and practical, between the *Comunión Tradicionalista* and FE de las JONS, concluding that 'the tendency towards the formation of a single force is undeniable'.[56]

In February 1937, Franco's brother-in-law, Ramón Serrano Suñer arrived in Salamanca, having escaped from Republican-held Madrid in October 1936.[57] He has generally been regarded, by Falangists and others, as the 'great atificer' of the final development and implementation of Franco's embryonic plan to unite all exisiting parties – *Falange*, *Comunión Tradicionalista*, *CEDA*, and *Renovación Española* – in a single entity.[58] As Franco's political advisor, as an experienced politician, and as a man with personal knowledge of the parties involved, Serrano probably played a part in finalising the project Franco had outlined to him shortly after his arrival in Salamanca,[59] but the idea itself undoubtedly dated from several months earlier.[60]

Whatever the exact weight of Serrano's contribution, the pace of events quickened in the period following his arrival in Salamanca. The atmosphere in the rebel rearguard became increasingly tense as two mutually antagonistic factions emerged within FE de las JONS and yet another crisis of leadership brewed. It was known, even if it had not been publicly admitted, that José Antonio Primo de Rivera was dead. For the *Falange*, it was therefore no longer a question of provisional, but of permanent party leadership. At the same time, since the possibility of political unification was by then common knowledge, 'party leadership' was understood to mean the representation of the *Falange* in what would foreseeably be a three-cornered contest between *Falange*, *Comunión Tradicionalista* and Franco for the domination of the resulting 'single party'. What was at stake was nothing less than the control of the socio-political and ideological structures of the post-war 'New State'.

Expectation grew in the first days of April 1937, as intra-Falangist relations deteriorated and rumours circulated that Franco would take advantage of the party's disorganisation to impose a new political order.[61] The *Junta de Mando Provisional*, incapacitated for united action by its internal rivalries, was engrossed in its factional conspiring until a meeting of the National Council was called for Sunday 25 April. The council meeting was hurriedly brought forward a week then a clash between rival groups of Falangists in Salamanca on the night of 16 April resulted in the death of two militants. Although Manuel Hedilla was elected National Chief in its first, highly conflictive session, on 18 April, the die was already cast for the *Falange*.[62] That same night, Franco announced in a radio broadcast his intention to unite *Falange* and *Comunión Tradicionalista*, dissolve all other political organisations and assume himself the national leadership of the new entity, which would be known as *Falange Española Tradicionalista y de las JONS* (FET y de las JONS). The terms of these measures were published as Decree 255 in the *Official Bulletin* of 20 April 1937.[63]

In later years, Falangists have expressed the opinion that the unification was motivated by purely immediate, pragmatic considerations:

> Franco acted to resolve the problem which had arisen in the political organisations. It was a circumstantial measure and a necessary one at the historical moment at which it occurred. It had its justification, which was to win the war.[64]

> In view of the clashes there had been and the irregularities in the rearguard, the Caudillo decided to unify all the political forces.[65]

Serious though the 'clashes' were, disciplinary not political measures would have seemed more appropriate to deal with them and, indeed, a Court Martial was subsequently held against those involved in the 16 April skirmish. Moreover, that incident was the result, not the cause, of possible changes in the party's structure and leadership.[66] Finally, the Right had always shown a tendency to close ranks when it perceived its interests to be threatened by a common enemy. It seems unlikely, therefore, that the *Falange* would have allowed internal divisions, however deep-seated, to jeopardise their possible victory in the war, for this would have meant the betrayal of the beliefs and objectives for which the insurgents had risen and to which the *Falange* had been explicitly committed since its foundation. Certainly, Decree 255 immediately altered the political status quo in the rebel zone. The crucial factor, however (as the Falangists surely knew), were its premeditated and long-term implications, in so far as it embodied Franco's will to implant a particular system of political organisation and expression in the 'national' zone and, ultimately, in the post-war 'New State'. So much was clear in the preamble to the Decree:

> Efficient governmental action, such as must be that of the new Spanish State . . . demands that the individual and collective action of all Spaniards be subjugated to its common destiny. This truth . . . is incompatible with the struggle of parties and political organisations which . . . waste their best energies in competition for the predominance of their particular styles or, what is worse, on questions of a personal nature, which give rise to petty discords within the organisations resuscitating old political intrigues and threatening with disintegration organisations and forces whose masses are moved by the impulse of the purest of ideals.[67]

The Decree, as University Professor Carlos Ollero wrote, on the fifth anniversary of the Unification, was 'an institutional act, the backbone of the regime.'[68] Its underlying political significance was that,

> after its implementation, there (was) no room in the new regime of the Fatherland for the existence, justification or free play of other political groups, for the principles which might inform them (had been) either incorporated in those of Falange Española Tradiciona-lista de las JONS, or (were) alien, when not opposed to the supreme values embodied by the National Movement.[69]

With Franco at its head, FET y de las JONS was, thus, the only political organism in legal existence. Within that hybrid entity, and as the 'authentic exponent of the National Rising initiated by our glorious Army on 17 July 1936'[70] *Falange* was to provide the fundamental principles of the new, one-party system, for, as the preamble to the Decree of Unification stated, 'the programmatic norm (of the New State) is constituted by the 26 Points of *Falange Española*'.[71]

The appointment of the members of the *Junta Política* of FET y de las JONS was published three days after the Decree of Unification.[72] Of the twenty members, half were to be elected by a National Council yet to be created and half directly nominated by Franco. On this occasion, he designated four Carlists and six Falangists, including the erstwhile, if short-lived, second National Chief of *Falange*, Manuel Hedilla. All was not well however, for it was known by 23 April that Hedilla had rejected his appointment.[73] On 25 April, he and a number of other Falangists were arrested. They were tried by Court Martial on 5 June 1937, charged with 'acts of mutiny against the Decree of Unification.'[74]

Hedilla and three other Falangists were sentenced to death; others received sentences ranging from life imprisonment to two years. The sentences were confirmed on 9 June, although the death sentences were later commuted to life imprisonment. On 7 June, a second Court Martial was held for the death of the two Falangists on the night of 16 April. Hedilla was again given the maximum penalty, as was one other Falangist. In this case, however, the death sentences were not subsequently confirmed, two of the accused were absolved and the remaining four sentences were reduced.[75]

Apart from the steps taken against Manuel Hedilla and those tried with him, the *Falange* passed with remarkable ease from its pre-April 1937 state of foundering independence to its new status as the largest single component in a quasi-single party under the control of a military dictator. Some comrades evidently suffered certain 'moral doubts'[76] but, nevertheless, had little difficulty in swallowing the Unification and their subsequent incorporation into the power structure of the post-war State. Only a small group around José Antonio Primo de Rivera's sister, Pilar, placed conditions on their cooperation in the new system, but even their apparently radical position did not entirely preclude collaboration with Franco's regime and their conditions – the establishment after the war of a national-syndicalist State – were satisfied with no more than verbal assurances. The *Falange* had seriously contemplated effecting a *coup* against the established Government at earlier moments of greater numerical and political weakness, yet now a nascent military dictatorship was readily accepted and Primo de Rivera's forebodings with respect to the dangers of such an eventuality were forgotten or ignored.[77]

Falange accepted the Unification because it had, after all, sub-scribed to the war as a means to the destruction of the Popular Front, and the image of the common enemy was ultimately more powerful than the issues involved in internal disputes. Moreover, the *Falange's* entire career had been characterised by its willingness to ally with any force that could offer it survival, including certain sectors of the Army. The acceptance of the unification was therefore historically coherent. It was also ideologically justified, for it represented the 'final thrust for the conquest of the State' envisaged by the last of the *Falange's* original 27 Programmatic Points. Although the 'conquest' thus attained left FE de las JONS with less than the supreme power it had aspired to, no dissenting voices were raised, for the Falangists knew that they had never before been so close to the corridors of power and were unwilling to risk that triumph for the sake of excessively rigid doctrinal interpretations.

To consolidate the political fusion, measures were immediately taken to erase separate identities. The uniform for all was a combina-tion of the Falangist blue shirt and the Carlist red beret. The party symbol was the Falangist yoke and arrows. The Falangist salute was adopted as the national salute on 24 April 1937.[78] On 30 April, equal representation of *Falange* and *Comunión Tradicionalista* on provincial amalgamation committees was ordered and, on 8 June Falangists and Carlists were instructed to use the same premises in towns of less than ten thousand inhabitants.[79] When information was received in May that 'in spite of the Unification decreed by the *Generalísimo*, a series of armed groups continue(d) to exist in the rearguard', Franco issued orders which indicated that not the slightest deviation from what he had decreed would be tolerated.[80]

At the same time, the work of building a power structure and an ideological system around Franco began. As yet, it was a slow process, for the outcome of the war was far from decided and political organisation was not, therefore, the most urgent of the *Cuartel General's* preoccupations. Nevertheless, the complexities of controlling an ever-expanding rearguard, of feeding its population, of financing the war and of assuring continued external and internal political support could not indefinitely be covered adequately by the *Junta Técnica*, limited as it was in its size, capacity and authority. Moreover, it was necessary to make provision for the future – assuming, as the rebels did, that 'the future' in Spain would not, in any way, resemble the Republican past. As part of that preparation, on 4 August 1937, the Statutes of FET y de las JONS were published, laying down the guiding principles for the party's main political bodies – the *Junta Política* and the *Consejo Nacional* – and regulating the construction of a corporativist trade union system and party services. The formation of the first National Council was completed on 19 October 1937 and it held its inaugural session in Burgos six weeks later, on 2 December.

At that meeting, Franco appointed the first Secretary General of the unified party: Raimundo Fernández Cuesta, the first secretary of *Falange Española* in 1933.[81] With regard to his appointment, Fernández Cuesta commented,

> The problem arose of whom to appoint as Secretary General: Serrano Suñer, who was Franco's brother-in law (and then the best of relations existed between them) or me. The mass of Falangists wanted it to be me. Franco wanted Serrano Suñer, because he had more confidence in him, whereas he didn't know me, Serrano was his brother-in-law and completely trusted by him. Realising that the atmosphere at the time was entirely in my favour, Franco resolved the dilemma by appointing me.[82]

There were in effect, a number of factors which militated in favour of Franco's choice. Although he had imposed his will in the April crisis and the majority of *Falange's* leaders had accepted that imposition, both the *Cuartel General* and the party hierarchs were concerned lest rearguard political manoeuvres should provoke a protest withdrawal by Falangists at the front line. Since there were several thousands of these, such an occurrence would have been militarily and politically very serious. Since Serrano Suñer was considered, rightly or wrongly, to be responsible for the Unification, his appointment as Secretary of FET y de las JONS might have been the 'last straw' for the front-line Falangists.[83] The designation of Fernández Cuesta, by contrast, not only provided a soothing sense of continuity for the Falangists, but also lent weight to the notion that they were, as they had aspired to be, at the top of the political pyramid. Moreover, Fernández Cuesta had been a member of *Falange* since its foundation in 1933, whereas Serrano had been a member if the now-extinct CEDA. Finally, whilst both men could claim close friendship with the Primo de Rivera family, Fernández Cuesta did not have Serrano's family ties with Franco and it appeared, at first, that he might show a certain independence from the *Generalísimo* and from the *Cuartel General* clique.[84]

On 30 January 1938, the composition of Franco's first government was published in the official Bulletin. Serrano Suñer was appointed Minister of the Interior and National Chief of the Press and Propaganda section of FET y de las JONS. As such, he 'looked in the *Falange* for men to work with (him)' and appointed Dionisio Ridruejo as Director General of Propaganda, José Antonio Giménez Arnau as Director General of the Press, Antonio Tovar as Head of Radio Services and Ramón Garriga as Head of Press Information.[85] Falangists were also appointed to two important ministerial posts. Raimundo Fernández Cuesta became Minister of Agriculture (as well as party Secretary) and Pedro González Bueno was designated Minister for Syndical Organisation and Action.

By the end of 1937, all formal manifestations of political groups other than *Falange* had disappeared. With the formation of the 1938 Cabinet, sworn into office at an elaborate ceremony in Burgos on 2 January 1938, the take-over bid was complete. With the consent and cooperation of all but a handful of its leading members, *Falange* now prepared to embark on a new career as partner in the joint enterprise of the nascent Franco regime.

Notes

1. The heading of the first part of letter written by José Antonio Primo de Rivera from prison in Madrid, in May 1936 (see below, pp. 30–1).
2. In spite of the scorn and venom directed against CEDA militants in *Arriba* throughout 1935, they were nevertheless admitted as members of *Falange*

after Feb. 1936. It is not known whether they were actively advised or encouraged to join FE de las JONS, but they evidently were not *prevented* from doing so. Cf. Preston, P., *The Coming of the Spanish Civil War.*, pp. 185–9.

3. For details of the conspiracy see, e.g. Sueiro, D., 'Sublevación contra la República' in *Historia 16*, nos. 89, 90 & 91 (Sept., Oct. & Nov. 1983) and 'La conspiración' in *Historia 16 (Julio 1936: España en guerra)* no. 100, Aug. 1984; Cardona, G., *El poder militar en la España contemporánea hasta la Guerra Civil*, siglo XXI (Madrid, 1983) pp. 219–47.

4. One of Primo de Rivera's professional assistants, Rafael Garcerán Sánchez, acted as intermediary between them (Falangist Diego Salas Pombo, interviewed on 14 Mar. 1978. The writer's efforts to interview Rafael Garcerán, in 1978 and again in 1985, were unsuccessful).

5. Bravo, *HFE*, p. 165.

6. Primo de Rivera, *Obras completas*, p. 667.

7. Reproduced in Jato, D., *La rebelión de los estudiantes* (Madrid, 1975) pp. 332–3.

8. Primo de Rivera, 'Carta a los militares de España' in *Obras Completas*, pp. 669–74.

9. Ibid., p. 672.

10. Ibid., p. 672.

11. Primo de Rivera, *Obras completas*, pp. 969–72.

12. Ibid., p. 970.

13. Ibid., p. 973.

14. In later years, Falangists have maintained that, had Primo de Rivera been free, Franco would not have been able to attain the position of unipersonal domination he did, in effect, achieve. Whilst it is arguable that Primo would have aspired to share power with the military, the nature of his political career up to July 1936 makes it seem unlikely that he would have gone so far as to rival or, even less, to oppose military authority.

15. Personal testimony given in Payne, S.G. op. cit., p. 121–2.

16. Other volunteers came mainly from the Carlist *Requeté*, but also from *Acción Popular* and its youth movement, JAP; Casas de la Vega, R. *Las milicias nacionales en la guerra de España* (Madrid: Editora Nacional, 1974) p. 59. The present writer was refused access to the Archive of the National Militias, but the archive of the *Servicio Histórico Militar* in Madrid (hereafter, SHM) contains numerous documents pertaining to the recruitment, training, organisation and deployment of volunteers. See, e.g.: *Armario* (hereafter, A) 16/ *Legajo* (hereafter, L) 1/ *Carpetas* (hereafter, C) 1, 10, 26, 57 & 944; A15/ L3/ C15 & 17; A18/ L1/ C11; A23/ L1/ C12; A96/ L4/ C12.

17. SHM. A15/ L1/ C44/ Document 1.

18. Ibid., Document 2.

19. Casas de la Vega, R., op. cit., p. 84.

20. Jackson, G. op. cit., p. 305; Thomas, H., *The Spanish Civil War* (Harmondsworth: Penguin, 1965) pp. 218, 223.

21. See e.g.: Jackson, G., op. cit., pp. 299–303 and refs: SHM, A15/ L3/ C17, A16/ L1/ C10, A18/ L1/ C11; Thomas, op. cit., pp. 221–3, 242; Casas de la Vega, op. cit., p. 91; Gibson, I., *The Death of Lorca* (London: Paladin,

1974) pp. 81, 124–5, 163–5; Brenan, G., *La faz actual de España* (Buenos Aires: Losada, 1952) pp. 112–28; Ridruejo, D., *Escrito en España*, (Buenos Aires: Losada, 1962) pp. 91–8; Gallo, M. op.cit., pp. 65–6.

22. Fernández Cuesta, R. in *La historia del franquismo*, Diario 16, Vol. I, (1984–85) p. 23.

23. Widow of JONist Onésimo Redondo. Allegedly killed by a Republican commando in rebel-held territory, it has been suggested that Redondo was, in fact, killed by Falangists of a rival faction (Diego Salas Pombo, interview 21 Nov. 1977; 'Falange española auténtica' in *El Pais* (Madrid, 28 May 1978).

24. Thomas, op. cit., p. 445, n.3; Giménez Caballero, E. *La Infantería española* (Madrid: Ediciones de la Vice-Secretaría de Educación Popular, 1941) pp. 62–3. For a detailed account of the creation of *Auxilio Social* and the disagreement between Sanz Bachiller and Pilar Primo de Rivera over its political character, see Gallego Méndez M.T., *Mujer, Falange y Franquismo* (Madrid: Taurus, 1983) pp. 47–75. See also Primo de Rivera, P., *Recuerdos de una vida* (Madrid: Ediciones Dyrsa, 1983) p. 103.

25. In a celebrated confrontation with General Millan Astray in Salamanca University on 12 Oct. 1936, Unamumo said, 'You will vanquish, because you have more than sufficient brute force. But you will not convince. To convince, one must persuade. And to persuade, you would need something you lack: Justice and Right in the struggle.' (Thomas, H., *La guerra civil española* vol. II (Barcelona: Grijalbo, 1978) p. 549.

26. Cf. Fontsere, C., *Los carteles de la Guerra Civil Española* (Madrid: Ediciones Urbión, 1981).

27. García i García, M. in the *Catalogue of the Exhibition 'La Guerra Civil Española'* (Madrid: Ministry of Culture, 1981) pp. 45–6. The Falangist film company, 'Patria Films', was created in Morocco in September 1936 and produced a number of documentaries depicting the party's participation in the war.

28. The rebel edn of *ABC* was published in Seville. *Arriba* was published in Pamplona as *Arriba España*.

29. Cadenas, V. *Actas*, p. 31.

30. Ibid., p. 20.

31. Ibid., pp. 17–62. Cadenas drew his inspiration for the scheme's 'departments and services, from the Ministry of Propaganda in Germany'. After the war, the Franco regime did in effect have the four official departments envisaged by Cadenas. The difference was that they were State, not party, organisms.

32. See note 23 above.

33. A number of accounts exist of the attempts to rescue Primo de Rivera, who had been transferred, with his brother, Miguel, to Alicante prison on 5 June 1936. See e.g.: Ximénez de Sandoval, F., op. cit., pp. 485–6; García Venero, M., *FGE*, pp. 200–4; Southworth, H.R., *Antifalange*, p. 150–3; Gibello, op. cit., pp. 370–4; Viñas, A. in *Historia 16*, nos. 1 & 2 (May & June 1976). Ernesto Giménez Caballero expressed the view that the Republican Government made a serious political and tactical error in not releasing the Falangist National Chief (interview, 11 July 1977) although, as noted earlier, it is by no means certain that this would have

altered significantly the course of the conflict.
34. Joachim von Knobloch, then honorary German Consul in Alicante and a party to the attempt, interviewed on 14 Jan. 1978. Von Knobloch added that, when he counted the money, some 200 000 pesetas were missing. Asked for an explanation, Aznar replied that the money had been used for 'expenses' in Seville.
35. Viñas, loc. cit. Confirmed by J. von Knobloch, loc. cit., and by A. Aznar in an unpublished account written by him and given to the present writer in Nov. 1976.
36. Viñas, loc. cit and personal conversation with one of the participants in the attempt, Pedro Gamero del Castillo, in Madrid, 4 Mar. 1978.
37. Viñas, loc. cit.
38. Even after the publication of the evidence indicating Franco's implication in the abortion of the attempt to rescue Primo de Rivera, Falangists interviewed by this writer were reluctant to admit its veracity.
39. For details of the trial, see Ximénez de Sandoval, op. cit., pp. 489–501; Gibello, op. cit. pp. 383–94; Mancisidor, J., *Frente a frente* (Madrid: Editorial Almena, 1975) *passim*; Bravo, F., *José Antonio ante la justicia roja* (Madrid: Ediciones de la Vice-Secretaría de Educación Popular, 1941) *passim*.
40. Detailed and frequently conflicting accounts of this important meeting are given by the following sources: Hedilla Rojas, M.I. in *Historia Internacional*, 12 (Madrid: Mar. 1976); García Venero, M., *HU*, pp. 83–4 and *FGE*, p. 190–1; Hedilla Larrey, M., *Manuel Hedilla, Testimonio* (Barcelona: Ediciones Acervo, 1972) pp. 219–22; Payne, op. cit., pp. 123–4; *Historia de la Cruzada Española*, 8 vols (Madrid: Ediciones Españolas, 1940–44), vol. III, pp. 395–9. The basic sequence of events was confirmed to this writer in interviews with Falangists Juan Aparicio (June 1977) and Jesus Suevos (Nov. 1977).
41. Roberto Reyes Morales, interviewed 29 Nov. 1977.
42. Angel Alcazar de Velasco, interviewed 15 Feb. 1977.
43. See e.g. the correspondence between Army Generals in Castile and Hedilla, signed by the latter as 'Chief of the *Junta de Mando Provisional*' and in which he refers to 'my importance in the Falange', SHM, *Ejército del Norte*, A15/ L2/ C63/ Document 1 and A16/ L10/ C16/ Document 9.
44. Ricardo Nieto Serrano, interviewed 15 Mar. 1977.
45. Manuel Valdés Larrañaga, interviewed 22 Nov. 1977.
46. The *Junta de Defensa Nacional* was replaced by the *Junta Técnica* after Franco's designation as Head of State on 1 Oct. 1936.
47. Hedilla Larrey, M. *Testimonio*, p.369.
48. SHM, A16/ L10/ C16/ Document 9.
49. Ibid., A15/ L1/ C94/ Document 1.
50. Casas de la Vega, R., *Las Milicias Nacionales*, 2 vols. (Madrid: Editora Nacional, 1977) vol. I, p. 301; Falangist Diego Salas Pombo, interviewed 26 Dec. 1977.
51. Hedilla Larrey, *Testimonio*, p. 362.
52. Cf. Morodo, R. *Acción Española: orígenes ideológicos del franquismo* (Madrid: Ediciones Tucar, 1980) pp. 39–40. This view was echoed by Juan Velarde Fuertes, interviewed in Madrid, 13 June 1978.

53. *BOE*, 30 Sept. 1936; Suárez Fernández, L. *Francisco Franco y su tiempo* vol. II (Madrid: Ediciones Azor, 1984) p. 107.
54. Serrano Suñer, R., *Entre Hendaya y Gibraltar* (Madrid: Ediciones y Publicaciones Españolas, 1942) p. 29 and *Memorias*, p. 184. See also, Suarez Fernández, L. op. cit., vol. 2, ch. VII, 'El camino hacia la unificación pólítica', pp. 169-95.
55. Ximénez de Sandoval, F. interviewed 14 Dec. 1977; Hedilla Larrey, *Testimonio*, pp. 364-5. In his autobiographical *Casi unas memorias*, Dionisio Ridruejo writes (Barcelona: Planeta, 1976, p. 65) that in the same month of Nov., General Yagüe suggested the idea of amalgamation in the Segovia press.
56. *Arriba España* Pamplona, 6 Jan. 1937. The same edn carried an Editorial by the Falangist priest, Fermín Yzurdiaga, also on the subject of the fusion of the two organisations.
57. Serrano recounts the vicissitudes of his escape in his *Memorias*, pp. 19-46 and 143-54 and, in less detail, in *Entre Hendaya y Gibraltar*, pp. 19-20.
58. See e.g. Alcazar de Velasco, A., *SDS*, p. 283; Payne, S.G., op. cit., p. 168; Cierva, R. de la, *La historia se confiesa*, p. 251; Ridruejo, D., *Casi unas Memorias*, p. 103; Thomas, H., op. cit., p. 532. A first unification had already occurred voluntarily: in Jan. 1937, the members of the extreme Right wing *Partido Nacionalista Español* (Spanish Nationalist Party) joined the *Comunión Tradicionalista* (Gil Pecharroman, J., 'Albiñana, el rey de los ultras' in *Historia 16*, no. 45 (Jan. 1980).
59. Serrano Suñer, *Entre Hendaya y Gibraltar*, p. 29. Serrano himself is disappointingly brief with regard to his rôle: 'My task was to write the Decree of Unification' (ibid., p. 31). See also, Saña, H., *El franquismo sin mites. Conversaciones con Serrano Suñer* (Barcelona: Grijalbo, 1982) pp. 77-79.
60. Falangist Narciso Perales Herrero, friend and contemporary of Serrano Suñer, states that Franco's legal advisor, Martínez Fusset, probably played a more active part than Serrano in the development of the idea itself and the elaboration of its Juridical aspects (interview, 24 Dec. 1977).
61. Cf. García Venero, *HU*, pp. 182-3, 188; Alcázar de Velasco, *SDS*, pp. 107-13, 125-34; Southworth, *Antifalange*, pp. 10-12, 37; Ridruejo, D. in *Destino*, Madrid, May-June 1974, and *Escrito en España*, pp. 13-15.
62. Details of the complex and far from clear events surrounding the summoning and proceedings of the Council meeting are given in: Alcazar de Velasco, *SDS*, pp. 91-105, 123-282, *Serrano Suñer en la Falange*, pp. 55-76 and *La Gran Fuga* (Barcelona: Planeta, 1977) pp. 16-28; Cadenas Vicent, *Actas*, pp. 66-156; Cierva, R. de la, *La historia se confiesa*, no. 43 (2 Dec. 1976); Hedilla Rojas, M. I. in *Historia Internacional*, nos. 11 & 12 (Feb. & Mar. 1976); Hedilla Larrey, M., *Testimonio*, pp. 443-94. The account given by one of the participants, Sancho Dávila, in Dávila, S., *José Antonio, Salamanca . . . y otras cosas* (Madrid: Afrodisio Aguado, 1967) pp. 125-33, is very incomplete. Two other witnesses, Agustin Aznar and Rafael Garcerán, refused to answer questions on the episode.
63. See also, *Fundamentos del Nuevo Estado* (Madrid: Ediciones de la Vice-

Secretaría de Educación Popular, 1943) pp. 11–21 and *El Adalento*, Salamanca (21 Apr. 1937).

64. Manuel Valdés Larrañaga, interviewed 22 Nov. 1977.
65. Jesus Suevos Fernández, interviewed 22 Nov. 1977.
66. Suárez Fernández states that the decision to proceed immediately to the unification of political forces, rather than wait until the war was over, was taken on 11 Apr. 1937 (op. cit. vol. 2, pp. 187–8). That he commented on the idea to Carlist leaders on 12 Apr. is corroborated by García Venero, *HU*, p. 189.
67. Preamble to Decree 255, *Boletin Oficial del Estado* (hereafter, *BOE*) 20 Apr. 1937. Neither the text of the preamble nor that of the Decree nor, as we have indicated in preceding pages, the history of the idea of unification, support Ricardo Chueca's contention that it 'was not the point of arrival of a political process . . . but, more pragmatically, the solution, in the form of a decree, to a problem of "order" within the political ranks of the insurgents' ('FET y de las JONS: la paradójica victoria de un fascismo fracasado' in Fontana J. (ed.), *España bajo el franquismo* (Barcelona: Crítica, 1986) p. 64).
68. 'En torno a una fecha histórica: sentido de la Unificación' in *Arriba*, 19 Apr. 1942.
69. Ibid.
70. Preamble, Decree 255, *BOE*, 20 Apr. 1937.
71. Point 27, which referred to Falange's reluctance to pact with other forces, had been eliminated.
72. *BOE*, 22 Apr. 1937. As we have indicated elsewhere, 'the new party adopted the same hierarchical structure, as *Falange*, with a single, charismatic leader; an executive committee, the *Junta Política*; and a consultative body of party delegates, the National Council' (Ellwood, S. in Blinkhorn, R. M., *Spain in Conflict* (London: Sage Publications, 1986).
73. García Venero, M. *HU*, p. 216. Juan Velarde Fuertes (interviewed 13 June 1978) expressed the view that Hedilla accepted the unification at first, thinking that Franco, as a military man, would delegate all civil power in the party leaders.
74. Hedilla Larrey, *Testimonio*, pp. 529–33. Among the 'acts of mutiny', apparently, was a telegram supposedly sent by Hedilla to Provincial Chiefs of Falange. The text of a telegram shown to this writer by Hedilla's son as the missive in question, reads as follows: '*Generalísimo* orders your possible modifications via supreme command *Falange*. I will severely sanction personal initiatives any *Falange* leader re fusion Decree. Acknowledge receipt urgently. National Chief, Hedilla.' Even if, strictly speaking, Hedilla was no longer 'National Chief', it is difficult to see 'mutiny' in this message.
75. It has always seemed to the present writer that the sentences pronounced at the first Court Martial were disproportionately savage, if the basis of the charges were Hedilla's refusal to form part of the *Junta Política*. Since it is not possible to consult primary sources pertaining to the trial (attempts made by the writer over a period of eight years have been consistently unsuccessful), the accounts given by contemporary writers are the only source available as to what Hedilla was accused of and these are at best,

fragmentary, See e.g. Alcazar de Velasco, A., *La gran fuga*, pp. 29–44; Serrano Suñer, R., *Memorias*, p. 191; García Venero, M., *HU*, p. 221; Ridruejo, D., *Casi unas memorias*, p. 99. From documents apparently belonging to Franco's personal archive, Suárez Fernandez indicates that Hedilla was accused of attempting to raise a Falangist rebellion against Franco (op. cit., vol. 2, pp. 202–3).

76. Ricardo Nieto Serrano, interviewed 15 Mar. 1977.

77. According to Suárez Fernandez – again, on the basis of the 'Archivo Francisco Franco' to which only he has had access – 1459 Falangists were arrested on account of their disagreement with the Unification. This information is not corroborated by any other source known to the present writer (op. cit., vol. 2, p. 198, n. 3).

78. Decree 263, *BOE*, 25 Apr. 1937.

79. Payne, S. G., op. cit., p. 191.

80. SHM, A15/ L2/ C106/ Documents 1 & 2.

81. Raimundo Fernández Cuesta, interviewed 15 July 1977. He was exchanged for Justino Azcárate, brother of Pablo Azcárate, then Republican Ambassador in London. Raimundo Fernández Cuesta gives details of his exchange in *Testimonio recuerdos y reflexiones* (hereafter, *Testimonio*), (Madrid: Ediciones Dyrsa, 1985) pp. 108–9, 117–19.

82. Ibid., see also, Fernández Cuesta, R., *Testimonio*, p. 149–52.

83. As we have noted earlier, the measures taken in 1936 to distribute party militia volunteers throughout the Army would have made a concerted and coordinated action of this nature difficult, but not impossible.

84. It was soon clear, however, that Fernández Cuesta was in favour of total submission of political to military matters. The hopes which some Falangists had pinned on his strengthening the *Falange* within the conglomerate FET y de las JONS proved to be illusory.

85. Serrano Suñer, *Memorias*, p. 260.

Part II
Falange Realised

3 1939–41

Apologista of the *Falange* would argue that the party created in April 1937 had little or nothing to do with the *Falange* founded in October 1933. Clearly, FE differed from FET y de las JONS in so far as the latter did not operate in a context of democratic competition; in that it could not aspire to the absolute control of State power; and in that its mechanisms of recruitment were based on automatic and obligatory, as well as voluntary, membership. However, to consider, on the basis of these factors alone, that the new situation was tantamount to a complete break with the past, is to overestimate the solvent power of the Decree of Unification and to underestimate the degree to which many of the differences which had existed between Right-wing groups before the war were carried over to the post-war period, albeit within a changed social and political framework.[1]

In principle, as we have noted in the preceding chapter, Decree 255 imposed the formal disappearance of all political parties as they had existed prior to 19 April 1937. Nevertheless, their respective militants still felt themselves to be – and, what was perhaps more important, recognised *each other* as being – Falangists, Carlists, Alphonsine monarchists, *CEDistas*, or whatever.[2] Their parties' formal structures had been eliminated, but neither the particular interests nor the convictions of those who had formed them had done a similar 'disappearing act'. On the contrary, they remained alive, if dormant, because although 'their' Army had destroyed the Republic it had not also brought the achievement of their ultimate goals. The monarchy had not been restored, nor had national-syndicalist totalitarianism been implanted. In the Spring of 1936, no one had envisaged that Franco would replace Azaña as head of the Spanish State; yet, in 1939, no one was prepared to unseat him, for fear of the 'reds' returning.[3]

Franco was well aware of the existence of various coteries within his own ranks and, as a soldier above all else, distrusted civilian politicking. At the same time, however, he was also head of a State and of a Government and could not dispense with politics, nor with politicians. The problem of how to make use of their civilian skills without losing control of ultimate power was resolved partly by involving them in the post-war repression (thereby establishing what, in the 1940s, came to be called 'the covenant of blood'[4]); partly by making them the beneficiaries of the post-war spoils system; and partly by employing the tactic of 'divide and rule', playing one group off against another. Ever present, too, were two infallible resorts: the threat of the use of force and the image of the common enemy. As part of this system, the Falangists worked alongside their erstwhile competitors on the Right, in what resembled the National Counter-revolutionary Front they had refused to join in December 1935.

As time went by and the regime adapted itself to changing circumstances within and beyond Spain's geographical frontiers, the Falangists began to complain that their particular representation in the corridors of power was undeservedly small. They were forgetting, however, that it was of the essence of Francoism not to allow any one group to occupy the centre of the stage for too long nor, even less, to hold a monopoly of power. They were also overlooking the fact that, until the defeat of the Axis powers in 1945, it was the Falangist component of FET y de las JONS which was always in the foreground, setting the ideological tone of the New State.[5] Finally, the Falangists who minimised their participation in the Franco regime were limiting their assessment to political power calculated in terms of governmental posts. Thus, they chose to ignore the power reflected in the fact that no other group (with the exception of the Catholic church) was permitted to retain its pre-war structure, title, symbols, lexicon, etc., nor to project them on society as Falange did throughout the Franco regime. That the fluctuations of national and international politics caused the Falangist ideology progressively to become irrelevant to the development of key areas, such as the economy or foreign affairs should not obscure the fact that, in other spheres, the *Falange's* hold remained formally intact until after the Dictator's death in 1975.[6]

In the distribution of fields of operation amongst the forces that had successfully undertaken the destruction of the Republican regime in 1936, it was essentially the socio-political areas which corresponded to the *Falange*. In particular, *Falange* exercised control over the mass of the population through the media, through the trade union organisation and through the vast, bureaucratic structure of the central and local Administration. In addition, the only women's organisation of a non-religious character allowed was Falangist, the *Sección Femenina* (Women's Section) and, although education was primarily the pre-rogative of the Church, *Falange* also inculcated its values in schools, through the teachers who trained in its colleges (*Escuelas de Mando*) and through the texts used in the classroom. Few Spaniards now recall anything of the Carlist of Alphonsine monarchist credos from the days of the Franco regime, but almost everyone over the age of 25 has childhood memories of having to sing the Falangist hymn every morning in school or going to a Falangist summer camp. As late as 1974, a Spanish girl of 18 could expect to do an obligatory period of 'social service' under the auspices and tutelege of the *Sección Femenina*.

Whilst the *Falange* acted in the areas of its control as a vehicle for the power of the Franco regime, it should not be considered that the party was unilaterally instrumentalised by the regime. The relationship was, rather, one of mutual support and benefit. In the same way that, in return for political inhibition or para-military services, the pre-war *Falange* had continuously sought the patronage or numerical strength of forces outside its own ranks, it now accepted the patronage of the Franco regime in return for an active contribution to the latter's consolidation and perpetuation. Contrary to what present-day Falangists affirm, the Falange was not an innocent and helpless bystander to the 'usurpation' of its symbols, style and ideals. Falange had been on the verge of disappearing in February 1936. Its adoption as the ideological basis of the Franco regime guaranteed that it would never again be without finance or militants.

The money was provided by the State budget. A large part of the membership was formed by State employees – such as Army officers, civil servants, trade union officials and the staff of the many ramifications of the party secretariat – for whom, under the terms of the Statutes of FET y de las JONS, party membership was an automatic and/or obligatory attribute of their posts. A prominent Falangist, Dionisio Ridruejo, wrote with respect to this form of recruitment, "One was not a political official (*funcionario político*) because one was a party militant, but *vice versa*."[7] It should be noted, however, that his comment is that of the renegade whose critical view of the regime stemmed from its failure to be more specifically Falangist in content and form. The imposed identification between party membership and power élite was a way of avoiding the excessive protagonism of any one group, as it was also a means of limiting the destabilising effect of possible conflicts between them. Looked at from a different angle, the fact that anyone who held an official post had to swear fidelity to the "26 Points of *Falange*", was a mechanism which ensured the control and discipline of the political class; a ritual in which it was made clear that ultimate power lay only at the top of the hierarchical pyramid and that the first duty of the underlings was obedience.[8]

As part of the attempt to disown their participation in the Franco regime, Falangists argue that this artificial increase in members, like the February 1936 influx, debased *Falange's* ideological purity. Yet, as we have indicated in preceding chapters, the *Falange's* history was liberally punctuated with occasions on which 'ideological purity' had been sacrificed for the sake of survival. Moreover, whilst many of those who received a party card may not have been convinced Falangists, their willingness to swell the party ranks, however passively, was the reverse side of their *un*willingness to question the whole system of which FET y de las JONS was part, lending it and the regime the weight of acquiescence which helped both to survive for almost forty years.

FET y de las JONS was not, however, entirely composed of those who passively accecpted automatic militancy. It also contained a considerable number of voluntary members. Some of these were people who found themselves without any alternative channel for their desire to be politically active.[9] Others were those who joined the party genuinely motivated by political conviction.

Consequent with its decision to support the military rising in July 1936, the *Falange* continued consciously to render its services both when the *coup* turned to war and after the war, not because it was 'deceived' into doing so, but because its interests and beliefs demanded that it should. As long as there existed any vestige of Marxist internationalism in Spain, any possibility, however remote, of Left-wing ideas walking abroad, the *Falange* would support the forces opposing such currents. That the balance of power among those forces lay in Franco's hands, not in those of the party, meant the frustation of *Falange's* supreme ambitions, but it did not mean that its basic, impelling credo, nor the class interests from which it arose, were altered.

The Franco regime was the result of a rising driven by the desire of a property-owning oligarchy to eliminate what it saw as the threat to its interests represented by a politically conscious and organised working class. The nature of the system created to replace class-based trade unions for the organisation and control of the working masses is therefore closely linked to that of the regime itself. Officially designated as the master of the official trade union organisation, it was in this area that the *Falange* identified itself most closely with the aims and interests of the regime.[10]

Although not formally created until January 1938, the Francoist trade union organisation had its origins in the first days of the Civil War. Decree 108, of 13 September 1936, issued before Franco's appointment as head of State, declared illegal, all parties and political and social groups which, since the announcement of the elections held on 16 February of this year, have participated in the so-called Popular Front. Likewise, all organisations which have taken part in the opposition to the forces which cooperate in the National Movement.[11]

The express application of this Decree, in January 1937, to the CNT, UGT, STV, and 'all other entities, groups, affiliated parties or groups analogous to those indicated',[12] left the Falangist *Central Obrera Nacional Sindicalista* (CONS) (Workers' National Syndicalist Union) as the only trade union organisation in legal existence. A second Decree, issued on 25 September 1936, stated that, for the duration of hostilities, 'all political activities' were prohibited, although

professional guilds may be formed, subject exclusively to the authority of this National Defence Committee and its delegates.[13]

Under the provisions of this Decree, and in response to the existence of the CONS, a similar body was created for employers: the *Central de Empresarios Nacional Sindicalista* (CENS) (Employers' National Syndicalist Union). With priority being given to the war effort, however, neither of these organisms as separate entities was developed further than their existence on paper.

The publication of the Party Statutes in August 1937 gave a clear indication as to what would be the form of the trade union system in the post-war State. In particular, the essential role to be played by Party militants was explicitly stated:

FET y de las JONS will create and maintain the syndical structures appropriate to the organisation of labour and production, and to the distribution of goods. The leaders (*"mandos"*) of these organisations shall proceed from the ranks of the Movement and the organisations shall be formed and guided by their leaders as a guarantee that the Syndical Organisation will be subordinated to the national interest and imbued with the ideals of the State. . . . The National Leadership of the Syndicates shall be conferred on a single militant and their internal structure shall be graduated in a vertical hierarchy, in the manner of a creative, just and ordered Army.[14]

Thus, the crusading spirit of the war, and of the Falangist militant in his double role of 'half monk, half soldier', was to be carried over to peace-time and imposed on the organisation of civilian society.

With the formation of the 1938 Cabinet and the subsequent Law of State Administration,[15] the Ministry of Syndical Organisation and Action came into being, directed, as we have noted, by the Falangist Pedro Gonzalez Bueno. The Ministry was divided into five departments (or 'Services'): Syndicates, Labour jurisdiction, Housing, Statistics and Emigration. Between them, they were responsible for dictating the 'norms of organisation, functioning and action of the Syndicates in the economic and social order'.

One of the first tasks of this Government was the elaboration of the Labour Charter (*Fuero de Trabajo*). The importance of this piece of legislation cannot be overestimated, for it constituted the basis of all subsequent labour legislation during the Franco regime and, in particular, the basis for the organisation of the official trade union system, the only one permitted until the death of Franco in 1975. This wide-ranging Decree encapsulates, perhaps better than any other Francoist law, the contribution of the *Falange* at a critical moment in the formation of the regime and precisely in one of its most sensitive areas: the economic organisation and socio-political control of the working classes.[16]

Two projects were drawn up. The first was prepared by the Minister, González Bueno, and a group of technical experts. It was rejected by the Cabinet and strongly contested by the Party's National Council. The second project was drafted by Dionisio Ridruejo and the members of a 'kind of technical office or study committee', set up by the Secretary General of the Party, Raimundo Fernández Cuesta. It was also rejected, in this case on the grounds that it was too radical and excessively influenced by national-syndicalist ideas. On the suggestion of Ramón Serrano Suñer, the crisis threatened by this confrontation between the more conservative and the more revolutionary elements of the Cabinet was resolved by shelving both projects and drawing up instead, in collaboration, a declaration of general principles, rather than a concrete socio-political programme.[17] The resulting *Fuero*, which came into being on 9 March 1938, was a compromise measure and had almost an air of provisionality about it. Nevertheless, it was given the status of Fundamental Law of the State. The radical Falangists were not content with the document, but accepted it in the hope that, once the war was over, they might be able to impose changes more in line with their totalitarian concepts. The process of the elaboration of the *Fuero del Trabajo* is a good example of the balance continually maintained between the various political currents present in the regime, in the interest of the stability beneficial to all. The Falangists had not been allowed to elaborate the *Fuero* alone, but the final text, reiterating the Statutes of FET y de las JONS, explicitly stated that 'the hierarchy of each syndicate will necessarily be staffed by militants of *Falange Española Tradicionalista de las JONS*'.[18] In practice, the organisation and administration of the trade union movement of the New State was the preserve of the Falangist component of the party, to an almost exclusive degree that does not appear ever to have been questioned by any of its other components.[19]

In addition, the text incorporated much of the Falangist lexicon and tenets. Indeed, the very notion of a State whose economic and social organisation was to be based on State-run, lay, non-class based, obligatory unions of workers and employers was essentially Falangist, differentiated from the corporativist ideas of other components of the Movement – former members of the CEDA or *Acción Española*, for example – by its laicism and the absence of any monarchical context. The definition of the State given in the preamble to the *Fuero* clearly owes more to Ramiro Ledesma Ramos than to Catholic nationalists such as Gil Robles or José Calvo Sotelo, or to Carlists like Victor Pradera:

National, in so far as it is a totalitarian instrument at the service of the integrity of the Fatherland, and Syndicalist, in so far as it represents a reaction against liberal capitalism and marxist materialism.[20]

A month after the publication of the *Fuero del Trabajo*, by a Decree of 21 April 1938, the hitherto separate workers' and employers' unions, CONS and CENS, were merged into a single body, to be known as the *Central Nacional Sindicalista* (CNS) (National Syndicalist Centre). Such professional organisations as the Catholic *Confederación Nacional de Sindicatos Católicos Obreros* (National Confederation of Workers' Catholic Unions), not previously declared illegal, were now also incorporated into the CNS.[21] Through this body, which gave physical expression to Ledesma Ramos' idea of a country organised as 'a huge union of producers . . . ordered as militias', and which subsequently grew into a vast bureaucracy with ramifications all over Spain, *Falange* was to exercise its official monopoly over the entire working population. This was a far cry from only five years earlier, when the CONS organised by Ledesma had virtually collapsed for lack of members and funds.

Whilst the Party's energies were partially absorbed in laying the foundations of the future trade union system, and in spite of the fact that the continuation of the war imposed the need for unity in the nationalist camp, latent animosity between Falangists and Alphonsine Monarchists came to the surface in a governmental crisis in June 1938. As in April 1937, the crisis was resolved via the imposition of Franco's personal authority and, also as in 1937, the Falangists not only accepted this solution, but accepted it at the political expense of some of their own comrades.

With the object of restructuring the Party, the *Consejo Nacional* had designed a Study Commission headed by Falangists Dionisio Ridruejo and Pedro Gamero del Castillo, and Carlist Juan José Pradera. The proposals put forward by the Commission were aimed at increasing the power of the Party within the State and also suggested that the Falangist militia be made autonomous. They encountered strong opposition from other members of the *Junta Política*, particularly from the Alphonsine Monarchist Minister of Education, Pedro Sainz Rodríguez, on the grounds that what was being proposed was the establishment of a totalitarian State. Ridruejo replied that, indeed, such was precisely the intention. Franco, presiding over the meeting in which this confrontation occurred, accused Ridruejo of lack of confidence in his leadership. To this, Ridruejo replied that, on the contrary, in seeking to strengthen the role of the *Falange*, whose National Chief was Franco, the proposed restructuring also sought to strengthen Franco's position. It was an agile reply and sufficient to save Ridruejo from any reprimand more serious than the rejection of his proposals, but Franco was not the man to tolerate any kind of rebelliousness within the ranks of his followers and almost certainly took note of Ridruejo as a discordant element.

The affair also had immediate repercussions for other members of the *Falange*, for it had sensitised Franco to possible sources of disloyalty within the Party. On 23 and 25 June 1938, two other members of the National Council, Agustín Aznar and Fernando González Vélez respectively, were arrested on suspicion of preparing a plot against Franco.[22] Falangist Narciso Perales, who, since February 1938, had been working in Granada under the direction of the party Secretary, Fernández Cuesta, was also implicated. He had organised a public meeting in Córdoba, which was attended by, among others, Aznar and González Vélez. Through them, news leaked out of what had occurred in the *Junta Política* meeting a few days earlier. They were arrested shortly after the Córdoba gathering. Nothing was proved against them but, as in 1937 with Manuel Hedilla, Franco's decision to exercise his authority went unquestioned by the rest of the *Falange*. Perales asked to be relieved of his duties as Extraordinary Delegate in Granada, not so much in solidarity with Aznar and González as in dissent from Fernández Cuesta, who maintained that the moment was not propitious for putting the *Falange's* original programme into practice. Perales transferred first to Málaga, in order to avoid arousing Franco's suspicions again, then joined the battle-front at Teruel in July 1938.[23] His was the only gesture of protest, limited as it was.

Similarly, the *Falange* did not object when, on 16 November 1938, the regime appropriated the date of the death of José Antonio Primo de Rivera, declaring it an annual day of national mourning. By that time, the end of the war was thought to be imminent and a Francoist victory assured. It would not have been politic to risk losing post-war rewards for the stake of one day a year.

Falangist hopes of increasing their stake in the governmental apparatus were realised when the war ended in 1939. The reorganisation and expansion of the Cabinet and central Administration carried out in August of that year reflected not only the need to develop governmental structures no longer conditioned by the necessities of war, but also the desire to give the impression of a regime in harmony with those of fascist Europe.

A considerable contingent of *camaradas* was added to those Falangists already occupying ministerial posts. They were given posts of lower hierarchical category but which, nevertheless, were important for the possibilities they afforded of manipulating people and re-sources. Pedro Gamero del Castillo was appointed Minister without Portfolio and Vice-secretary General of the Party; Rafael Sánchez Mazas was also made Minister without Portfolio; José María Alfaro became Under-Secretary for Press and Propaganda and member of the *Junta Política*; Miguel Primo de Rivera was appointed Provincial Chief of the Movement for Madrid and member of the *Junta Política*; and Manuel Valdés Larrañaga became Under-Secretary for Labour. General Agustín Muñoz Grandes, who was not a Party militant but was known to have strong Falangist sympathies, replaced Raimundo Fernández Cuesta as Secretary General of the party.[24] Ramón Serrano Suñer took over from Pedro González Bueno as President of the *Junta Política*.

This last appointment may appear to have been disadvantageous to the *Falange*, since Serrano had never been a member of the party founded by Primo de Rivera in 1933. It was, however, at the height of Serrano's political career that the *Falange* too was at the height of its visible power and through his presence that FE seemed to have most possibilities of promoting its men and its ideology within the conglomerate Movement. Precisely that attempt made an important contribution to Serrano's ultimate downfall.

Shortly after the August Cabinet changes, in September 1939, the first National Head (*Delegado Nacional*) of the Syndical Organisation was appointed. The post was assigned to Falangist Gerado Salvador Merino. Merino had been *Falange* chief in the province of La Coruña and was, according to his colleague and personal friend, Pedro Gamero del Castillo, 'well situated politically, in so far as his relations with Ramón Serrano Suñer were good'.[25] As head of the CNS, which was a department of the Party Secretariat, Merino collaborated with Party Vicesecretary Gamero in the elaboration of a Law which determined 'the mode of incorporation of extant economic and professional bodies into the Syndical Organisation'[26] and laid down that,

> the Syndical Organisation of FET y de las JONS is the only one recognised by the State – which will admit the existence of no other with similar or analogous aims – as having personality sufficient to bring to the State the needs and aspirations which, in the socio-economic order, may be felt by the producers of the nation and is, at the same time, the vehicle whereby the economic directives of the State reach the producers.[27]

The Law proposed to unite workers, technicians and entrepreneurs in a single, 'classless' organisation divided only according to sectors of production, not according to ideological or social differences. Gamero states that the fundamental aim of the project was

> to cement at the social level the healing of the wound, caused by the Civil War, being worked at the intellectual level by such enterprises as the magazine *Escorial*, in which people of very different opinions participated.[28]

This altruistic view should not obscure the reality that the reason for setting up a trade union organisation at all was that, through it, the greater part of the populace could be controlled in an area of prime importance: its working life.

It has been maintained that Merino's Falangist radicalism as Syndical Delegate and, especially, his capacity and opportunities for organising the workers *en masse* alarmed conservative and military elements in the Government.[29] In effect, the Law of Syndical Unity aimed at increasing the weight of the trade union system at political, as well as socio-economic levels and at strengthening the exclusive character of the *Falange's* control thereof. Certainly, too, the large contingent of well-drilled, blue-shirted 'producers'[30] who took part, for example, in the Victory Day parade in Madrid on 30 March 1940 could, as representatives of the different *Sindicatos*, be considered Merino's men. As such, it is possible that those who were hostile to the creation of trades unions were also made uneasy by the sight of large numbers of civilian 'recruits' behaving in such military fashion. Both suggested the resurgence of an organised working class, this time under the direction of the *Falange*. Franco, however, had no such fears. On the contrary, says Gamero del Castillo, he liked the workers' parades, for they represented a popular claque for his leadership.[31] Furthermore, if the first post-war manifestation of genuine worker feeling had appeared in a down-tools in Barcelona in 1940, the repressive apparatus was more than equal to the task of restoring order.[32]

In fact, Merino had aroused the hostility of certain members of his own party, who based their objections to men like himself or Gamero del Castillo on the contention that, as people who had joined *Falange* after 1936 ('New Shirts'), they could not be the legitimate interpreters of the Falangist ideology. This was the view of *Falange* 'legitimists' such as Pilar and Miguel Primo de Rivera, Sancho Dávila, Agustín Aznar and José Antonio Girón. In reality they were anxious to oust the likes of Merino in so far as he was a rival for positions of social, economic and political power to which they themselves aspired. Merino was denounced[33] as a former member of a Masonic Lodge – a far more powerful weapon against him than nebulous accusations of Falangist revisionism. As a result, Merino was dismissed from his post in the CNS and exiled to the Balearic Isles, in July 1941.

The demise of Merino was part of a dismantling operation carried out on the group around Serrano Suñer, whose star began to decline in 1941. Some of those Falangists (the 'legitimists') who, since the time of the Unification, had relied on Serrano as their only 'real link between the authority of Franco . . . and the aspirations of the Falangists',[34] became disillusioned or impatient with their intermediary and began to seek ways of dealing directly with the *Caudillo*. At the same time, encouraged by such 'Old Shirt' Falangists as Party Secretary José Luis Arrese Magra and those conservative and military elements within the regime who felt no affection for *Falange*, Franco began to doubt the loyalty of a man who 'took upon himself the representation of a collective will, that of the *Falange*, different to his own personal will'.[35] Any manifestation of independent or spontaneous activity was liable to arouse the *Generalísimo's* mistrust and, by 1941, it was beginning to seem to him that Serrano Suñer and his collaborators were trying to force the pace of post-war reconstruction too fast. Gamero del Castillo quotes four, rapidly-succeeding events in this connection: the creation of *Escorial*; the foundation of the Institute of Political Studies; the Law of Syndical Unity; and the Law of the University Students' Union (SEU).[36] All of these were, in fact, initiatives in favour of the regime, designed not to replace Franco, but to broaden the socio-political foundations on which the military victory rested. Franco, however, saw in them an excessive desire to promote the *Falange* and, therefore, a potential threat to his hegemony. Serrano Suñer was seen as the prime mover of that threat.

Consequently, when a series of Cabinet changes were made in May 1941, the *Falange* 'legitimists' gained ground at the expense of Serrano. The latter, who had also been appointed Minister of Foreign Affairs in October 1940, was replaced in the Ministry of the Interior by Valentín Galarza, considered extremely anti-Falangist. The appointment, for once, caused a furore among the Falangists. The publication of an anonymous article (later attributed to Dionisio Ridruejo), entitled 'The Man and the Pipsqueak', in defence of Serrano Suñer, provoked a reply in the 12 May 1941 edition of the national daily, *Madrid*, which claimed that the Falangists were 'incompatible' with the new Minister. The Falangists responsible for Press and Propaganda, Ridruejo (then Director of Propaganda), Antonio Tovar (Under-Secretary for Falangist Press) and Jesus Ercilla (Director General of Press), were dismissed from their posts and Miguel Primo de Rivera resigned as Civil Governor and Party Chief of Madrid, as did Arrese, then Civil Governor in Málaga.

Serrano Suñer, thinking it his duty to show solidarity with what appeared to be a token of protest from the 'legitimist' group with which he had actively sympathised since 1937, also submitted his resignation to Franco. The *Generalísimo* refused to accept it and Serrano would have insisted, had he not learned that three of the Falangists whose position he was defending were about to accept Ministerial posts. In effect, Miguel Primo de Rivera was appointed Minister of Agriculture; Girón, minister of Labour; and Arrese, Minister Secretary General of the Party.[37] In addition, Agustín Aznar, rehabilitated after his political pecadilloes of 1938, was appointed as the Party's National Delegate for Health, whilst, in October 1941, veteran *JONSista*, Juan Aparicio, took over as Director General of Press.[38]

Serrano Suñer remained in his posts as Minister of Foreign Affairs and President of the *Junta Política* for over a year after this episode, but the damage was done, in that he had revealed his hand and part of his erstwhile support had gone over to the highest bidder – Franco. With the incorporation of Girón, Arrese, Primo de Rivera and Aznar into the official rewards system, success was assured for the absorption process initiated in December 1936, with the militarisation of the *Falange* militias, and made irreversible by the 1937 Decree of Unification.

Up to 1943, continuing Axis victories in the Second World War favoured the consolidation of the mutually beneficial links between the Party and the personal power of the *Caudillo*. The former sought to extend its influence at the expense of other elements in the Movement, whilst the latter sought to consolidate his somewhat isolated position via the international connections of *Falange*, via the Party's ability to provide an entourage of loyal and grateful followers, and via its coercive and cooptive roles with respect to the mass of the population.

In this context and, perhaps, in the wake of the Merino affair, on 24 November 1941, the Minister Secretary General of the Party, José Luis Arrese, ordered a Party purge to be initiated. No new admissions were to be made for six months, except from the Party youth organisation, the *Frente de Juventudes* (Youth Front). Expulsions were to be made on a national scale for a variety of social, political or moral reasons and for having passed from 'militant' to merely 'supporter' status. The criteria according to which expulsions would be made were numerous: former Masons, communists and anarchists; former officials or sympathisers of the Popular Front; former supporters of separatist movements; anyone who had 'attempted to prevent the success of the Movement'; anyone considered, publicly or privately, 'immoral'; members of pre-Unification political groups attempting to revive the same; anyone considered to have scoffed at, or ridiculed, the Catholic faith; and anyone judged guilty of crimes 'incompatible' with Party principles.[39] Such were the guide-lines of a witch-hunt of which almost anyone might fall foul and whose double objective was not increased efficiency or 'energetic social action', but simply the reactionary elimination of radicals within the ranks and the increase of pro-Francoist fervour.[40]

The purge, organised by one of the departments of the Party

Secretariat, the National Delegation of Information and Investigation, was financed and executed by a body set up for the purpose, the Inspectorate of Purges (*Inspección de Depuración*).[41] The public explanations given maintained that it was essential to the 'dignity and confidence' due to the Party, especially in the circumstance of international war, and in preparation against 'everything which, out of the present external conflagration, might turn into an obstacle for the existence and development of the national-syndicalist Movement'.[42] In similar vein, the Party's Provincial Chief for Madrid, Carlos Ruiz, told militants at a meeting called in Madrid on 26 November 1941 that the purge was necessary to 'quell external criticism of the doctrine and integrity of the Party'.[43]

From the point of view of the national context, Party leaders expressed their support for the purge in the interests of 'unity, hierarchy and discipline',[44] and exhorted unquestioning obedience to 'the leadership, or whomsoever the leader might designate,[45] by, which, of course, they referred to themselves. The Falangist Press also made its contribution to the campaign in support of the purge. Thus, *Arriba* referred to it as the guarantee given by *Falange* itself that the task entrusted to it would be carried out with the utmost seriousness,[46] whilst *El Alcazar* linked it to the desirability of close collaboration between the *Falange* and the Armed Forces. These, it continued, together with the *Caudillo*, constituted the foundations of 'the security and expectations of Spain'.[47] The object of cleansing Party cadres, added *El Alcazar*, was to guarantee the inclusion of *Falange* in the trinity which, in 'brotherhood, harmony and solidarity' would provide and preside Spain's prosperous future.[48] Only five years earlier, José Antonio Primo de Rivera had warned against the risks inherent in subscribing to the 'political plans of the military men'.[49] Yet, now, the *Falange* had assumed precisely the status which Primo de Rivera had then rejected, that of 'auxilliary shock troops', 'the chorus', for the real holders of power, the Armed Forces. Far from finding this role offensive as Primo had urged, the Falangist leaders in 1942 were anxious to consolidate it.[50]

Notes

1. The argument that the 'real' *Falange* died in 1937 was frequently used by Falangists anxious to dissociate themselves from the Franco regime as a prior step to finding a place in the transition to post-Francoist democracy.

2. The various 'families' identified by sociologist Amando de Miguel as the socio-political components of the Franco regime have their origins in the pre-war parties (*La herencia del Franquismo*, Cambio 16, Madrid 1976).

3. Cf. Escobar y Kirkpatrick, I. *Testimonio sobre una gran traición*, typewritten pamphlet, undated (1978?): 'None of us who supported the 18 July rising thought the end result would be a personal régime headed by Franco'; and R. Salas Larrazabal, interviewed in Salamanca, 1 August 1984: 'even the dissatisfied preferred Franco to the "reds".'

4. Carr, R. & Fusi, J.P., *España, de la dictadura a la democracia* (Barcelona: Planeta, 1979) p. 30.

5. Cf. Jerez Mir, M., *Elites políticas y centros de extracción en España* (Madrid: Centro de Investigaciones Sociológicas, 1982) pp. 49–175. A comparison of the most important pieces of early Francoist legislation with texts such as the writings of Primo de Rivera or the '27 Doctrinal Points' indicates that many of the concepts and much of the vocabulary of the former were culled from Falangist sources.

6. In practice, and particularly from the 1960s onwards, it was increasingly questioned and by-passed, by social and political groups outside and inside the regime. The alternatives they advocated, however, were illegal. Legality was constituted by the system which began to be established in 1937 and which was not entirely dismantled until the first democratic elections were held in 1977.

7. Ridruejo, D. quoted in Ros Hombravella *et al.*, *Capitalismo español: de la autarquía a la establización* (Madrid: Edicusa, 1978) p. 77.

8. As time went by, this requirement became little more than a formality. In the foundational years of the regime, however, it had a very real sense. Access to the ranks of a uniformed élite constituted immediate public recognition of being on the 'right' side – by no means unimportant at a time when the 'crusade' against anything and everything outside the regime was far from over.

9. A former Falangist (and, subsequently, member and ex-member of the Spanish Communist party) commented to the writer, with respect to his joining the Falange in the 1950s: 'What else could you do? If you had any urge to participate in politics, you had no other way to do so other than by joining the Falange – in much the same way that, later, if you wanted to be part of the anti-Francoist opposition, you had to join the PCE. There was nothing else.'

10. Cf. Velarde Fuertes, J., interviewed 13 June 1978: 'In the Franco regime, the *Falange* can be seen particularly in the social and labour policies applied from the Ministry of Labour and the Syndical Organisation.' For a monographical study of the Francoist trade union system, see Aparicio, M.A., *El sindicalismo vertical en la formación del Estado franquista* (Barcelona: Eunibar S.A., 1980) *passim*.

11. Decree 108, *BOE*, 16 Sept. 1936.

12. Order of 10 Jan. 1937, *BOE*, 13 Jan. 1937.

13. *BOE*, 28 Sept. 1936. The National Defence Committee (*Junta Nacional de Defensa*) was formed on 25 July 1936.

14. Ibid., 7 Aug. 1937. *Estatutos de FET y de las JONS*, Articles 29 & 30.

15. Ibid., 31 Jan. 1938. Ley de Administración del Estado.

16. According to the Syndical Organisation itself, it constituted the 'basic norms of all the dispositions which subsequently shaped our syndicalism'; quoted in Oficina Internacional del Trabajo, *La situación laboral y sindical en España* (Geneva 1969) p. 127.

17. Serrano Suñer, R., *Siete discursos* (Bilbao: Ediciones 'FE', 1940) p. 25; Ridruejo, D., *Casi unas Memorias*, p. 195. See also: Mayor Martínez, L., *Ideologías dominantes en el sindicato vertical* (Madrid: Editorial Zero, 1972) p. 111; Aparicio, M.A., op. cit., pp. 79–83 & 108–10 and 'Aspectos políticos del sindicalismo español de posguerra' in *Sistema*, no. 13 (Apr. 1976).

18. *Fuero del Trabajo*, Declaration XIII, 'National Syndicalist Organisation', Point 4, *BOE* (10 Mar. 1938)

19. This is not to say that they did not, on occasions, question the line followed by particular Falangists within the trade union system. See below, p. 67.

20. Preamble to the *Fuero del Trabajo*, *BOE*, 10 Mar. 1938.

21. *BOE*, 24 Apr. 1938. For details of the structure and functioning of the CNS at national and provincial levels, see Iglesias Selgas, C., *El sindicalismo español* (Madrid: Doncel, 1974) pp. 9–20 & 45–6; Oficina International del Trabajo, op. cit., pp. 129–30; Legaz Lacambra, L. and Gómez Aragón, B., *4 estudios sobre sindicalismo vertical* (Zaragoza, 1939); Ludevid, M., *40 años de sindicato vertical* (Barcelona: Editorial Laia, 1976).

22. Ridruejo, D., *Casi unas memorias*, p. 127. Aznar had been relieved of his post as Chief of the Party militias, but was organising militants in 'work units', which were considered highly suspiciously non-Falangists.

23. Narciso Perales Herrero, interview 31 Dec. 1976.

24. Narciso Perales states (interview 31 Dec. 1976) that he was in close personal contact with Muñoz Grandes during the forties and that he was 'an austere, mature man, who could have taken over from Franco. But, above all, he was a professional soldier and could not, therefore, participate actively in politics. Despite his agreement with the Falangist theses, his professionalism, his sense of discipline and hierarchy, prevented him from being *actively* in agreement. Hence the fact that, although he maintained relations with members of *Falange*, he could never commit himself to acting alongside *Falange* and not alongside Franco'. As far as is known, the General never found himself obliged to choose between the two.

25. Pedro Gamero del Castillo, interview, 4 Mar. 1978.

26. From Declaration XIII, Point 9, *Fuero del Trabajo*, *BOE*, 10 Mar. 1938.

27. Law of Syndical Unity, *BOE*, 31 Jan. 1940.

28. Pedro Gamero del Castillo, interview, 4 Mar. 1978. The 'Editorial Manifesto' of the magazine, whose Editor was Dionisio Ridruejo, and which first appeared in November 1940, stated that it was not 'a propaganda magazine, but honorably and sincerely a professional magazine devoted to culture and letters'. Nevertheless, its political character was also clear: 'the *Falange* has for a long time been interested in creating a magazine which might be the meeting place and viewing point of Spanish intellectuals . . .' and which would 'offer to the Spanish Revolution and to its

mission in the world, one more arm and one more vehicle, be it modest or valuable'.

29. Payne, S.G., op. cit., p. 220.
30. It is probable that not all of the participants were genuinely 'workers', except in the sense that, in accordance with the Falangist division of the active population into employers, technicians and workers, anyone who did not fall into either of the first two categories automatically fell into the third. Thus students could be paraded as 'producers'. The authenticity or otherwise of the characterisation, however, was not what concerned some observers. What mattered was that here was a show of organised force, potentially at Falangist command.
31. Gamero del Castillo, loc. cit.
32. Serious incidents also occurred in Cádiz in 1941, Mataró (Barcelona) in 1942 and Valencia in 1944. Cf. Barba, B., *Dos años al frente del Gobierno Civil de Barcelona* (Madrid, 1948); Ferri, L. *et al.*, *Las huelgas contra Franco* (Planeta, Barna., 1978).
33. According to Falangist Narciso Perales (interview, 24 Dec. 1976) and ex-Falangist Ceferino Maestu (interview, 14 Dec. 1977), Merino was denounced by a Falangist comrade, although neither was willing to disclose the name of the person concerned.
34. Serrano Suñer, R., *Memorias*, p. 197.
35. Ibid., p. 201. Arrese was appointed to the post, which had been vacant since Nov. 1940, in May 1941 (see below, pp. 68–9).
36. This represented the realisation of a project conceived in 1934, whereby three student organisations (SEU, FEC and AET) would be amalgamated. The opposition of the Traditionalist AET frustrated the plan in 1934, but it was revived in 1940–41 and culminated in the Law which made the Falangist SEU (*Sindicato Español Universitario*) the only, and obligatory, union of students.
37. Serrano Suñer, R., *Memorias*, pp. 200–1; *Arriba* (8 May 1941); *Madrid* (12 May 1941); Narciso Perales, interview, 31 Dec. 1976.
38. By that time, this Department had been taken out of the Ministry of the Interior and transferred to the Vice-Secretariat of Popular Education, in turn part of the General Secretariat of FET y de las JONS.
39. *El Alcazar* (Madrid, 25 Nov. 1941).
40. Cf. Ridruejo, D., *Escrito en España* (Buenos Aires: Editorial Losada, 1962) p. 87: 'It was a measure of adaptation to the general criteria, with a view to pacific enjoyment of privileged positions which the mistrust of other political powers might place in jeopardy'.
41. Ibid. The National Delegation of Information and Investigation carried out intelligence services parallel to those of the Police Forces and was, thus, part of the regime's repressive apparatus. A report published by the department itself in 1941 stated that it then had 693 agents, and that during 1941, it had provided 570 000 reports 'for the Party and State organisms' and had approximately 6 000 000 references in its files (*Arriba*, 8 May 1942).
42. *El Alcazar*, 25 Nov. 1941.
43. Ibid., 27 Nov. 1941.

44. The Civil Governor and Party Provincial Chief of Sevilla, at a meeting of Old Guard Falangists in Sevilla on 18 Jan. 1942 (*Arriba*, 19 Jan. 1942).
45. Miguel Primo de Rivera, ibid.
46. Editorial, *Arriba* (5 Jan. 1942). See also editions of 3 and 8 Jan. 1942.
47. *El Alcazar* (8 Dec. 1941).
48. Ibid.
49. Primo de Rivera, J.A., 'Circular to all Territorial and Provincial Chiefs' (24 June 1936), in *Obras Completas*, pp. 970–1.
50. Up to the end of the purge in June 1945, some 4000 militants were expelled from the party. Admissions recommenced in Nov. 1943, however, and, by that same date (June 1945) about 3000 new members had been admitted (*Boletín Oficial del Movimento*, 1942–45).

4 1941–43

It was not only in the upper echelons of the body politic that the *Falange*, more than any other political group, made its presence felt. In the years in which the New State was being established on the basis of the Falangist ideology and through the channels of the Party apparatus, the *Falange* permeated every level of day-to-day existence.

It appeared in the provincial tours of Ministers and Party officials, not to mention those of Franco himself; in the mass gatherings and parades of 'producers' who turned out to listen to the VIPs; and in the Movement Press which provided lengthy and graphic reports of these events. Thus, in 1942 alone, the national dailies *Arriba* and *El Alcazar* and, where appropriate, the provincial Press, reported in eulogistic terms on no less than fourteen major tours or gatherings and innumerable minor Party meetings and celebrationas throughout the country. Of the former, the most important was Franco's visit to Cataluña from 26 to 30 January 1942, accompanied by Secretary General Arrese and the Minister of Defence, General Varela, during which Franco watched a parade of 400 000 workers from the balcony of the CNS in Barcelona, wearing the uniform of the National Chief of the *Falange*.[1] Other important events were the 1942 Victory Day parade in Madrid, presided over by Franco, the Cabinet and a numerous contingent of Party officials;[2] the parade of 60 000 workers arranged in Madrid by the Syndical Organisation to commemorate the rising of 18 July 1936;[3] and the two 'massive Falangist demonstrations' watched by Franco and Arrese in Vigo and La Coruña in August 1942.[4] Also worthy of ample coverage were the open-air meetings organised to commemorate the death of the first Falangist 'martyr', Matías Montero, in February 1934;[5] or the fusion of *Falange* and JONS in January 1934;[6] a three-day visit by the Minister of Labour, Girón, to the Basque Country, where he addressed numerous gatherings on the shop-floor;[7] or the same Minister's tour of Andalucía where, among other events, he presided at a parade of 20 000 miners in Jaen.[8]

Then there were the *Falange's* symbols (five arrows joined horizontally by a yoke) at the entrance and exit to every town and village, large or small; the heads of Franco and Primo de Rivera stencilled on the walls, along with the *Falange* slogan '¡Arriba España!'; the local premises of 'Social Aid', the Women's Section, the Syndical Organisation and the Party, *proprement dit*. There was the national ritual of the annual commemoration of the death of José Antonio Primo de Rivera, like that of 1941, when a mass of 28 000 marched from Madrid to El Escorial (some 60 km), to lay a wreath on the tomb of *Falange's* founder;[9] and there were the plaques and street names commemorating the lives or deaths of other Party heroes. There were the magazines and books; the Youth Front meetings, outings and summer camps;[10] the Falangist 'consultancies' set up in working-class districts, like Madrid's Vallecas;[11] the campaigns for the collection of waste paper organised by the Women's Section; and the Party representatives in every block of flats, every group of blocks and every suburb.[12] No other political current was permitted this massive and continual propagandistic 'bombardment' of the populace, such that what Primo de Rivera had described in 1933 as the essence of *Falange* had, with the *Falange's* connivance, become a reality: 'our movement is not only a way of thinking, it is a way of being'.[13]

Falangists may maintain, now that Franco is no more, that, in all this, their power was more apparent than real. For the mass of the contemporary population, however, it was very apparent indeed and constituted their reality. The *Falange* had hoisted itself on to the bandwaggon of post-war opportunism, its hopes kindled by promises like that made by the *Caudillo* during his visit to Cataluña in January 1942. Addressing a reception given by the 'Social Service of Higher Economic Culture' (*Servicio Social de Alta Cultura Económica*) in Barcelona, he said:

> We have said (that civilian life will run along the path traced by *Falange*) as an indispensible premise for the administrative organisation of the Nation, so that the feeling and the heat of the producing classes and other national sectors may reach us through hierarchical and specialised channels. . . . You have a channel and a way (to make your initiative, your complaint or your advice reach the State): the Syndical channel, the Syndical hierarchy. . . . No one and nothing will divert us from these directives. The watchword has been given to the Nation: civilian life is going to flow through the organisation of the *Falange*, with its syndicates, its CNS, and with all the activities it is in charge of organising.[14]

The Party organ, *Arriba*, triumphantly interpreted the speech as stating 'loudly, clearly, and unequivocally, the guarantees offered by Franco, confirming the *Falange* as the political base of the State and channel of civilian life in Spain'.[15]

In return, the anniversaries of *Falange* brought an impressive crop of telegrams of 'unshakeable fidelity' to the *Caudillo*, and newspaper articles lauding his mandate at the head of FET y de las JONS. Thus, for example, Giménez Caballero's piece, 'The Spanish Dilemma: Total Unification or Total Communism' on the occasion of the fifth anniversary of the 1937 Unification, in which he praised Franco as the 'beloved programmatic executor of José Antonio Primo de Rivera'.[16] When not directly in praise of Franco, the manifestations were expressions of solidarity with the Armed Forces – which was tantamount to solidarity with their *Generalísimo* – linking *Falange* and Army in terms of the values embodied and the objectives pursued by both. On 'Infantry Day' (8 December) 1941, *El Alcazar* reproduced passages from Primo de Rivera's 'Letter to the Military Men of Spain'.[17] The same edition carried an article entitled 'Catholic and Military Roots of *Falange*', in which it was stated that externally and internally the Movement was inspired by Catholic and military principles, that the unity of *Caudillo*, Army and *Falange* was essential for the security of Spain, and that

> the politico-military bloc has the solidity of granite. The fragmentation of one of those elements will always be impossible, as will the fragmentation of the unmovable and enduring unity of all three, with the desire for a vital destiny and the rejection of other, vanquished or superceded things.[18]

Finally, the reports which were published on 'Victory Day' (1 April) each year, and the attendance of Party officials at the parade, represented the high point of the anxiety to identify the *Falange* with the Armed Forces. *Arriba's* headlines on 1 April 1942 are typical: 'The Army and the *Falange* maintain the heroic spirit which initiated the universal enterprise against Communism'.[19]

The Party Press thus clearly shows that the *Falange's a posteriori* contention that it was, at best, a reluctant camp-follower in the Franco regime, is manifestly untrue.

Whilst the *Falange* worked hard to consolidate its position as part of the socio-political fabric of the New State in domestic terms, it did not neglect the opportunities offered by external situations and events to assert and assure its status as the only permitted representative and spokesman, at a non-governmental level, of the Spanish State and people. Although little is known of the work of the *Falange's* 'Foreign Department' (*Servicio del Exterior*), nevertheless, it undoubtedly constituted an important facet of Falangist activity in so far as it represented the bridge-head established in different countries for the subsequent diffusion of the Falangist ideology. The prime targets for such 'missionary' work were, naturally enough, the Latin American countries (always referred to as the Hispano-American countries in the Falangist lexicon). It was proposed that, through *Falange*, these would form a close and mutually beneficial association with the mother country, a vast hispanic community. It was in this way, rather than through expansionist invasion of foreign territory, that imperialism manifested itself in the Falangist credo.[20]

It is unlikely that there was ever any possibility that this imperialist dream could have been realised, and none at all once the Second World War had broken out. Nevertheless, the placement in various countries of groups of Francoist partisans could clearly have its uses in terms of information, channelling funds or arms, or subversion of the established order. A phrase from one of the Foreign Department's own publications suggests that, in effect, this particular part of the organisation was of use in more than strictly Party affairs: 'The national syndicalist doctrine had to create organs of unity and cohesion for expatriate Spaniards, which would, in different spheres, act in collaboration with diplomatic and consular agents'.[21]

Although, in the early 1940s, the possibilities of creating an empire were remote, the *Falange* nevertheless did what it could to take advantage of the international situation, to extend its field of operation outside Spain. Besides the space devoted to the military aspects of the Second World War and, especially, to the progress made by the Axis powers, the Falangist Press also reported all other connections between Spain and the Axis in minute and enthusiastic detail. In this context, for 'Spain' we can read '*Falange*' for, as the Spanish Ambassador in Berlin stated to the German Press in late 1941, 'the *Falange* has been the principle bond in the friendly relations between Germany and Spain'.[22]

There were, for example, innumerable exchanges of delegations of one section or another of each country's respective Party. In 1940, a delegation led by Ramón Serrano Suñer, accompanied by Pilar Primo de Rivera, Manuel Halcón, Demetrio Carceller and others, visited Germany. In November 1941, they were decorated by the German Ambassador in Madrid, who also sent special regards to Dionisio Ridruejo and Manuel Mora Figueroa.[23] Italian and German delegates were present at the fifth National Council of the SEU, held between 9 and 16 December 1941, during which, Spanish students were urged to be 'the youth of gun and book, like the youth advocated by Mussolini'.[24] In February 1942, a mission from the Education and Leisure Department of FET y de las JONS visited *'la casa del fascio'* in Venice while, on 27 March of that year, in Madrid, the Vice-secretary General of the Party, José Luna, visited 'the Italian fascist centre, at the invitation of the Fascist Officer in Spain, Conde Asinari de San Marsano'.[25] The Falangist organ, *Arriba*, regaled its readers in April 1942 with the entire text of a speech made by Hitler in which, among other things, the *Führer* praised Franco and the Spanish volunteer force, the Blue Division,[26] whose Commander in chief, General Muñoz Grandes, was decorated on 9 April 1942 with the German Iron Cross.

In the same month, readers were informed of the *Falange's* activities in Italy. Almost all of the six hundred Spaniards resident in Rome were affiliated to *Falange*, said the report, observing that 'contrary to what people might suppose, the Spanish colony in Italy is very small'.[27] Nevertheless, the Italian branch of the *Falange* enjoyed relations with the Fascist Party which were 'characterised primarily by their cordiality, and, in preference to the normal diplomatic channels, acted as the intermediary for the latter's invitations to Spanish commissions to visit Italy.[28]

Whilst the first contingent of Spanish emigrant workers was on its way to Germany in June 1942, a delegation of adolescents led by Pilar Primo de Rivera, attended a meeting of European youth in Florence and, later in the year, the National Delegate for the *Falange* Youth Front, Antonio Elola Olasa, spoke at the Congress of European Youth in Vienna.[29]

Inside Spain, too, Hispano-Italian relations were nourished and cherished through the *Falange*. In May 1942, for example, Italian Fascist officials were received by the Vice-secretary of *Falange*, Luna, and taken on a tour of Extremadura, amid expressions of fraternity and political coincidence. In Madrid, meanwhile, a delegation of Fascist trade unionists were entertained by their Spanish colleagues and the *Sección Femenina* was 'At Home' to *its* Italian counterpart.[30]

Gone were the days when Falangists could maintain that they had no connection with European totalitarianism.[31]

By far the most important and ostentatious of the *Falange's* contributions to the strengthening of relations between Spain and the Axis powers was the volunteer force created in 1941, on Serrano Suñer's initiative, as an integral part of Spanish foreign (and military) policy.[32]

The Blue Division – so-called on account of its almost exclusively Falangist composition – was created specifically as a force to be sent to fight as part of the regular German Army. As such, it was also one of the most paradoxical of the Falangist enterprises of the early 1940s. Many volunteers felt that, in enlisting, they were rebelling against the ideological and material disappointments of Francoism and striking a blow for doctrinal radicalism in the form of active solidarity with the Axis. In fact, they were allowing themselves to be used as a key piece in the delicate diplomatic game being played in order to avoid greater Spanish commitment in the conflict. It was clear from the article published by Serrano Suñer in the organ of the Hitler Youth movement, *Will und Macht*, in August 1942, that this was the function of the Blue Division with respect to external relations and situations. Serrano recognised the 'importance for all' of the world war, but reaffirmed the Spanish attitude of non-belligerence on the grounds that Spain had already contributed to the struggle against communism with the Spanish Civil War, and continued to do so through the volunteers of the Blue Division.[33] In effect, as well as aiding and abetting the foreign policy of the regime, the explicitly anti-communist nature of the Blue Division was entirely consonant with the very essence of Francoism.

Finally, the Blue Division served as an exercise in xenophobia, uniting against a common foreign enemy sentiments which might otherwise have been directed against leaders at home. Leaving aside the question of political repression, directed exclusively against those who had not supported the Nationalist cause, the years immediately following the Civil War were years of tremendous hardship for the mass of the working population, irrespective of political sympathies. The members of the lower and middle classes who had supported the Nationalists in the Civil War could not easily understand how their participation was now followed by shortages of basic necessities and an atmosphere of general misery, as if they had been on the losing side. Annual average *per capita* income, for example, had been around 8000 pesetas in 1935 and had fallen to some 6500 pesetas in 1940.[34] Wages, no longer negotiable between workers and employers but controlled by the State, were maintained during the period between 1939 and 1945 at only 25% of their pre-war levels in urban areas.[35] Production, particularly of agricultural goods, had fallen between 30% and 40% on pre-war levels, provoking shortages, price increases and massive corruption and abuse.[36] The State body whose mission was the collection and marketing of cereal crops, the *Servicio Nacional del*

Trigo, admitted that almost 40% of the 1942–43 wheat crop was sold on the black market;[37] whilst a British survey estimated that this illegal channel may have supplied up to 50% of national demand for all goods in 1940.[38] Ration books were introduced in May 1939 and were not withdrawn until 1952.

The talk of Man as 'the bearer of eternal values' and of 'one great brotherhood of producers', from well-fed Party officials in safe positions was far-removed from the day-to-day realities of hardship between 1939 and 1945. Those same officials added their seal of approval to the policies of the regime by acquiescing in, and repeating publicly, the official justifications of the difficulties. They explained the food shortages as due to the world situation, which caused supplies to be interrupted, and attributed to the outbreak of the world war the fact that the revolutionary aspects of the national syndicalist doctrine had not been able to go ahead as rapidly as they would have wished. Thus, the Vice-secretary General of the Party, José Luna, in a speech made in November 1941, regretted that the war was preventing *Falange* from devoting its full attention to the trade unions, which, consequently, he said, were not 'in the hands of the best men, as *Falange* would have wished', but 'infiltrated' by others of lesser category.[39] Considering, in the first place, that the trade union system was specifically the exclusive domain of the *Falange* and, in the second, that Spain was not an active participant in the war, it is difficult to understand, let alone accept, the logic of Luna's argument.

Summing up the year 1941, the *Arriba* editoralist admitted that the Syndical Organisation had not managed to transform the economy, improve the standard of living of the working classes, or structure itself adequately. Nevertheless, he continued, the CNS could feel satisfied with itself because 'the masses are organised and subject to discipline, the anarchic economy is under control, and a brake has been put on abuse'.[40] In other words, the relatively comfortable economic position of the ruling classes had been secured at the expense of the working classes. The reference to the brake applied to corruption was a straightforward untruth, as the official admissions of the operation of the black market clearly showed.[41]

The Secretary General of the Party, José Luis de Arrese, spoke in similar vein to the *Arriba* journalist at the Sixth Congress of the *Sección Feminina*:

It is true that the circumstances of our Civil War and the present war suppose an obstacle in our way. It is true that some organisms of the

Falange, set up in haste, cannot yet yield as much as they would have done had they had a slower period of gestation.[42]

He also recognised popular disbelief in the Falangist revolution, general apathy with regard to the possibilities of effecting it, and the loss of unity present in the initial Falangist euphoria. Such references to reality were brief and marginal, however, and the solutions proposed did not for one moment question the validity of the structural context. On the contrary, the remedy proposed by Arrese was already familiar and entirely in keeping with the style of the regime: greater discipline, within the framework established between 1936 and 1939.

While it was relatively easy to silence or ignore popular dissatis-faction, it was not so easy to obviate the threat to internal stability posed by Falangists discontented at the slow progress of their revolution (1941, it will be remembered, was the year in which syndical leader Merino was ousted and in which the Party purge was initiated). It was therefore necessary to find a means of diverting attention and uniting support once more around the dual image of national heroism and the common enemy; to give politically and socio-economically dissatisfied Francoists an outlet for their discontent; and to provide Falangists with a token means of participating in the world war, in lieu of the mass intervention from Spain for which they were anxious.

Such was the mixture of sentiments which could be discerned in Serrano Suñer's celebrated 'Russia is to blame' speech, delivered from the balcony of the General Secretariat of the Party in Madrid, on 13 June 1941.[43] A month later, on 14 July 1941, the first contingent of several thousand volunteers left for Germany, amid a tumultuous send-off from Party officials, relatives and Falangist comrades. On arrival at their destination, they did not constitute a distinct Spanish unit with their own uniform, as they had expected, but were incorporated into the German army and kitted out as German troops. Nor could they immediately set about fulfilling their mission against the 'Russian monster', for the need to train them after German military style kept them in the rearguard for several weeks. When they did finally reach the battlefront, they soon encountered the hardships of the Russian winter, which took their toll on the Blue Division, in spite of the training some of its members had recieved during the Spanish Civil War on the Teruel front.[44]

At home, the Women's Section in several provinces organised a campaign of subscriptions to provide clothing for the volunteers in Russia. Collections were taken to send food to them, and Falangists organised themselves into groups which would visit the homes of volunteers on Christmas Eve, as a 'testimony of brotherhood'. Even Franco sent a consignment of brandy and tobacco to be distributed among the troops, an event which was enthusiastically reported as a demonstration of the *Caudillo's* magnanimity by the Nationalist ex-servicemen's organisation, the *Confederación Nacional de Ex-combatientes*, of which the majority of members were Falangists.[45]

Throughout 1941 and 1942, in a campaign aimed as much at foreign observers as at the domestic reader, the efforts of the Falangist Press to convey the significance and heroism of the Blue Division were unstinting. Leading Party members – most of whom did not, however, go so far as to actually enlist – lost no opportunity to express support for the noble sacrifice being made by their compatriots in Russia and to reiterate the status of the volunteers as Spain's representatives in the world war. Thus, on 3 November 1941, *El Alcazar*, reported 'what the German Press says about our glorious Blue Division': that it represented the return of spain to the international scene on a war-footing, 'the image of Spain's return to Europe to participate in the common mission of Europe'. The following day brought a similar report, taken from *Il Corriere della Sera*, which laid emphasis on the character of the volunteers as the representatives of the traditional, imperial and military strength of Spain.

Falange's Provincial Chief in Toledo, Alberto Martín Gamero, wrote a eulogistic piece entitled 'The Spanish Princes of the Blue Division' towards the end of 1941,[46] whilst the obituaries which soon began to appear spoke in terms of 'heroes gloriously fallen for the Fatherland' and the 'glorious crusade against Communism'. Some volunteers did, indeed, receive a hero's burial. For example, the funeral on 17 January 1942 of Vicente Gaceo del Pino,[47] was attended by three Ministers, four Under-Secretaries, two National Delegates, four National Councilors and a dozen other assorted Syndical chiefs, military men, diplomats and municipal officials.[48] The concession of such honours was, however, the exception, not the rule.

Whilst the reasons which motivated men to set off for an unknown country, probably not to return, are as diverse and as inaccessible in the case of the Blue Division as in that of the International Brigades five years earlier, it seems likely that, for the Falangist volunteers, patriotism or a strong ideological impulse moved only a minority. It is doubtful whether the idealistic vision of their motives described, for example, by Minister of Labour José Antonio Girón, bore any resemblance to reality: 'the attraction of combat, the desire for sacrifice, the Spanish understanding of pride and of showing itself before the world as race and as imperialism'.[49]

Such high-sounding phrases were more appropriate to the public-relations operation which surrounded the Blue Division than to real political or material motivations. Apart from the escape from frustration or other domestic problems, the incentives for joining the Blue Division were scarcely overwhelming. At most, there were vague promises of unspecified powers: 'The combatants must organise Spanish society and productive activities; they will control syndical action';[50] exemption from registration and examination fees in the University (though no mention was made of where the rest of the money necessary to complete a course was to come from);[51] and the concession of 'certain advantages in official competitions and examinations'.[52] Nevertheless, in the two years of its existence thousands of men passed through the ranks of the Blue Division, thereby lending themselves voluntarily to a national and international manoeuvre designed first and foremost to ensure the stability of the Franco regime.[53]

Partly in rebellion against the way in which the *Falange* had been utilised in the person of the Blue Division volunteers, a group of Falangists was the protagonist of an incident which occurred in the Basque Country in the summer of 1942. The affair, in which certain returning Blue Division volunteers were involved, had the makings of a major political crisis. The *Generalísimo*, however, rode it out with the by then familiar mixture of insouciance and authoritatianism. In the entire course of its development, the *Falange* shows a remarkable incapacity to learn from its own history; the 1942 crisis was yet another occasion on which Falangist purism was betrayed by Falangist realism and demonstrated that neither José Antonio Primo de Rivera, nor Manuel Hedilla, nor Salvador Merino had taught the Falangists anything.

On 16 August 1942, a special mass was to be celebrated in the church at Begoña, near Bilbao, for the souls of Carlist soldiers of the Our Lady of Begoña *tercio*, killed in the Civil War. Already, on 25 July 1942, the Carlists had organised a special mass in the church of San Vicente at Abando (Bilbao), for the souls of 'the monarchs of the legitimate dynasty and all the Vizcaya Carlists and *Requetes* killed in the crusade'.[54] The religious service was followed by a demonstration through the streets of Bilbao. This event, as in the case of other, similar commemorative services in Moncada, Montserrat, Poblet and Valladolid, was silenced by the Press. In view of its potential size and popularity, it was intitially considered advisable to cancel the Begoña mass. No such measure was taken, however, and, worried by the strength of the Carlist forces, Vizcaya Falangist and local chief of the Old Guard, Maíz, asked for Falangist reinforcements to be sent from Valladolid, Santander and Vitoria.[55]

On 15 August 1942, an official car left the Party provincial headquarters in Valladolid, occupied by the head of the Vizcaya SEU, Eduardo Berastegui Guerenliain, and Falangist Hernando Calleja García. They drove to San Sebastian, where they collected Falangist comrade Juan Domínguez Muñoz,[56] and the party then proceeded to Bilbao, where they stayed the night. On the following day, accompanied by a second party car, they left for Begoña and, on arrival at the church, they waited on one side, 'making use of the insignia and official uniforms they were wearing, accompanied by three comrades under the protection of a group of policemen who were there'.[57]

Inside the building the mass was already under way, presided by the Minister of the Army, Enrique Varela. As the Carlists left the church, one of the Falangists threw a small bomb, which hit the portico, but did not explode. A grenade was then thrown into the crowd outside, which, although knocked to one side as it fell, nevertheless wounded more than a hundred people.[58] The public, most of them Carlists, would have overwhelmed the Falangists, but for the intervention of the police, who protected Dominguez and his comrades from the angry crowd, put them into the official cars they had come in and drove them away, evidently under arrest.[59]

Franco was informed of the incident by Arrese, who was staying with the *Caudillo* at the latter's Summer residence in Galicia. Franco's initial inclination towards taking no action was typical of his use of 'wait-and-see' tactics, and of his capacity to maintain control by allowing possible sources of opposition to spend their strength in skirmishes against each other. He concluded that what had occurred was the reaction on the part of the Falangists who chanced to be in the area to subversive, anti-Francoist slogans shouted by the Carlists. General Varela, however, in conversation with Franco on 24 August 1942, denied this, maintaining that the incident had been an attempt on his life.[60] In official circles, the affair was silenced. In its 19 August edition, *Arriba* merely indicated that 'on 16 August, a mass was celebrated for 136 dead of the *Tercio* of Our Lady of Begoña, attended by more than 5000 people, and presided by the Minister of the Army and the Under-Secretary of the Interior'. There was not even room for reading between the lines in this hermetic report, and it is only with the wisdom of hindsight that there is any special significance to be attached to Franco's speech at La Coruña on 25 August 1942, or to the *Arriba* Editorial of the following day, both of which laid particular emphasis on the importance of unity between the *Falange* and the Army.

Neither the Carlists nor the Falangists, however, were prepared to allow the matter to be buried in official silence. Each party issued an inflammatory leaflet denouncing the other.[61] Ten Carlists resigned from their posts in the Movement and, unbeknown to Franco, Varela and the Minister of the Interior, Valentín Galarza, sent notes to all the Captaincies General in the country, presenting the incident as an attack on the Army as an institution.

Franco was prepared to induce his collaborators to reveal their political hand, but he was not the man to tolerate any outright indiscipline, least of all when a major crisis might be the outcome. An example had already been made of Hedilla and Merino, and a further example was now made of the perpetrators of the Begoña incident. The harshness of the punishment meted out to the Falangists, whilst the Carlists' part in the confrontation was ignored, indicates that, although absorbed into the Movement, Franco still saw in the *Falange* a potential threat to the delicate balance of his house-of-cards regime. Juan Domínguez Muñoz and six Falangist comrades were tried before a Court Martial in Bilbao. Domínguez and Hernando Calleja were sentenced to death. Jorge Hernández Bravo, Luis Lorenzo Salgado, Eduardo Berastegui Guerenliain, Virgilio Hernández Rivadulla and Eugenio Moretón Soriano were given prison sentences. Calleja's sentence was commuted to a prison term, on account of his being a war cripple. He and the other five prisoners were subsequently pardoned by a Decree issued by Franco in 1945.[62] Juan Domínguez's sentence, however, was confirmed.

Led by Falangist and former comrade-in-arms of Domínguez, Narciso Perales, a campaign was mounted by a group of Falangists to save Domínguez's life. They may have been motivated by humanitarian considerations, but they were principally concerned by their view that the survival or demise of the *Falange* as a credible political force depended on the success or failure of their attempt. If Domínguez were shot, the *Falange* would lose an important round to rival forces within the Movement. If he were saved, *Falange's* influence in high places would not only be proved, but even strengthened. Perales, then Civil Governor of León, spent a week in feverish efforts to convince fellow Falangists of the long-term importance of the case, and to whip up support for Domínguez in official circles. He spoke with Arrese, Girón, Ridruejo, and Serrano Suñer, who promised to intervene before Franco on Domínguez's behalf.[63] Serrano achieved nothing, however, and it was clear that Arrese and Girón were only prepared to give moral support, not to risk their posts by active disagreement with the sentence. Serrano promised to make fresh attempts to sway Franco's decision, but, before he could do so, Domínguez was shot 'in the ditch surrounding the prison at Larrínaga (Bilbao), in the early hours of 2 September 1942'.[64]

It was unlikely that he could have been saved from the firing squad. Apart from the internal political factors involved in the affair, Domínguez was also suspected of being a British spy.[65] Perales had obtained information from Domínguez's address book which indicated, rather, that he was working as a German agent, but this hardly improved the situation, for his role as such was evidently to provoke an internal conflict which would lead to the dismissal of the anglophile Varela and the subsequent entry of Spain into the war in support of the Axis.[66] A passage in J. M. Doussinague's book, *España tenía razón*, echoes this version and indicates, furthermore, that the Ministry of Foreign Affairs was already aware of Falangist-German machinations when the Begoña incident occurred:

> An attaché of the German Embassy in Madrid left the capital by car one day for France and, having stopped for lunch in Burgos, exchanged opinions with one of his companions on the projected conspiracy (an attempt at a *coup de main* by Falangists and SS people in order to take over the Government and allow the Germans to reach Gibraltar via Spain). They were overheard by someone who knew German well and who listened to the conversation, which provided some very interesting details. From 15 (sic) August onwards, when a tragic incident occurred after mass in the church at Begoña, Bilbao, certain Spanish elements of very low calibre, and in the pay of the German Embassy, were being tracked down and one of them was shot as responsible for that incident.[67]

Domínguez's 'Testamentary message for national-syndicalist posterity'[68] suggests clearly that, in effect, the Begoña incident was at once a Falangist protest against what was considered to be part betrayal, part political error, on Franco's part, and a deliberate attempt to correct the *Caudillo's* line. Whilst Franco's foreign policy had not yet taken a decidedly pro-Allied turn, the Falangists considered that it was not, and never had been, sufficiently pro-Axis either. Thus, Domínguez wrote shortly before his execution that Franco, in these moments of hesitation improper of the path traced by José Antonio, has – unconsciously, perhaps – joined our secular foreign enemies, but he will answer to God and to History for debility improper in a General who wears the Cross of San Fernando and who wrote in letters of gold a page of national ressurection.[69]

From the standpoint of their Falangist logic, Domínguez and those who tried to save his life undoubtedly acted in good faith. They believed that the national-syndicalist revolution had not been implemented in accordance with the doctrine elaborated by José Antonio Primo de Rivera, and that *Falange's* position in the regime was not hegemonic, because of the influence exercised on the *Generalísimo* by elements contrary to *Falange* and to the Falangist interpretation of the historic tasks of Spain.[70]

What they did not seem to understand was the objective role of the *Falange* as an integral part of the system established by means of the Civil War. As such, it was charged with the execution of the socio-political aspects of an overall plan designed for the promotion of those interests whose protection had made the civil War 'necessary' and possible, and in which the *Falange* itself participated. Any attempt by a fraction of the *Falange* to assume any other than the executive function assigned to it would be crushed by the combined efforts of the other forces present in the regime and, ultimately, by the holders of supreme power, the Armed Forces, headed by Franco.[71]

The corollary to this particularly bitter bout of political in-fighting was made public at the beginning of September 1942. The headline of *Arriba* on 4 September left no doubt as to Franco's determination to show that he alone would decide where leadership and the balance of power were concerned: 'The *Caudillo* and National Leader of *Falange* assumes the Presidency of the *Junta Política*.' The front pages of all the national dailies that day were devoted to a series of important Cabinet and other changes. Serrano Suñer was removed not only from the Presidency of the *Junta Política*, but also from the Ministry of Foreign Affairs, where he was replaced by General Gómez Jordana. General Varela ceded his place as Minister of the Army to General Asensio Cabanillas, thereto Chief of the Central General Staff. The National Delegate for Law and Justice, Falangist Blas Pérez González, succeeded General Galarza as Minister of the Interior and José Luna was replaced in the General Vice-Secretariat of the Party by Manuel Mora Figueroa. Rodrigo Vivar Téllez was appointed as the new Civil Governor of Vizcaya on 6 September 1942 and, on 12 September, José

Porres was dismissed as Civil Governor of Valladolid – two changes which support the allegations made in the Carlist leaflet to the effect that the Begoña affair was prepared with the connivance of Party officials in these two provinces.

Franco's intention in making these changes was clear from the comments printed in the Movement Press in the first half of September 1942: absolute unity of command (*'unidad en el mando'*) was as necessary in peace-time as in war-time and, in internal politics, 'the severest discipline in observance of the Law' would be imposed inexorably, in order to preserve that unity.[72] The dismissals represented a mere 'changing of the guard', wrote *Arriba*, which in no way meant that there would be changes in national or international policies, nor that the essence of the regime's principal institutions, the Army and the *Falange*, would alter. The nominal holders of power might vary, concluded the official Editorialist, but the permanent essence of the totalitarian State remained and the only real government, that of Franco, did not change at all.[73]

Varela and Galarza had clearly over-reached themselves in sending their notes to the Captaincies General after Franco had already taken the measures he considered sufficient to compensate the Army for the affront allegedly received in Begoña. The Party officials involved in the changes were suspected of being implicated in an affair which could well be interpreted as a demonstration of disagreement with Franco's leadership and such an act of defiance could not go unpunished. Only those who obediently toed the line were safe. Girón, Arrese and Valdés kept *their* positions because they did precisely that.

The reasons behind Serrano's ouster are not so immediately comprehensible, although it may be said at once that a change in foreign policy was not among them. In his memoirs, Serrano himself writes:

The fact that Franco eliminated Varela from the Government because of the internal political situation, in spite of the excellent relations that the twice-decorated General then maintained with the British Ambassador, Sir Samuel Hoare, is a further demonstration of the fallaciousness of the official story, concocted *a posteriori*, that my dismissal was for reasons of a shrewd rectification in our external policy.[74]

Dionisio Ridruejo echoes Serrano's judgement:

The fact that, months after (Serrano's) fall, the Axis' star began to fade, served to weave the legend of the astute foresight of the dictator – a legend which any explorer of newspapers archives will, with little effort, see refuted.[75]

In effect, the Movement Press maintained its pro-Axis tone for several months after the September 1942 crisis. In January 1943, *Arriba* published front-page reports of the summary of 1942 made by Hitler, giving an outstanding position to one of the *Führer's* phrases in particular: 'A nation is sinking, and it is not Germany. Alas for Europe if the Jewish–bolshevik–capitalist conspiracy triumphs!'[76] Falangists Arrese, Valdés Larrañaga, Aznar and Arias Salgado visited Germany in the same month; Arrese was received by Hitler and the two held 'a long coversation characterised by the spirit of frank amity which exists between Germany and Spain'.[77] The leading article in the 24 January 1943 edition of *Arriba* was entitled 'Russia is the enemy', whilst exactly six months after Serrano Suñer's dismissal, on 2 February 1943, the front page of the same paper proclaimed that 'the initiative has not been taken out of Axis hands'.

Notes

1. *El Alcazar, Arriba* (27, 28, 29 & 30 Jan. 1942).
2. Ibid. (2 Apr. 1942).
3. Ibid. (19 July 1942).
4. Ibid. (21 & 25 Aug. 1942).
5. Ibid. (10 Feb. 1942).
6. Ibid. (9 Mar. 1942).
7. Ibid. (22, 23 & 24 Feb. 1942).
8. Ibid. (3 May 1942).
9. *El Alcazar*, 19 November 1941.
10. According to a Law of 6 December 1940, membership of the *Frente de Juventudes* was obligatory, in order that Spanish youth should 'receive the formative influence of the *Falange*'. As of December 1941, the Youth Front had 943 951 members, both male and female, between the ages of 7 and 18, according to a report published in the 3 December 1941 edition of *El Alcazar*. At present, there exists no monographic study of this section of the *Falange*, which undoubtedly exerted a significant influence on postwar Spanish youth, except Alcocer, J. L. *Radiografía de un fraude*, Planeta, Barcelona 1978.
11. *El Alcazar*, 17 November 1941.
12. *Arriba*, 16 March 1943 published the following figures referring to the

capital city of Madrid: 22 000 block representatives, 1800 representatives of groups of blocks, and 120 suburb representatives.

13. Foundational speech, 29 October 1933, in *Obras Completas*, p. 24.
14. *Arriba* (29 Jan. 1942).
15. Ibid. (5 Feb. 1942).
16. Ibid. (19 Apr. 1942).
17. See above, pp. 87–88.
18. 'Raíz católica y militar de la Falange' in *El Alcazar*, 8 December 1941.
19. See also the Editorial in *Arriba*, 26 August 1942 and the speech made by Franco in La Coruña on 24 August 1942, in which he stated that 'nothing is closer to things military than our *Falange*, and nothing more Falangist than the virtues of an Army'.
20. This is not to say, however, that territorial gains were absent from the *Falange's* aspirations; see, for example, Ledesma Ramos, R., *Discurso a las Juventudes de España*, pp. 90–1, 101–7; Primo de Rivera, J. A., *Cortes* speech, 2/10/35, in *Obras completas* pp. 397–406; Redondo, O., 'Castilla en España' in *JONS*, no. 2 (June 1933); Aparicio, J., 'Imperio o anarquía' in *JONS*, *Antología*, pp. 211–13; Areilza, J. M., & Castiella. F., *Reivindicaciones de España* (Madrid: Instituto de Estudios Políticos, 1941) *passim*. Cf. also, Southworth, H. *Antifalange*, pp. 13–19, 29–41, 48–61; Costa Morata, P., 'La idea del Imperio' in *Historia internacional*, no. 11 (Feb. 1976) pp. 51–5 and refs.
21. Servicio Exterior de FET y de las JONS, *FET y de las JONS en el exterior*. *Revista hispánica moderna* (New York, 1939), quoted in Southworth, H., *Antifalange*, p. 154. The only existing monographic study of the Falangist Foreign Department is Allan Chase, *Falange: the Axis' Secret Army in the Americas*, (New York: G. P. Putman, 1943).
22. *El Alcazar*, (7 Nov. 1941).
23. Ibid. (10 Nov. 1941). The Nazi party had a centre and representatives in Spain at this time. When their leader, Thomsen, left Spain in February 1943, he was presented with a leather-bound volume containing the signatures of several hundreds of Falangist 'producers' (*Arriba*, 24 Feb. 1943).
24. *El Alcazar*, 11 Dec. 1941.
25. *Arriba*, 15 Feb. and 28 Mar. 1942.
26. Ibid., 28 Apr. 1942. On the Blue Division, see below, pp. 80, 82–4.
27. Ibid., 29 Apr. 1942.
28. Ibid. It also acted as the channel for such matters as a request to Spanish vintners to send wines and spirits for distribution among the wounded in Roman hospitals.
29. Ibid. (10 May 1942).
30. Ibid. (27 June & 18 Sept. 1942).
31. Even although, as we have discussed in Chapter 1, the assertion was untrue.
32. Franco was always mistrustful of the spontaneous initiatives of his collaborators. The fact that this was a quasi-military initiative probably fostered even further his suspicions with respect to Serrano's desire to promote the *Falange*.
33. *Arriba* (15 Aug. 1942).

34. Ros Hombravella *et al.*, op. cit., p. 61.
35. Esteban J. in Preston, P. (ed.), *España en crisis* (Madrid: Fondo de Cultura Económica, 1978) p. 163.
36. Ibid., p. 161.
37. Servicio Nacional del Trigo, *Cosechas, Comercio y Consumo de Trigo durante las veinticinco campañas 1939–1940, 1963–1964* (Madrid: Ministry of Agriculture, 1964) quoted in Ros Hombravella op. cit., p. 57.
38. Walker, J. *Spain, Economic and Commercial Conditions*, Overseas Economic Surveys (London: HMSO, 1949) quoted in Esteban J., loc. cit.. p. 161, n. 53.
39. *El Alcazar* (10 Nov. 1941).
40. *Arriba* (1 Jan. 1942).
41. See notes 37 and 38 above. In 1942, indeed, a Falangist, José Pérez de Cabo, was shot precisely for his apparent involvement in black market dealings in eastern Spain.
42. Ibid. (12 Jan. 1942).
43. Serrano Suñer had already indicated the convenience of mobilising popular sentiment against the communist enemy in a speech made at a Falangist gathering in Mota del Cuervo on 3 May 1941. He repeated the idea in the meeting of the Council of Ministers held on 25 June 1941. Cf. *Arriba* (4 May & 26 June 1941).
44. Ridruejo, D. *Los cuadernos de Rusia* (Barcelona: Planeta, 1978) pp. 10–14. See also, Esteban Infantes, E., *La División Azul* (Madrid: Editorial AHR, 1965). Esteban Infantes was Supreme Commander of the Division between Dec. 1942 and Dec. 1943.
45. *El Alcazar* (15 Nov. 1941).
46. 'Los infantes españoles de la División Azul' in *El Alcazar*, 21 December 1941.
47. Gaceo had been a member of the first National Council of *Falange Española*, Chief of the Press Office of the Party Secretariat, and journalist on the staff of *Arriba*.
48. *Arriba* (18 Jan. 1942). According to Serrano Suñer (*Memorias*, p. 191), Gaceo was accused *en rebeldía* in the Court Martial held against Manuel Hedilla and others on 5 June 1937, which implies a good deal of cynicism, or hypocrisy, on the part of Gaceo and no less on the part of those members of the Establishment who buried him as a hero.
49. Girón J. A., 'The transcendence of the Blue Division', in *Arriba* (2 Jan. 1942).
50. Francisco Franco, speech made in Terrassa (Barcelona) in Jan. 1942, and quoted in *Arriba* (7 Feb. 1942).
51. *BOE.* (5 Feb. 1942).
52. Ibid. (8 May 1942).
53. Cfr. Ridruejo, D., *Los cuadernos de Rusia*, p. 13. Esteban Infantes, E., op. cit., p. 25, gives the figure of 17 406 volunteers, although it is not clear whether this includes replacements and does not include the airmen of the 'Escuadrilla Azul'.
54. According to a Carlist pamphlet, *El crimen de la Falange en Begoña*, dated 17 Aug. 1942, of which a copy was kindly lent to this writer by D. Miguel Alvarez Bonald. Cf. Marquina Barrio, A., 'El atentado de Begoña' in

Historia 16, no.76 (Aug. 1982).

55. *El Crimen de la Falange en Begoña*. The request was made to the Party Vicesecretary, Luna. It is not known whether the Secretary General, Arrese, was informed of these movements.

56. David Jato Miranda, interview (7 July 1977). Jato was among a group of Blue Division volunteers on their way home whom Domínguez tried to persuade to accompany him to Begoña.

57. *El crimen de la Falange en Begoña*. Neither the origin of the second car, nor the names of its occupants are given.

58. An unpublished list compiled by Carlists who visited the hospitals where the wounded were attended, given to this writer by D. Miguel Alvarez Bonald, gives the names of 117 people, two of whom ultimately died of their injuries.

59. This is the Carlist version. The Falangist version, as given to this writer by Falangists Perales and Jato, claims that the Falangists were arrested when they went to report the Carlists to the police.

60. David Jato, interview, 7 July 1977. Lopez Rodó, L., *La larga Marcha hacia la monarquía* (Barcelona: Noguer, 1977) pp. 29, 503–5.

61. The Carlist leaflet has already been mentioned. The Falangist reply was evidently dated 18 Aug. 1942 and written by a SEU official. The present writer has been able to find no trace of its text. Cf. Payne, op. cit., p. 235.

62. *BOE*, 26 Nov. 1945.

63. Narciso Perales, interview, 31 Dec. 1976.

64. Taken from an unpublished account of Domínguez's final moments, written by the priest who heard his last confesion, Fr. Eusebio G. de Pesquera, and shown to this writer by Narciso Perales. Notice that the execution had taken place was published in a discreet corner of the Monarchist daily, *ABC*, and, without any detail whatsoever, in *Arriba*, on 3 Sept. 1942. Cf. Serrano Suñer, R., *Memorias*, pp. 366–7.

65. Falangist Manuel Valdés Larrañga was said to be responsible for the report denouncing Domíguez as a British spy. When questioned by this writer (interview, 22 Nov. 1977), Valdés was prepared only to say that it was 'a matter without any importance'.

66. David Jato, interview, 7 July 1977; Narciso Perales, interview 31 Dec. 1976 and in *Personas*, Madrid, 11 Dec. 1976.

67. Doussinague, J. M., *España tenía Razón* (Madrid, 1950) p. 127. Doussinague was General Director of External Policy in the Ministry of Foreign Affairs and his account can therefore be considered as having a semi-official character.

68. This unpublished document, loaned to the present writer by Dr Narciso Perales, was written in Larrínaga prison, 'at 22 hours and 1 minute of September 1942'.

69. Ibid.

70. Similar sentiments are frequently expressed in the internal organ of the Blue Division, the *Boletín de la Hermandad de la División Azul*: whilst the volunteers were away saving Spain from Communism, comrades with less altruistic motives had stayed at home to enrich themselves personally and to climb up the socio-political and professional ladders.

71. As has been noted earlier (p. 31), Primo de Rivera *had* realised what

might be the role of *Falange* in a State established by a military coup. His confidence that the risk was eliminated if the coup was prepared by 'a very capable minority which exists in the Army', was not confirmed by the use made of his party during the Franco regime.

72. *Arriba* (4 & 22 Sept. 1942). See also the edns of 5, 6, 10 & 12 Sept. 1942.
73. Ibid. (4 Sept. 1942).
74. Serrano Suñer, R., *Memorias*, p. 372.
75. Ridruejo, D., *Escrito en España*, p. 85.
76. *Arriba* (2 Jan. 1943).
77. Ibid. (20 Jan. 1943).

5 1945–57

The political demise of Serrano in September 1942 represented another important stage in the process of the absorption of the *Falange* into the fabric of the regime. With his departure from active politics, the hopes which Falangists like Perales and Ridruejo had cherished of being able, through him, to secure independent power for their party also disappeared. The direction of the *Falange* was, henceforth, more than ever in the hands of men who were, first and foremost, subordinate to, and identified with, the objectives and interests of the regime, adapting their particular beliefs and interests to these.

In international terms, this meant the acceptance of the de-fascistization of the regime's façade after 1945. In national terms, it meant being aware of, and adaptable to, the presence and ambitions of political rivals more acceptable in the post-world war international context. The most dangerous of the competitors in the political race were the Alphonsine Monarchists, allied to whom were what the Falangists termed 'Christian-Democratic elements', who felt that an Allied victory in the war would oblige Franco to renounce his position as Head of State.[1]

Some of Franco's own supporters also considered this a likely possibility and even had the temerity to write a collective letter to Franco, in June 1943, in which they suggested that he cede his place to the Alphonsine Pretender, D. Juan de Borbón.[2] In fact, however, the Allies had no intention of interfering in the internal affairs of Spain to restore the monarchy, nor had Franco any intention of bowing out gracefully. On the contrary, a deliberate policy of isolation was practised against Spain by the victorious Allied powers and the Franco regime took advantage of this circumstance to adopt an equally deliberate independentist posture, which had its politico-economic expression in the period of autarchy which lasted until the 1950s.[3]

Nevertheless, after 1945, and in a context of international ostracism which contributed in no small measure to the long-term prospects of survival of the regime, Franco began to move slowly but unremittingly towards a monarchical solution to the as yet remote, but inevitable, question of the preparation of the post-Franco era. In spite of this being in contradiction to the anti-monarchical doctrine of José Antonio Primo de Rivera which the Falangists professed to defend, they lent their support to this operation as the only possible means of securing their own political survival.

In the thirty years which stretched from the end of the Second World War to the death of Franco in 1975, there were four occasions which revealed with particular clarity the Falangists' disposition to accept whatever the *Caudillo* proposed: the Law of Succession, passed in 1947; the signing of the Hispano-American 'Pacts of Madrid', in 1953; the Law of the Fundamental Principles of the Movement, elaborated over a period of two years, between 1956 and 1958; and the process of the selection of Franco's successor, between 1966 and 1969. In each of these critical moments, FE clearly demonstrated its identification with the regime, even to its own detriment, and with the continuation of Francoism, even in the form of a monarchy. The regime, for its part, showed its disposition to continue providing the *Falange* with its livelihood and its political *raison d'être*, in return for the Party's services in the structures of the administrative and socio-political bodies which, via a mixture of repression, coercion and cooption, guaranteed the state of popular inertia which permitted the untroubled development of the regime and the tranquil gestation of the provisions for its continuation in the event of Franco's death, incapacity or retirement.

On 28 March, 1947, the Spanish Government formally decided to submit to the *Cortes* a project for a Law of Succession. The project was made public on 31 march 1947, the eve of 'Victory Day', in a radio broadcast of the text of the Law. This was preceded by a speech in which Franco pointed to the need to 'confront the ultimate definition of our State, inseparably linked to the statute of succession in its highest echelons'.[4] For the first time since the liquidation of the Second Republic, Spain was explicitly recognised as a kingdom. Nevertheless, the *Caudillo* retained for life the leadership of the State, the right to designate the members of the Council of the Realm to which any future monarch would ultimately be responsible, and the prerogative of nominating a Council of Regency which, in the event of the *Caudillo's* demise, would act as his substitute until such time as a successor could be appointed. Most important of all, Franco retained the right to designate his own successor, as King or Regent. No alusion was made, in either the Law or Franco's speech, to the *Falange* as a separate entity. On the contrary, also for the first time, it was made juridically specific that the political basis of the regime, the *Movimiento*, was to be an amalgam of forces, not the prerogative of any one in particular.[5]

The Law of Succession pleased neither the Monarchists nor the

Falangists. The Alphonsine Pretender, D. Juan, issued a manifesto condemning it on 7 April 1947. He made no secret of his opposition and conceded an interview to the *Observer* on 13 April 1947, which was also broadcast by the BBC and reproduced by the *New York Times*.[6] The *Falange* was much more discreet in its opposition, of which the spokesman was José Luis Arrese, who had been relieved of his post as Secretary General of FET y de las JONS in July 1945, but who was still a member of the *Junta Politica*. Arrese's criticism was contained in a document for internal consumption only, entitled *Notes on the Law of Succession: to the Cortes, but not as a private motion (Anotaciones a la Ley de Sucesión: a las Cortes, sin pretensión de voto particular)*. As the title indicates, Arrese wished his opinions to be considered as nothing more offensive than a few notes, and he was not prepared to commit himself as far as a private member's vote on the subject. Such caution was characteristic of Arrese at that time. In the same year, 1947, he published *Capitalismo, Cristianismo, Comunismo,* in which the chapter dealing with 'A Scheme for the Possible Organisation of the State' avoids all mention of the monarchy and does not touch on the clearly crucial question of what form the leadership of the State should take.[7]

As Arrese and his Falangist comrades realised, whilst Franco was not prepared to release *Falange* from its contract with the Movement,[8] it was not his intention, either, to allow the Party to impose its aspirations of being the primary element in an institutionalised regime. They had little room to manoeuvre and Arrese's half-hearted dissent was the expression of that of no more than a small minority within the Movement *Falange*. The majority quickly 'suffocated, overcame and distorted'[9] the objections raised by Arrese, who claimed to consider the regime 'non-existent',[10] yet continued to participate in it. The view of a Falangist critic sums up the *Falange's* performance with respect to the Law of Succession: 'we must conclude that the *Falange*, at least through its most important ideologue of that time (ie. Arrese), cannot be considered to have played a very brilliant role, because of its reticent and vacillating attitude.'[11]

If Arrese was 'reticent and vacillating', the majority of his comrades were not. The projected Law was approved by the *Cortes* on 7 June 1947, and a popular referendum was called for 6 July. 'The provincial and local official organs of the Movement', in which most of the career Falangists were employed, 'set to work to achieve the greatest possible success for the referendum'.[12] In spite of the Law being against the anti-monarchical tenets of the Falangist credo, the Party Press lent itself wholeheartedly to the campaign:

The basic Laws included in the norms for the Succession indicate the constitutional status achieved by the régime and how far a system of permanence and continuity is indispensable.[13]

The National Government and its eminent leadership, in a magnificent act without equal in the political present or in the history of the most worthily-titled democracies, places a limit on itself, taking a Law to approval by national referendum.[14]

We are pleased to say that we affirm the Law of succession and we would affirm unconditionally any other proposed by the *Caudillo* . . . . For the *Falange*, to vote "Yes" – and not only to vote "Yes", but simply to vote – is something as primary as its active appearance in the streets and fields of Spain in its first days.[15]

We waged a war of Liberation to wrest the Fatherland from the claws of communism . . . if you do not wish to endanger all this, vote YES in the referendum.[16]

Their efforts were rewarded with a predictably large majority in favour of the Law: 14 145 163, as against 1 074 500 negative votes and spoiled ballots.[17] This was hardly surprising, given the vast programme of propaganda which had recommeneded the 'Yes' vote, the prohibition on propaganda advocating a 'No' vote or abstention, and the sanctions which would be imposed on those who did not go to the polling stations. These were formidable indeed in a context of socio-political repression and economic hardship. A certificate was issued to each voter at the polling stations, which it was necessary to present in order to collect wages. In addition, ration cards had also to be stamped on voting and any card not stamped was subsequently invalid. Ballots were to be completed at home, thereby enabling spot-checks to be made on polling day, and the Catholic Church threatened to refuse absolution to anyone who did not vote 'Yes'. 'The weightiest factor', however, 'was that there was nothing else to be done, that it was impossible to fight or to abstain either individually or collectively.'[18]

The Falangist voice was among those which enthused over the result: 'the whole of Spain ratifies with its vote the independence of the nation and the powers of Franco. . . . Polling day was an example of enthusiasm and political morality'; 'if the *Caudillo* had only this to his credit, it would be sufficient to make him worthy of the highest historical glory. . . .'[19] As the *Falange* had not dared to risk opposing the Unification of political parties in 1937, so in 1947 it did not dare to risk opposing this new limitation on its present status and future prospects. However, the succession was hedged round with a complex set of controls and was, as yet, a matter for an indeterminate future. It was therefore still possible to hope that there would yet be opportunities to influence the course of events to the benefit of *Falange*. In 1947, *Falange* had nothing to gain from opposing the succession, but it still had a good deal to lose.

Events in 1948 seemed to prove Party leaders correct in their assessment of the situation. In the first place, and in terms of national politics, the tension already existing between D. Juan de Borbón and Franco became more acute in that year, in spite of the apparently cordial meetings on board the *Generalísimo's* yacht.[20]

In the second place, the international situation had changed by 1948, strengthening the Franco regime with external support thereto denied to it. Winston Churchill's Fulton speech of 5 March 1946 had insinuated that the anti-communism of the Spanish Nationalists was politically acceptable and morally justified. By 1948, the Cold War was well under way. Given the strategic position of the Iberian Peninsula, it was now both convenient and necessary for the Allies to court Spanish favour, and to ensure the stability and permanence of a strong, friendly regime. Under such circumstances, the condemnation of two years earlier must be waived and Spain re-admitted to the West European fold. With material and ideological defence of the West the prime consideration, the democratic or non-democratic nature of one of the strategically most important defenders was of less concern. In 1945, it had been considered necessary by the regime to reduce the visible presence of the *Falange*, in order not to offend the representatives of liberal democracy. Now, three years later, it was possible to restore the second most important post in the Party[21] without a murmur from those same liberal democrats, because the *Falange's* anti-communism more than compensated for its anti-democratic character.

The first steps were now taken towards lifting the international blockade. In 1948, supplies of oil and petroleum, plus military and para-military equipment, began to arrive from the United States via the Standard Oil Company. 1950 saw the arrival in Madrid of United States Economic and Military Missions and a Mission from the financial departments of the US Senate and Chamber of Deputies. In the Spring of 1951, Ambassadors from France, Great Britain and the United States presented their credentials to the *Generalísimo*, whilst the Ex-Im Bank made a first grant of $86.5 million. In 1952, Spain was admitted as a member of UNESCO.[22]

The political about-face on the part of the Western democracies was inspired, as we have noted, by essentially pragmatic motives. The Franco regime's willingness to consort with powers which, until very recently, had been total anathema, was equally based on considerations of political and economic realism. By the end of the 1940s, the impracticability of economic self-sufficiency was manifest and, consequently, the socio-political stability of the regime which had adopted autarchy as its economic line was at risk.

The situation of shortages and poverty, characteristic of the years immediately after the end of the Civil War, stagnated and, in some respects, even deteriorated in the second half of the decade. By 1949, agricultural production, on which the policy of autarchy relied almost entirely to feed the population, had fallen even below its 1942–43 subsistence levels, as a result of lack of seeds and fertilisers, extremely low levels of mechanisation, and adverse climatic conditions.[23] Industrial production in 1949 was only 30% higher than it had been in 1929, and, in 1950, only 18% higher than in 1935, conditioned as it was by the difficulties in obtaining raw materials and mechanising antiquated production processes, and by shortages of fuels and electricity. In an attempt to contain growing economic inflation, restrictions were imposed on credit facilities in the Autumn of 1947, which not only failed to stop the inflationary trend, but also caused investment to stagnate and the number of enterprises declared bankrupt to increase.

In spite of ferocious repression and the implications of being indexed ('*fichado*') in the files of the Ministry of the Interior, the people least able to defend themselves against the effects of economic autarchy, the working classes, showed increasing external signs of their discontent in the latter half of the 1940s and the first years of the 1950s. Sporadic protests against working conditions and the rising cost of living in Cataluña and Vizcaya in 1946 and 1947, had grown by the Spring of 1951 to much more serious conflicts in Madrid, Guipúzcoa, Vizcaya and Cataluña. In Barcelona, a full-scale general strike took place on 12 and 13 March 1951 and a down-tools affecting some 250 000 workers occurred in Bilbao and San Sebastian on 23 and 24 April of the same year. The strikes were motivated primarily by economic hardship, but their political implications were clear – as, indeed, the regime itself recognised, denouncing the strike movement as the work of communist agitators.[24]

In these circumstances, if the Western bloc needed Spain as an anticommunist ally, the Franco regime was more than willing to accept, in return, the life-line offered in the form of economic aid and international recognition. The process of *détente* culminated in the signing, on 26 September 1953, of the Hispano-American agreement known as the 'Pacts of Madrid'. In socio-economic terms, this meant the end of autarchy and the beginning of the conversion of Spain into a modern, consumer society. In political terms, it meant a reinforcement of the status quo. This was a paradigmatic example of the peculiar capacity of the Franco regime to effect important changes at the economic and social levels without altering substantially the political super-structure.[25]

In view of the nationalist and anti-liberal democratic emphasis of its doctrine, it might have been expected that the *Falange* would organise some kind of opposition to such mortgaging of the Fatherland to foreign powers. Once again, however, political survival coupled with opportunism took precedence over ideological consistency. Throughout the period leading up to the 'Pacts of Madrid', the Party Press conducted a campaign in favour of the new understanding reached between the two countries, laying emphasis on the anti-communist aspect of their mutual interests.[26] One month after the signing of the treaty, a further occasion arose for the *Falange* to voice its support to the regime's foreign policy. In October 1953, coinciding with the twentieth anniversary of the foundation of *Falange Española*, the First National Congress of FET y de las JONS was held in Madrid. It was organised and presided over by Raimundo Fernández Cuesta, Minister Secretary General of the Movement since 1951, and held in spite of 'strong opposition from other members of the Government, who said it was madness to give this sensation of revitalisation of the *Falange*'.[27] Franco, however, approved of the exercise and his approval was far more important than the grumblings of the sceptics. He even presided at, and addressed, the mass gathering of Falangists in the Chamartín sports stadium on the final day of the Congress, to the enthusiastic acclaim of the assembled comrades.[28]

As in 1948, when the cooling of relations with the Alphonsine monarchists had been accompanied by the restoration of the post of Secretary General of FET y de las JONS, *Falange* was now again visibly promoted to maintain the internal balance of power.[29] In spite of the international political successes of the preceding three years, the regime was being criticised by a certain sector of the Monarchist camp, and Franco looked to the *Falange* for public support. The Falangists, ever sensitive to opportunities to score over political rivals, organised the Congress (the first and only one in the history of the unified Party, and held sixteen years after the latter's creation) as an attempt to save the force, opinion and doctrine of the *Falange* and to harmonise them with the political line being followed by Franco, which (was) directed towards saving the contemporary situation of Spain.[30]

The resolutions adopted and the speeches made in the course of the Congress revealed both *Falange's* identification with the regime and its determination not to yield any ground to any force which might threaten to disrupt a balance of power then favourable to *Falange*:

> Those comrades who fought on the battlefield, achieving by their effort and sacrifice the nationalist victory, will continue to be organised in Delegations of Ex-Combatants, a heroic reserve unit always prepared to become a combative force, lest, at any time, hesitation or betrayal should endanger our Revolution.[31]

> The *Falange* will act severely against any liberalising deviations which may occur within or outside its ranks, reducing to silence any discordant voice which attempts to attack the Unity of the Victory.[32]

> The *Falange* maintains an alert and resolute vigil against attempts at the surreptitious organisation of political parties and certain tendencies which, whether they be Rightist or Leftist, would mean opposition to the unity of the Movement. Under no circumstances will the *Falange* permit the illegitimate action of cliques which aspire to undermine its condition of sole source of the political inspiration of the State, thereby also undermining the authority of *Falange's* Chief and *Caudillo*.[33]

The speech made by Party Secretary Fernández Cuesta on 28 October 1953 contained a direct attack on the Alphonsine Monarchists' notion of establishing a 'third force', a 'social monarchy', in Spain:

> Falangism . . . energetically rejects all accusations of anachronism or senility and opposes the effective strength revealed by the presence of one hundred and fifty thousand comrades, to the supposed existence in Spain of a third force.[34]

With regard to the recent alliance with the United States, far from being critical, or even mildly disapproving, the *Falange* repeated its wholehearted support for the idea of creating a West European bulwark against the communist 'threat':

A new and necessary mission, a new and imposing reason, broaden our horizons and accelerate our pace. Our national mission, ever ongoing, grows and spreads to become a universal mission. Spain has associated herself, decisively and contractually, with the defence of Europe. For us, this is above all the defence of Western Christianity. We defended it in our Homeland as the prime *raison d'être* of our Falangist being and we shall have to defend it in the world. Now the dead of our Blue Division form the vanguard of the defence of Europe.[35]

At most, Fernández Cuesta alluded discreetly to unspecified risks involved in Spain's new international role:

Falange continues to constitute the core of the unity of the Spanish people, of its incorruptible dignity and its national sense of independence, all the more important to maintain and proclaim, the more intense our international relations and the more possible outside influences.[36]

This ostentatious and carefully orchestrated operation of mutual support and admiration need not have irritated the *Falange's* opponents nor encouraged excessively its partisans, for Franco was no more prepared now than he had ever been to promote any single sector of his following to sole power. The support publicly afforded to FET y de las JONS in 1953 was one more 'stroke' in the game of maintaining the balance of internal power whereby the regime contrived to survive and prosper. In so far as the *Falange*, like the other players, participated voluntarily in the game, accepting the rules, the risks and the method of play, it also contributed to the survival and prosperity of the whole system.

When convenient in the short term to counterbalance Monarchist pressures, the *Falange* was temporarily elevated to the position of protagonist of the political moment. It had been made clear in 1947, however, that the institutional framework of the regime was not to take totalitarian form, and it was therefore not politic in the long term to alienate non-Falangist support by excessive promotion of the Falangist component of the Movement. Thus, in spite of the tensions frequently existing between the regime and the exiled monarchy, the partisans of the Alphonsine Pretender were allowed to participate in the municipal elections held in November 1954 and, in December of the same year, Franco and Don Juan met on the estate of the Conde de

Ruiseñada, in the province of Cáceres. They had already exchanged letters in the course of the year regarding the education in Spain of Don Juan's son and heir, Prince Juan Carlos. 1955 was punctuated by declarations of mutual understanding which suggested that the question of the succession was settled and even relatively imminent.[37]

Some of the younger members of *Falange* were incensed by the Monarchist advance, and voiced their anti-royalist feeling in shouting abusive slogans at the periodic gatherings of the *Frente de Juventudes*.[38] More significant for future developments than the mere vociferating of the rank and file, however, was the attitude adopted by a group of students who then comprised the leading ranks of the official union of students, the SEU: Manuel Fraga Iribarne, Gabriel Elorriaga, Rodolfo Martín Villa, Miguel Ortí Bordás, Antonio Castro Villacañas, Jorge Jordana Fuentes, and Miguel Sánchez Mazas.

The turnover of members in the *Frente de Juventudes* was very rapid and the political, or doctrinal, level low. The majority of long-term militants, except those who went to the 'José Antonio Training School' ('Escuela de Mandos José Antonio') subsequently staffed the lowest grades of the Party and administrative structures in their adult professional career. The SEU, on the other hand, although not providing any kind of autonomous stimulus to student politics as such, was the training ground for a significant number of those who were later to hold positions of political responsibility at a national level.[39]

The position of the SEUists in the 1950s was not merely of resigned acquiescence in the regime, but of active support for its continuance through the combination of the legacy of the Civil War – Francoism – with an institutional structure appropriate both to Spanish traditions and contemporary national and international needs and convenience. Neither the republican nor the totalitarian models fulfilled all these conditions. Besides, Spain had been declared a kingdom in 1947 and the *Falange* had supported that declaration. To oppose the monarchist option now would have offered the double difficulty of going against Franco's will and of finding an alternative, neither of which were within the bounds of possibility for the SEU leaders.

They accepted what was, in theory, contrary to Falangist principles because they knew that the monarchist die was irrevocably cast. They were realistic in their appreciation of the contemporary situation and rejected any attempt to impede change simply by ignoring it. 'There is no way of eluding the historical situation at any given point in time', declared the SEU magazine, *Juventud*, in an article which discussed the relationship between the Movement and the Monarchy.[40] Whilst its assessment of that particular 'given point in time' led to the conclusion that Spain needed a political structure other than the Movement, it nevertheless still advocated an institutional framework applicable to a country 'saved from the Communist invasion by the rising of 18 July 1936'.[41]

Unlike the older generation of *camisa vieja* Falangists, the SEU leaders of the early 1950s were more concerned with the conservation of the political and ideological content of the regime than simply with the preservation of its structural form. Their attitude earned them the label of 'leftists' from the *Falange's* self-styled purists.[42] They certainly belonged to the first post-war generation of Falangists, but they could not – and did not wish to – be considered as 'leftists'.

Beneficiaries of the Nationalist victory, but not participants in the war; upholding the values of Fatherland, Catholicism and anti-communism, but aware of the need for a certain flexibility in order to adapt to the immense social, political, economic and cultural changes brought about by World War II and its aftermath, they considered it not only possible but also necessary to combine 'revolution' with 'restoration', since theirs was a Lampedusian concept of change.[43] In them, for reasons of age, social background, political affiliation and professional ambition, lay the human basis for the transition from Francoism to Monarchy under Juan Carlos I. The combination which they incarnated, of political conservatism and socio-economic liberalism, made them ideal occupants for those positions of power from which it could be ensured that the transitional opeation would take place without upheaval, without any power-vacuum, and without significant immediate change. It was, to a significant degree, through them as Ministers, Under-Secretaries, Director Generals and so on, that Franco made certain the realisation of his own forecast with regard to the institutional situation immediately after his death: 'The future of our Fatherland is tied up and well tied up.'[44]

Clearly, this assessment is made in the light of events subsequent to the period under consideration here. In fact, however, it was possible from the 1950s onwards to distinguish where the political future of the 'SEU generation' might lie. Their publications, their involvement with the contemporary student movement and their desire for professional success were explicitly identified with Franco and the *Falange*: 'The *Falange* is with Franco . . . and Franco believes in Spain because he believes in the *Falange*';[45] 'the mention of (José Antonio's) name is sufficient for those of us who seek in him our roots, our human model and the inspiration for new enterprises'.[46] Whilst they were forward-looking in their attitude towards the social and political development of Spain, their starting point was the conservation of the Nationalist victory in 1939. 'Continuity is a political virtue of the first order',[47] affirmed *La Hora*, while *Alcalá* published the following eulogistic lines on the political figure of Franco:

> The Spanish régime born of the rising of 18 July 1936 has been consolidated, enjoys an indisputable prestige, and has achieved, for the first time in centuries, an independent political line for the Spanish people. . . . The figure of Francisco Franco, and his political talent like his military talent before, have made possible a situation in which we may look to the future with optimism. Precisely for that reason, it is urgently necessary to consolidate the present and to make definitively sure of the future.[48]

In similar vein, Rodolfo Martín Villa wrote that 'few things can inspire us with as much hope as the vitality and desire for continuity that we find in the *Sindicato Español Universitario*'.[49] He was right in pointing to the significance of the fact that his contemporaries in the SEU, young men who hankered after 'an idea, a myth, an archetype around which to group themselves' and who found attractive the idea of 'the habit of conquest', were those who were 'being trained for their role as the professionals of the future'.[50]

Both the aggressive Falangists of the *Frente de Juventudes* and the more rational comrades of the SEU were, however, frustrated in their eagerness to effect their 'revolution' by the attitude of their elder comrades, ensconced in the Movement structures. The willingness of these Falangists to subordinate their own political line to 'whatever revisions life might demand',[51] was accompanied by an explicitly threatening attitude towards 'certain foreign interests, which sometimes aspire to finding internal echoes',[52] by which they meant as much those Falangists whom they termed 'leftists' as their traditional enemies, the socialists and communists.

So much was clear from the opposition of the Minister of the Interior, Blas Pérez González, and the Vice-secretary General of the Movement, Tomás Romojaro, to a 'Congress of Young University Writers of Spain', planned for November 1955 and organised by, among others, Falangists Dionisio Ridruejo and Pedro Laín Entralgo (then Dean of Madrid's Central Univeristy), with the participation of a 'reformist' group within the SEU.[53] Three months later, in February 1956, a serious incident occurred in the Madrid University campus which demonstrated even more clearly that the main fear of the Movement Falangists was not that the *Falange* would not set a revolutionary process in motion, but precisely that it might. On this occasion again, fidelity to Franco was placed before solidarity with Falangist comrades, when the two came into conflict with each other.

9 February is the anniversary of the death of the Falangist proto-, martyr, Matías Montero, commemorated annually by his comrades. On their way back from the commemorative events of 9 February 1956, a group of Falangists encountered a group of student opponents in one of the main thoroughfares of the student quarter in Madrid.[54] A violent clash ensued, in the course of which a young Falangist, Miguel Alvarez Pérez, was seriously wounded by a bullet in the head. He was taken to hospital and underwent emergency brain surgery, being suddenly converted into the focus of the tension between the most reactionary elements in the regime and those who aspired to seeing even the mildest breeze of change blow through its structures.

Predictably, the response of the former was repressive and, in Ridruejo's opinion, absurdly exaggerated.[55] The governing body of the University immediately announced the suspension of classes. The Secretary General of the Movement, Fernández Cuesta, was urgently recalled from an official visit to Brazil and Santo Domingo. The meeting of the Council of Ministers held on 10 February decreed the suspension for three months of Articles 14 and 18 of the *Fuero de los Españoles* (Spaniards' Charter), which guaranteed, repectively, free-dom of movement within 'the national territory' and release or prosecution within seventy-two hours for anyone arrested.

The Monarchist daily, *ABC*, added to the violence of the atmos-phere with an Editorial in the 11 February 1956 edition entitled 'Patriotic alert', in which it declared its solidarity with 'the Falangist faith' and warned against the 'hidden hand' which supposedly controlled 'the authors of the crime'. Responsibility was implicitly laid at the door of the exiled Socialist leader, Indalecio Prieto, who was quoted as writing in a recent issue of *El Socialista*, 'I think the moment has arrived again to stimulate and cultivate from outside the noble attitude symptomatic of the young people inside Spain'.

Even though Alvarez was still alive, *Arriba* headlined its 10 February 1956 edition, 'They've killed Matías Montero again', while *El Español*, published by the Ministry of Information and Tourism, carried an article entitled 'The conspiracy has names' ('La conjura tiene nombres propios'). The piece constituted a violent attack on certain students, whom it accused as 'Communist intriguers', and denounced the proposed 'Young Writers' Congress' as a typical *agit-prop* tactic, strongly condemning the participation of 'people from inside our own house'.[56]

In Falangist circles, the most extreme comrades were thirsting for vengeance and a 'night of the long knives' was feared if Alvarez should, in fact, die. The orthodox members of the SEU and the extreme Right-wing Falangist organisation the *Guardia de Franco*, then under the leadership of Dr Luis González Vicén, were on the alert for any new developments and their premises were placed under Army surveillance in order to forestall any attempt at reprisals.[57] In the event, Alvarez survived, with severe brain damage. His official compensation was the Falangist medal for bravery and the income from a small, open-air bar in the centre of Madrid.[58]

The net result of the February 1956 crisis was that the attempt to reform from within the University in general, and the SEU in particular, had come to nothing and was even counter-productive. The Cabinet changes which took place immediately afterwards, and in clear reaction to what had happened, removed the would-be reformers Laín Entralgo, Joaquín Ruiz Jiménez (then Minister of Education) and Manuel Fraga (then General Technical Secretary for Education, and considered 'progressive'). The new Minister of Education, Jesus Rubio, was an 'Old Shirt' Falangist with almost twenty years of service in the Educational Depatment of FET y de las JONS. Fraga Iribarne's successor, Antonio Tena Artigas, was the former Head of Radio Services in the Party Propaganda Secretariat for the province of Madrid. There were also important changes for the most reactionary members of the *Falange*. Fernández Cuesta was replaced as Secretary General by José Luis Arrese, and Romojaro as Vice-secretary by Diego Salas Pombo.[59] The 'incompetence' of those dismissed was thus castigated without making too great a concession to the anti-Falangist supporters of the regime.

The political significance of what occurred in the Universities in the first half of the decade of the 1950s was, of course, far deeper than the changing of Cabinet posts in 1956 implies. Indeed, the analysis of this critical period as a watershed for the entire Spanish political spectrum, both inside and outside Spain, goes beyond the limits of the present study. For the *Falange* in particular, however, it can be said that the crisis, and the solution provided by the regime, gave rise to a clarification of positions within the ranks from which two, or even three, currents emerged.

On the one hand, there were those whose dissatisfaction with the regime was radicalised by the events of 1955–56. Some left the *Falange* altogether others formed 'purist' Falangist groups, in order to 'rescue' the original doctrine from its 'usurpation' by the Movement. The emergence and development of these groups will be examined in Chapter 7.

On the other hand, there were those other Falangists who realised that, in a trial of strength between the forces of reform and those of conservatism, the latter would always win, if only for the simple reason that they held control of the means of physical repression. These Falangists, mainly to be found in the *Frente de Juventudes* and the SEU, were pragmatic and even reformist in their outlook but not, as we have noted earlier, leftist. Applying their pragmatism now to the political situation in 1956, they understood that, for the moment at least, the structural framework of the regime was not going to be changed. As Fraga Iribarne's dismissal intimated, the furtherance of their political careers depended not on advocating such change, as they had done at the beginning of the decade, but on installing themselves in the ramifications of the Establishment, in order to 'play the system'.

With the situation in the Universities once more under control, the new governmental team was commissioned to produce a blue-print for a revised version of the Party Statutes, for a Law of the Fundamental Principles of the State, an Organic Law of the Movement, and an Organisational Law of the Government. On the basis of this vote of confidence in the *Falange*, it prepared to reassert its presence and influence in the elaboration of what was conceived of as tantamount to a Constitution. A study group was formed, composed by Arrese, González Vicén, José Antonio Elola, Diego Salas Pombo, Rafael Sánchez Mazas and Javier Conde. Arrese's speech in Valladolid on 3 March 1956 referred to what the group, as representatives of the *Falange*, saw as their prime objectives: 'to win the man in the street and to structure the regime'.[60]

Although Salas Pombo comments that Arrese was far more concerned with the latter than with the former, at least at the outset Arrese laid emphasis on the need to increase *Falange's* popular appeal:

> The mission of the *Falange* is to root itself in the conscience of all Spaniards, in the knowledge that the future will not be uncertain whilst the *Falange* is firmly implanted, well-loved, and at one with the very existence of the Fatherland.[61]

Vice-secretary Salas held a similar view, believing that 'it is people who make institutions, and it is the popular foundation of a system which guarantees its permanence',[62] by which he meant the permanence of the regime through that of the *Falange*, and *vice versa*. Unlike Arrese, however, Salas Pombo was especially concerned with the question of broadening, or at least maintaining, the social base of the *Falange* at a time when 'Franco's peace' and the first tastes of the benefits of a consumer society were more attractive than political militancy to the middle classes which had formerly constituted *Falange's* active clientele. A certain process of 'proletarianisation' had even taken place, in so far as the upper middle class and aristocratic elements which had constituted an important part of the militant base of the pre-war *Falange* now formed part of the élite of the post-war single party, whilst rank-and-file militants now came mainly from the urban lower middle and service classes, swelled by immigrants from impoverished rural areas attracted by the relative prosperity of the urban centres.[63] Whilst the *Falange's* patron survived, the question of its independent strength scarcely arose. With an economically, socially, culturally and politically debilitated rank and file, however, the party's chances of survival without Franco, or some other form of official protection, were not good.

Salas Pombo was undoubtedly aware of this problem. Speaking in 1977 of the difficult two-year period in which he was active in the elaboration of the Law of Fundamental Principles, he commented:

> The institutionalisation of the Movement seemed to me far less important than the recovery of the vitality and strength that the *Falange* had progressively lost with the passage of time. The important thing was to recover the support, and restore the faith, of our people, who, as a consequence of inactivity and routine, no longer had the tension they had in 1939 or that they had maintained until 1953, when the Concordat with the Vatican and the pact with North America made people relax in the belief that everything was done now.[64]

Arrese, however, was intent on spearheading the 'institutionalisation of the Movement', and commissioned from the Institute of Political Studies a preliminary study for the three Laws which were to be prepared.[65] The report it duly produced made no reference to the monarchy, in spite of the fact that, in accordance with the 1947 Law of Succession, the institutional framework in which the Movement would be inserted was, *a priori*, that of a kingdom. On the contrary, increased importance was given to the role of the Movement in general and of the National Council and the Secretary General of FET y de las JONS in particular, within the context of the unspecified leadership of an undefined State. The question of the succession was left equally vague. The successor was referred to as 'the one called to the leadership', though it was not explained how the 'calling' was to be effected.[66]

The proposals met with the disapproval of Falangist Luis González Vicén, of Franco's close collaborator Luis Carrero Blanco, and of the Minister of Justice, Antonio Iturmendi. Carrero's comments spoke clearly of establishing a 'social monarchy', based on the Fundamental Laws and on the 'principles which inform the National Movement'. 'The fundamental elements of this system', he continued, 'must be the Crown, the Council of the Realm, the National Council of the Movement, the Cortes and the government'.[67] Neither the *Falange*, nor the Secretary General, as autonomous elements, entered into this scheme at all.

The criticisms made by Iturmendi were of a similar nature, and he went further. He commissioned from Laureano López Rodó, then General Technical Secretary to the Presidency of the Government and closely connected to Carrero Blanco by political, ideological and religious affinities, a 'study for the Laws, which would complete the constitutional organisation (of the State)'.[68] The 'thirteen dense pages' which López Rodó submitted in response to Iturmendi's request, and which formed the basis of a report presented to Franco entitled 'Ideas on the Fundamental Laws', were aimed quite clearly at limiting the powers of the Movement as an institution and at exalting the values of the Monarchy.[69]

In addition to the excessive importance they considered to be given to Falangist concepts, the objections to Arrese's project were based on what was seen as Arrese's tactic of 'taking the matter of the Fundamental Laws out of the Govenment's hands and placing it exclusively in those of the National Council and the *Junta Política*', thereby trying to give these bodies a new significance even before the Laws were passed.[70] In effect, it was Arrese's intention to present the Cabinet with a finished project, which would then follow the normal legislative procedure. The non-Falangist members of the Cabinet saw this as an attempt at a Falangist *coup de main* and, evidently considering such a thing a real possibility, expressed their total opposition.

At the same time, there was strong opposition to the Falangist proposals from the upper echelons of the Spanish Church hierarchy.

Franco received a group of Cardinals, who expressed the opinion that Arrese's proposals were inadmissible because of their 'totalitarian' nature and because they had been elaborated 'behind the back of the Government and of the social forces of the nation'.[71] Arrese instructed Salas Pombo to send a copy of his proposed Laws to all the Captains General of the Armed Forces, the Rectors of the Universities, and the most important Church dignitaries. The military men replied in terms which indicated that they were prepared to participate, with the contribution of their opinion, so that the project would be 'the product of the collaboration of all'.[72] The Cardinals, however, held firm, in spite of modifications introduced into the original draft. A speech made by Arrese in December 1956, in which he attempted to demonstrate that Falangist participation in the institutions of the State was minimal,[73] did not sway them either. The intense activity of Salas Pombo, who tried to persuade them of the non-totalitarian nature of Arrese's proposals, was equally in vain. The Falangists knew, moreover, that Franco was going to be more influenced on this occasion by the combined effects of Carrero's criticisms, the apprehensions of the Church's representatives, and the 'political reticence' of such prestigious military colleagues as the Captain General of Cataluña, Juan Bautista Sánchez, than by the insistence of Arrese and Salas Pombo.[74]

From the outset, there had been indications that Franco intended to control closely the process in hand. In July 1956, in a speech made before the National Council, he told the assembled Councillors that the Programmatic Points of the *Falange* were out of date and that a new formula must be found, more appropriate to the contemporary reality of Spain.[75] Salas Pombo relates the remarks made to him by Franco afterwards

> Speaking to me alone, explaining to me what he was going to do, and what he thought, he announced to me the Fundamental Principles which eventually came out in 1958. He said to me, 'Look, the 26 Points have done their time. One of them deals with separatism and says "The Republican Constitution in force, in so far as it threatens the unity of Spain, should be annulled. We demand its immediate annulment." It doesn't make sense to go on talking about the Republican Constitution when we've already annulled it years ago.'[76]

It was clear, then, that whilst a desire for ideological continuity underlay the decision to make the Falangists responsible for the Fundamental Principles project, it was not intended that the *Falange* itself should be converted into an institution. Like the young Falangists of the SEU, the regime was concerned to preserve its essential content whilst adapting its form to the needs of the socio-political moment, whereas the career Falangists around Arrese intended also to maintain and even strengthen the form of the preceding twenty years. Thus when, in January 1957, Franco told Arrese that, for the time being, his project must be left to one side, the official *Falange* was obliged to realise that it had lost the opportunity ('which we felt intuitively might well be the last'[77]) definitively to secure its own future as an integral and indispensable part of Francoism.

Since it had no viable alternative, the *Falange* was obliged to accept, as it had accepted other adverse situations in the past, the Fundamental Principles which were finally approved in May 1958 and which made no special provision for the role of the Party within the framework of the regime. Arrese's subsequent transferral from the Party Secretariat to the Ministry of Housing should not be seen as demotion, says Salas Pombo, but as testimony of Franco's gratitude for faithful service, which Arrese took with the same sense of duty, decorum and fidelity.[78]

Notes

1. For the development of the Alphonsine cause and of the relations between Franco and D. Juan de Borbón during the period 1939–1945 see Gil Robles, J. M., *La monarquía por la que yo luché* (Madrid: Taurus, 1976) pp.15–150; Sainz Rodríguez, P., op. cit., pp. 275–310; and López Rodó, L., op. cit., pp.13–70.
2. The text of the letter is reproduced in Lopez Rodó, L., op. cit., pp. 37–8. The Falangist signatories included Pedro Gamero del Castillo, Manuel Halcón, Juan Manuel Fanjul (then Vicesecretary General of the Movement), Antonio Gallego Burín and Jaime de Foxá.
3. For a detailed study of the period of economic autarchy, see Ros Hombravella *et al.*, op. cit., *passim* and the references given therein. See also, Esteban, J., loc. cit. A contemporary account of the general socio-political context of the early 1940s is given in Barba, B., *Dos años al frente del Gobierno Civil de Barcelona* (Madrid, 1948) and that of a foreign historian in Gallo, M., *Spain under Franco*, pp. 85–160.
4. *Arriba* (1 Apr. 1947); López Rodó, op. cit., p. 90. See also Suárez Fernández, L., op. cit., vol IV, pp.160–4.
5. The text of the Law was published in the 27 July 1947 edn of the *Boletín Oficial del Estado*.

6. *The Observer* (London, 13 Apr. 1947); López Rodó, L., op. cit. pp. 91–3.
7. Arrese Magra, J. L., *Capitalismo, Cristianismo, Comunismo* (Madrid: Ediciones Radar, 1947), ch. XVII, *passim*.
8. A letter written by Dionisio Ridruejo to Franco in Feb. 1947, suggesting the convenience of 'liberating' the *Falange* from its connection with the official structures of the regime, went unheeded as had a similar request made by Ridruejo in 1942 (Ridruejo, D., *Casi unas memorias* pp. 282–4).
9. Martínez Val, J.M., *¿Por qué no fué posible la Falange?* (Barcelona: Dopesa, 1975) p. 95.
10. Arrese, J. L., *Anotaciones a la Ley de Sucesión . . .*, quoted in Martínez Val, op. cit., p. 97.
11. Ibid.
12. Ibid.
13. 'La fiel historia', leading article in *Arriba* (8 Apr. 1947).
14. *Arriba* (10 June 1947).
15. 'La Falange y el Referendum', leading article in *Arriba* (22 June 1947).
16. Ibid. (25 June 1947).
17. Ibid. (27 July 1947). Cf. Preston, P. in *Historia 16*, Extra no. XXIV (Dec. 1982), who gives 3 033 649 as the total of 'no's', spoiled ballots and abstentions.
18. Gallo, M., op. cit., pp. 178–9; *BOE* (9 & 25 June 1947).
19. *Arriba* (8 & 23 July 1947).
20. For Franco's interview with Don Juan on board the *Azor* on 25 Aug. 1948, see López Rodó, L. op. cit., p. 106; Gil Robles, J. M., op. cit., p. 265; *ABC* (Madrid, 29 Aug. 1948).
21. The post of Secretary General of FET y de las JONS had been vacant since the dismissal of Arrese. It was now assigned (although as yet without Ministerial status) to Raimundo Fernández Cuesta, who, at the same time, was Minister of Justice.
22. Hovey, H. A., *U.S. Military Assistance*, Praegart, New York 1965, p. 175; Tamames, R. *Estructura económica de España*, Madrid 1964, pp. 564–6; Gallo, M., op. cit., pp. 202–6.
23. In October 1946, a commercial agreement concluded with Argentina provided for the import of 520 000 ton of cereals in 1947 and 400 000 in 1948. Further imports of basic foodstuffs were agreed on for a period of five years (although this agreement was revised in 1948 and the proposed imports from Argentina were substituted by produce from Mexico). Ros Hombravella, op. cit., pp. 165–6.
24. Ros Hombravella, op. cit., pp. 138–206; Gallo, M., op. cit., pp. 180–97, 207–14; Ferri, L., op. cit., pp. 74–194; Esteban, J., loc. cit., pp. 159–67; Soler, R., 'The New Spain' in *New Left Review*, no. 58 (Nov.–Dec. 1969) pp. 3–10; Calamai, N., *La lotta di classe sotto il Franchismo*, (Bari: De Donato Editore, 1971) pp. 11–14.
25. Cf. Miguel, A. de, *Sociología del franquismo* (Barcelona: Euros, 1975) *passim*.
26. See, for example, the following Editorials in *Arriba*: 'España y Norte-america', 5 July 1952; 'Intereses y Simpatías' (22 Aug. 1952); 'Línea anticomunista' (31 Aug. 1952); 'Advertencia a Occidente' (6 Aug. 1953); 'La amenaza de esta hora' (19 Aug. 1953); 'España no puede ser

indiferente a la defensa occidental' (1 Oct. 1953).

27. Raimundo Fernández Cuesta, interview, 15 July 1977; see also, Fernández Cuesta, R., *Testimonio*, pp. 237–8.
28. *Arriba, Pueblo* (29 Oct. 1953).
29. On his appointment and duties as Secretary General and the growing tensions within the regime, see Fernández Cuesta, *Testimonio*, pp. 233–8.
30. Raimundo Fernández Cuesta, interview, 15 July 1977.
31. *I Congreso Nacional de FET y de las JONS* (Minutes of the Congress) Madrid, Oct. 1953, p.104.
32. Ibid., p.101.
33. Ibid., p.167.
34. Ibid., p.175; *Arriba* (30 Oct. 1953). The idea of the 'social monarchy' and the 'third force' was proposed by the sector of Monarchist partisans whose most prominent spokesman was *Opus Dei* member Rafael Calvo Serer. It was first expressed by him in an article entitled 'The internal politics of Franco's Spain', published in *Ecrits de Paris*, September 1953, which constituted a joint attack on the *Falange* and the Chrisitian Democrats.
35. *I Congreso Nacional de FET y de las JONS*, p. 166.
36. Ibid., p.175.
37. López Rodó, L., op. cit., pp.115–17. On the Monarchist participation in the 1954 municipal elections, see González, A. A. '¿Pucherazo en Madrid?' in *Los domingos de ABC* (Madrid, 24 Dec. 1975).
38. Alcocer, J. L., op. cit., pp.16, 18, 30–8, 73–6; personal conversation with sociologist and former Falangist Angel de Lucas, (Madrid, 13 Mar. 1977).
39. I am grateful to the current Director of the Institute for Youth (Instituto de la Juventud) in Madrid, D. Juan Saez Marín, for his insights into the nature and functioning of the *Frente de Juventudes* and the SEU during the Franco period.
40. 'Instauración y Movimiento' in *Juventud* (Madrid, 28 Aug. 1952).
41. Ibid.
42. 'El juego de la reacción' in *Haz*, no. 4 (1 Mar. 1952). *Haz* was the official mouthpiece of the SEU.
43. Fraga Iribarne, M. 'Revolución y restauración' in *Alcalá*, no. 28 (Feb. 1953). Cf. Triguero, J. 'La generación de Fraga y su destino', in *Cuadernos de Ruedo Ibérico*, no. 1, (Paris: Ruedo Ibérico, June–July 1965).
44. Francisco Franco, speech made on 11 Nov. 1971, at the opening of the tenth legislature of the Spanish *Cortes*.
45. 'El juego de la reacción', loc. cit. (1 Mar. 1952).
46. Castro Villacañas, A., 'La organización del Estado en el pensamiento de José Antonio', in *Alcalá*, no. 45 (Madrid–Barcelona: 25 Nov. 1953).
47. 'Continuidad revolucionaria' in *La Hora*, no. 101 (Apr. 1954).
48. Arroita-Jaúrregui, M., '18 julio: punto de partida' in *Alcalá*, no.13 (25 July 1952).
49. Martín Villa, R. 'En el camino', in *24*, no.17 (Madrid, 1954). In 1960, Martín Villa was appointed National Chief of the SEU.
50. Ibid.
51. Fernández Cuesta, R., *I Congreso Nacional . . .*, p.178.
52. Fernández Cuesta, R., speech broadcast by *Radio Nacional* on 19 Apr.

1955 (28th anniversary of the Unification) and reproduced in Fernández Cuesta, R. *Continuidad falangista al servicio de España* (Madrid: Ediciones del Movimiento, 1955) pp.183–5.

53. Laín Entralgo, P., *Descargo de conciencia (1930–1960)*, (Barcelona: Barral Editores, 1976) pp.404–25; Arrese Magra, J. L. *Una etapa constituyente* (hereafter *UEC*) (Barcelona: Planeta, 1982) pp.7–10, 16–18; Ridruejo, D., *Escrito en España*, pp.116–20, 127.

54. Former Falangist José Luis Rubio Cordón, interviewed in Madrid on 23 Mar. 1979, states his opinion that the encounter was deliberately engineered by the Ministry of the Interior, in order to provoke a situation in which repression in the University would appear to be justified from the point of view of public order.

55. Ridruejo's analysis of the situation is contained in an unpublished report compiled for submission to the *Junta Política* of FET y de las JONS, dated 1 Apr. 1956. A copy was given to the present writer by D. Diego Salas Pombo. A slightly modified version, prepared, but not published, in 1957, is reproduced in Ridruejo, D. *Casi unas memorias*, pp.337–55. A complete 'dossier' of contemporary documents was published in 1982 by the Universidad Complutense, Madrid, compiled by Roberto Mesa, under the title, *Jaraneros y Alborotadores* ('Rowdies and Trouble-makers') – Franco's description of the dissident students.

56. *El Español*, Madrid 24 Feb. 1956, *ABC*, 4 Mar. 1956, reproduced the article with remarks of support for the line taken by *El Español* and of condemnation for the declaration made on 9 Feb. 1956 to *l'Humanité* by exiled communist Santiago Carrillo, in solidarity with 'the struggle of the intellectuals against present-day Spain'. Ridruejo, in his report for the *Junta Política*, states that the article in *El Español* and, indeed, the entire coverage given to the incident by the Press, was a deliberate, malicious and infantile fabrication of lies, designed to justify the imposition of official authority via the exorcism of a supposed communist bogey.

57. Narciso Perales, interview 7 Jan. 1977; José Luis Rubio, interview, 23 Mar. 1979; Enrique Múgica Herzog – one of those arrested in February 1956 accused of subversive activities – in *El País*, Madrid, 3 Oct. 1976.

58. Múgica Herzog, E., loc. cit.; cf. Arrese, *UEC*, p.29.: 'I made the General Secretariat buy him a small-holding in Barajas . . .'.

59. Fernández Cuesta gives a brief account of the Feb. 1956 crisis in *Testimonio*, pp.243–5.

60. Arrese Magra, J. L., *Hacia una meta institucional* (Madrid: Ediciones del Movimiento, 1957) p.118. See also, Arrese, *UEC*, *passim*, esp. pp.56–267, which gives a truly blow-by-blow account of the two years which the process of the elaboration of these Laws lasted.

61. Arrese, J. L., *Hacia una meta institucional*, pp.120–1.

62. Diego Salas Pombo, interview, 21 Nov. 1977.

63. Cf. Jerez Mir, op. cit., pp.101–33.

64. Ibid., pp.101–33.

65. Arrese, J. L., *Hacia una meta institucional*, p.214; *UEC*, pp.73–7.

66. From the draft of the Organic Law of the Movement, quoted in López Rodó, L., op. cit., p.126.

67. Ibid., p.127; Arrese, J. L., *UEC*, pp.79–80; González Vicén, L. in *Gentes*

(Madrid, 1 Aug. 1976) and *La Gaceta Ilustrada* (10 Oct. 1976).
68. López Rodó, L. op. cit., p.128.
69. Ibid., pp.128–32; Arrese, J. L., *UEC*, pp.84–5.
70. Salas Pombo, D. interview, 21 Nov. 1977; López Rodó, L., op. cit., pp.133–4.
71. Ibid., pp.133–4.
72. Salas Pombo, interview, 27 Dec. 1977 and unpublished correspondence in the possession of Sr. Salas which this writer was permitted to examine very briefly.
73. Arrese, J. L., *Hacia una meta institucional*, pp.212–13.
74. Salas Pombo, D., interview, 27 Dec. 1977; Arrese, J. L., *UEC*, pp.212–6, 251, 262–4.
75. Arrese, J. L., *UEC*, pp.98–103.
76. Salas Pombo, D., interview, 21 Nov. 1977.
77. Fernández Cuesta, R., interview, 15 July 1977; Arrese, J. L., *UEC*, p.259.
78. Salas Pombo, D., interview, 27 Dec. 1977; Arrese, J. L. *UEC*, pp.247–8.

6 1957-76

The rejection of Arrese's attempt to impose the Falangist stamp on the new Fundamental Principles of the State undoubtedly represented an important setback for the *Falange*. The Cabinet reshuffle effected in February 1957 further reflected the regime's awareness that, in the wake of the socio-economic changes initiated in the first half of the decade, the Falangist project was a political anachronism. The Falangist attempt to assert and assure its presence was quashed in preference for the ideas and image of up-and-coming post-war politicians, whose attraction lay not only in the non-totalitarian doctrine they preached, but also in the modern, international capitalism they represented. Arrese and Salas Pombo were removed from the Party Secretariat; José Antonio Girón from the Ministry of Labour; and Blas Pérez González from the Ministry of the Interior. The disappearance of these strategic figures was scarcely compensated for the *Falange* by the retention of Jesus Rubio in the Ministry of Education, and Gabriel Arias Salgado in that of Information and Tourism, nor by the substitution of the moderate Fermín Sanz Orio for the radical Girón, and the garrulous José Solís for Arrese. Most important of all was the incorporation of three 'developmentalists' into three key positions: Alberto Ullastres as Minister of Commerce, Mariano Navarro Rubio as Minister of Finance, and Pedro Gual Villalbí as Minister without Portfolio and President of the newly-created Council for the National Economy.[1]

The economy had never been the prerogative of the *Falange* in the distribution of fields of influence whereby Franco achieved the internal balance of power. However, whereas in the 1940s economic objectives were subordinate to political considerations, the position was to be reversed in the decade of the 1960s, and the incumbent of the politico-ideological sphere, the *Falange*, was relegated to a secondary position. The *Falange* reacted to this body-blow with inertia and the customary willingness to accept whatever the *Caudillo* dictated. The new situation, says Raimundo Fernández Cuesta, 'did not please' the Falangists, but there was no question of public protest.[2] On the contrary, the Secretariat of the Movement sent a circular to all the Provincial Delegations, in which it assured militants in soothing tones that,

The familiar lexicon, and the dearly-loved concepts contained in the Declaration of Principles, indicate clearly and perfectly what are the doctrinal sources from which the Movement's programmatic bases have been taken. The *Caudillo's* explicit declaration that these basic points are the same as those expressed in the Decree of Unification shows beyond all shadow of doubt that the initial programmatic norms have been definitively incorporated into the body of fundamental legal norms by which the lives of Spain and all Spaniards are to be ruled. . . . The promulgation of the Principles thus represents the first step towards the institutionalisation of the Movement, so often requested and now made reality.[3]

Besides, although it was the 'technocrats' (as the new occupants of the economic Ministries were termed by way of ideological identification) who concerned themselves from the end of the 1950s onwards with the economic future of Spain, it was still the *Falange* that was in charge of the socio-political control of the mass of the population which was to provide the man-power for, and bear the brunt of the inflationary effects of, 'development'.

In the first half of the fifties, as we have noted earlier, a combination of political convenience and economic pragmatism had obliged the regime to accept the reincorporation of Spain into the world capitalist system. The benefits of external aid undoubtedly went a long way to relieving the hardships resulting from the failure of autarchy and, at the same time, to easing the social pressures they generated. Nevertheless, and in spite of repression.[4] the grievances of a traditionally politicised and militant working class could scarcely be entirely satisfied by the withdrawal of ration cards (in 1952) or the return of the foreign diplomats withdrawn in 1946.

Carefully regulated escape-valves were therefore created within the structures established in 1939 (and commended, it will be remembered, to the *Falange*), to ensure continued control of the working masses. Thus, in 1947, a law was passed which provided for minimal worker representation on works' committees (*Jurados de Empresa*), to be created within the framework of the official trade union system. However, the law was not implemented until 1953 and the first committees could not begin to function until 1956. Strike action was taken in Navarra, Barcelona, Valencia and the Basque Country in 1956, in which the principle demand was a guaranteed minimum wage of 75 pesetas per day.[5] As a result, the Minimum Guaranteed Salary was introduced, fixing different minimum wages according to geographical area. In 1956, the highest wage fixed was 36 pesetas, in Madrid, which was not raised to 60 pesetas until 1963 – still 15 pesetas below the 1957 demand.[6] In a similar way, the Law of Collective Contracts passed in April 1958 constituted an ostentatious, but controlled, step in the direction of achieving negotiated, rather than dictated, conditions of labour. Such negotiations, however, were carried on within, and under the supervision of, the *Central Nacional Sindicalista*, and the apparent recognition given to the division existing between workers' and employers' interests was contradicted by the cooperative nature of the official trade union system.[7]

That it should be deemed necessary to refocus labour relations was part and parcel of the general reconsideration of policies, particularly economic policies, reflected in the Cabinet changes made in February 1957. On the basis of the credits provided by such international financial bodies as the Ex-Im Bank and the IMF, together with the investments of private foreign capital, Spain had embarked on a programme of rapid industrialisation in the mid-1950s. The concentration on industrial development, to the detriment of the hitherto dominant agricultural sector of the economy, had, as one of its many social consequences, the rapid increase of urban working populations which, in turn, meant that wages could be kept depressed. At the same time, the substitution of cheap man-power for quantitatively and qualitatively deficient capital goods, coupled to the relatively high cost of raw materials and the increased demand generated by the increased urban populace, resulted in low production levels and high prices.

Between 1939 and 1959, industrial production rose by 200%, but industrial prices rose by 676.8%.[8] Whilst the annual average increase in wholesale prices and the cost of living, between 1956 and 1959, was around 10%, the average annual increase in *per capita* income in the same period was approximately 5.5%.[9] In early 1958, strikes occurred in protest against the rising cost of living and the falling purchasing power of wages, in Asturias, Barcelona, the Basque Country, Madrid, Valencia and Zaragoza.[10] The official response was a mixture of coercion and cooption: suspension of Articles 14 and 18 of the *Fuero de los Españoles* and, subsequently, application of the collective bargaining procedures approved in April of that year, which invariably linked minimal wage concessions to productivity deals. Any optimism which the working classes might have felt in the light of the very limited gains made as a result of their organised protests was curtailed by the 1959 Stabilisation Plan which, for the working classes, meant a wage freeze; a prohibition on over-time which, according to a CNS official, cut workers' wages by an average of 23%;[11] and contraction of the labour market as a result of the brake placed on credit and investment facilities.

The Stabilisation Plan heralded a decade of determined, programmed, economic development in which Spain began effectively to fulfil her role not only as the recipient of external inputs, but also as a new, virtually untapped source of benefits for multinational companies, the profitability of whose operations lay in the exploitation, *in situ*, of local materials, labour, infrastructures and consumers. A corporativistic trade union structure was scarcely compatible with an economy increasingly based on the operation of the free market and, in truth, by the beginning of the 1960s, the CNS was visibly insufficient to its task. With the creation, between 1958 and 1963, of a number of illegal, though not always clandestine, class-based trade union organisations,[12] trade union pluralism was a reality and many employers who did not want to lose production time in resolving labour disputes began to prefer direct negotiation with the unofficial, but authentic, representatives of their workers to the slow and complicated arbitration channels of the CNS.

Nevertheless, the *Falange*, in the person of the National Delegate for Syndicates and Secretary General of FET y de las JONS, José Solís, struggled to maintain the relevance of its domain. In 1963, a year in which strikes were staged again in Asturias, Cataluña, Andalucía and the Basque Country,[13] Solís promised truly free and representative syndical elections. In the following year, a law was passed which provided for the sharing of organisation and decision-taking by workers and employers in any given enterprise[14] and, in that same year, 1964, the official organisation made a final attempt to give institutional form to the conflict of interests between workers and employers, with the creation of separate Workers' and Employers' Councils for the negotiation of wages and working conditions.[15]

By the mid-1960s, however, the aspirations generated by the increasing availability of consumer goods; by contact with other, more open societies through emigration, tourism and imported cultural products; and such liberalising measures as the 1966 Press Law or the revision of Article 222 of the Penal Code, which admitted strike action for 'professional' motives, were only partially satisfied in economic terms, and largely frustrated in political terms. By 1966, the political future of Spain had once more been brought to the fore by a combination of socio-political unrest, economic crisis, Franco's advancing age, and the desire of those economic and social forces which also constituted the most influential political forces for long-term solutions more effective and internationally acceptable than repression alone.

In response to these pressures, the penultimate step was taken in the attempt to guarantee the survival of the regime after Franco's death. On 22 November 1966, the Organic Law of the State was read before the *Cortes*. It was clear from the speech read by Franco as the introduction to the Law, that the military victory of 1939 continued to be the initial source of legitimation for the regime. The main concern, now, however, was to convey the notion that that victory, as the basis for 'growth' and 'progress' in material terms, was also to be the principle source of the regime's *continued* legitimacy.

In political terms, whilst 'acceptance of, and respect for a common denominator, a single field of play and a single set of rules . . .' were still necessary for the maintenance of the 'political order of unity, authority, justice and progress'[16] it was felt that certain modifications should be made with regard to the future. The new order, nevertheless, was to be one of continuity:

> In order that provision for the future be duly made, political action of continuity is necessary. . . . We are not talking about an emergency measure, but one of foresight. Today and for many years to come, stability is assured.[17]

'Valuable elements of permanent worth' would be retained from the Movement, but alongside 'flexible institutions capable of adapting to inevitable changes'. It was a question, Franco concluded, of 'following our path, the path which has saved Spain; and of continuing along it beyond any accidental event, safe from all threats'.[18] How far Franco intended that Spain should continue along the same path was clearly indicated:

> It is necessary to provide with precision the guarantees and formal procedures not only for the first succession, but also of those which will follow once the normal order has been installed.[19]

The *Falange* was not referred to once, even indirectly, in the entire text. Even within the limits imposed by the 'organic regulation of the totality of our institutions', the political life of the country, conceived of as 'the ordered concurrence of criteria', was a far cry, in November 1966, from the days when it had run through 'the sole channel of FET y de las JONS'.[20]

Nevertheless, even before the Law was published, the career Falangists had expressed their customary identification with the *Caudillo's* policy: 'We are all with the *Caudillo*. Leaving aside marginal political differences with regard to the form, we agree upon the essence of the content.'[21] Former SEUist Manuel Fraga, by then Minister of Information and Tourism, was unstinting in his enthusiasm:

> What does Franco propose? He proposes that we go forward in the great historic enterprise of making Spain one, great and free . . . a nation respected in the world. . . . A Spain at once traditional and modern. . . . We must maintain stability. We must cement the continuity of the régime. . . . Stability and continuity are the conditions necessary for true evolution, which presupposes permanent principles, sure channels and a prudent rhythm.[22]

His words were reminiscent of, and entirely in keeping with, the continuist line he had advocated in the pages of *Alcalá* fifteen years earlier. As in 1947 and 1958, so in 1966 the attitude of the Movement Falangists was based on a two-fold assessment of the situation in general and their own possibilities and interests in particular. Falangism in 1966 had no meaning if divorced from the regime born of the 1936 military rising. Furthermore, the changes envisaged were aimed at providing continuity, not revolution, and the prime consideration was the protection of the interests behind the regime, which the Falangists shared. One of the tutors of the future King Juan Carlos, and later, in 1969, Minister Secretary General of the Movement, expressed the Party point of view succinctly:

> The succession must be continuity. . . . the King must be the personification of the historico-national legitimacy incarnated in the Spanish State to which the rebellion of 18 July 1936 gave rise.[23]

In a similar way, the Secretary General of FET y de las JONS, José Solís Ruiz, had shown, before the public announcement of the Law, that the career Falangists like himself had perceived that their interest lay in accepting a measure designed to ensure continuity in change:

> We must say "Yes" to whatever Franco asks of us. It is a question of showing that we want continuity, in the interest of the well-being of the Fatherland.[24]

As in 1947, a referendum was to be held to submit the Law to popular approval. Once the pre-referendum campaign opened, the Movement *Falange* spared no efforts to ensure an overwhelming victory for the 'Ayes'. The referendum was to be held on 14 December 1966 and, between 13 November and 13 December, the indefatigable Solís addressed meetings of workers, employers, Movement officials, youth groups and trade unionists in no less than eleven different and widely-separatd towns. Speaking always in favour of the Law as the culmination of the labours of thirty years, and the basis for those of at least another thirty, his words to Movement officials and syndicalists in Avila were typical:

> The immense responsibility of achieving political continuity and of ensuring the succession, falls on the Spanish people. As the spiritual key to that continuity, we have the National Movement, in which are reflected the inalienable principles which have constituted the difficult task of achieving peace . . . Franco has spoken to us of that peace and of the Law and the national future like a father, asking us for unity, concord and understanding. He has convoked us on 14 December with his hopes set on the future. . . . The time has come when we must choose between greatness and freedom, or misery and oppression.[25]

In a letter to Party militants, Solís was equally unequivocal in his identification, as a Falangist, with the policy adopted with regard to converting the regime into an institution,

> We are about to give our approval to the Organic Law of the State; the Law which will perpetuate, beyond the life of Franco and beyond our own lifetime, the ideals of peace, unity and justice which we were the first to proclaim and defend and which we have been the most faithful in serving.[26]

The *Falange's* most important figures added the weight of their words to the efforts being made by Solís. The Vice-secretary General of the Movement, Alejandro Rodríguez de Valcarcel, qualified the Law as expressing the 'representative and democratic aims of the Spanish people'.[27] The man who had been Minister of Labour for a record term of eleven years, José Antonio Girón reappeared, after ten years of political absence, in a television broadcast in which he declared that 'the Law we are going to vote is a veritable constitution'.[28] Former Party Secretary Raimundo Fernández Cuesta was unhesitating in his analysis of the relationship between *Falange* and Franco: 'Since the rising on 18 July 1936, as now, the *Falange* has had only one, decisive aim: obedience to Franco. . . . We did, we do and we shall continue to do, whatever Franco orders.'[29]

As had occurred in 1947 with the referendum of the Law of Succession, the result of the 1966 referendum of the Organic Law of the State was massive approval. The Law consequently became part of the basic legislation of the State on 10 January 1967. The Falangists were, predictably, enthusiastic in their comments, though some evidently felt qualms sufficient to motivate public justification of their affirmative vote.[30] *Arriba*, the Party mouthpiece, went so far as to engage in a polemic with the Monarchist daily, *ABC* on account of an article the latter had published entitled 'La sucesión' and which *Arriba* saw as an attack on the Organic Law of the State.[31] It was certainly ironic that the representatives of a party which had once deemed the Monarchy 'gloriously defunct' should now be defending a Law which assured the future of the Monarchy against the criticism levelled by that institution's own supporters.

The Minister Under-Secretary to the Presidency of the Government, Admiral Luis Carrero Blanco, had affirmed, four days before the referendum, that the 'Organic Law of the State ends all speculation about the future of the regime',[32] and, in the decade following the approval of the Law, the preparation of the 'installation' of Franco's successor was of paramount importance. Indeed, it might be said that the death of Franco on 20 November 1975 occassioned no more than the succession as a juridical formality, whereas the transition as a *de facto* reality began in 1966. The logical conclusion and the culmination of the process of preparation of the post-Franco era came in 1969, with the designation of Prince Juan Carlos de Borbón as Franco's successor, 'with the title of King'.

In the preceding three years, the *Falange* had received several indications that, at least in its original form, it was considered outdated. In 1967, the 'Falangist General', Agustín Muñoz Grandes, was replaced as Vice-President of the Government by Admiral Carrero Blanco, whose political sympathies lay with the Monarchist cause. In the same year, changes were made to the *Fuero del Trabajo* which effectively cancelled *Falange's* thereto exclusive access to administrative posts in the Syndical Organisation.[33] 1968 saw the publication of the 'Regulations of the Movement' (*Reglamento del Movimiento*) in which *Falange* was not afforded a status any different to any of the other political tendencies represented in the amalgamous

Movement. Finally, in 1969, former SEUist Fraga Iribarne and Party Secretary Solís Ruiz were ousted from the Government in the wake of a financial scandal in which their only involvement was its discovery.[34]

Yet the Falangists voted in favour of the nomination of Prince Juan Carlos as future King. Some justified their action alleging that what they had approved was a new Monarchy, installed by Franco, not the old Monarchy, 'the caricature of the institution of Monarchy' known and condemned by José Antonio Primo de Rivera.[35] The official Falangist Press was favourable, if not effusive, in its reception of Juan Carlos as Franco's successor, and duly contributed, whenever the occasion arose, to the public relations operation designed to promote the Prince's image as Franco's legitimate heir. In so doing, the Falangists considered that they were doing no more and no less than they had always done: realise 'the politics which have put Spain where she is today'.[36]

There was, however, a defiant note in the Falangist Press of 1969, which conveyed the warning that the *Falange* was not yet a spent force. It was not without grounds, for it was during the decade of the 1960s that the young SEUists of the 1950s had been serving their political apprenticeship in Movement – and even, in the case of Manuel Fraga, ministerial – posts.

To a certain extent, the popular view that 'here, every Tom, Dick and Harry has been in *Falange* at some stage', was true. The obligatory nature of organisations like the SEU or the *Frente de Juventudes*, the lack of legal alternatives for organised political activity, and the pressure towards demonstrating Falangist membership as a security measure in a repressive regime, did indeed have the effect of exposing far more people to *Falange* than the party's founders could ever have hoped for otherwise. Although, as we have noted earlier, average permanence in the Falangist organisations was short, it was nevertheless long enough to leave a lasting mark on all of those who passed through Party hands and, in some cases, was consciously used as a trampolin to a career in national politics. Thus, the changes made in the Cabinet and Administration in November 1969, as well as incorporating such seasoned Falangists as Carlos Iglesias Selgas, José Utrera Molina and Torcuato Fernández Miranda, brought a number of post-war Falangists into important positions in the power structure. Miguel Ortí Bordás was appointed Vice-secretary General of the Movement; Rodolfo Martín Villa took over from Solís as leader of the Syndical Organisation; and a man who had not belonged to the SEU but who was of the same generation and who had come up through the ranks of the *Falange*, Adolfo Suárez González, was made Director General of the State radio and television broadcasting corporation.[37]

It was precisely these neo-Falangists who were to be entrusted with the task of effecting the transition from Francoism to democracy. Adolfo Suárez, for example, was Secretary General of the Movement from December 1975 to July 1976, and President of the Government in the crucial period from July 1976 to December 1980, in which the foundations of the post-Francoist Parliamentary democracy were established. Rodolfo Martín Villa, for his part, was Minister for Syndical Relations in the first Cabinet of the Monarchy and Minister of the Interior in the second (July 1976).[38] It was of these men that the *Arriba* correspondent Ismael Medina was thinking when he wrote in 1969,

The political future of Spain will depend, in the final analysis, on the creation of a Francoist school of understanding politics among those who will ultimately be responsible for the peaceful realisation of the succession process.[39]

Whilst the new generations of Falangists climbed up the politico-professional ladder, the old school Falangists nevertheless remained at the ready. Decadent, embittered and *démodé*, but surviving, their presence at the annual gatherings in homage to Franco, in the ramifications of an ever more inadequate trade union organisation, and in the offices of the Public Administration, helped to sustain a regime increasingly harrassed by the problems generated by its own immobile structures. Their uninterrupted and 'unshakable fidelity' in turn guaranteed that, while Franco lived, the *Falange* would not be completely pensioned off.

By the beginning of the 1970s, however, the official situation of political singularity had been superceded by a real situation of (as yet illegal) plurality. In the field of labour relations, for example, both employers and workers were anxious to be free of the encumbrance of the excessively slow and rigid Syndical Organisation, and had for some time been by-passing it, where possible, in negotiations. The Trade Union Unity Act of 1971, which permitted the formation of 'Professional Associations', constituted an eleventh-hour attempt to convert the CNS into an entity of representation and participation rather than of repression and control, in anticipation of the post-Franco era. This attempt to bring politicised conflict back into the orbit of the official channels and away from illegal opposition unions proved, ultimately, to be in vain. The organisation of free, spont-aneous trade unions was legalised in March 1977 and the official CNS lost its *raison d'être* after thirty-eight years of 'unshakably faithful' service to the Francoist cause.[40]

In the strictly political field, too, plurality of ideologies and organisations was a reality, as even the regime had been forced to admit, with the promulgation, in December 1974, of a Statute of Political Associations.[41] *Falange* stalwarts Fernández Cuesta, Girón and Blas Piñar López,[42] were quick to attempt to perpetuate *Falange's* existence in the new situation and to project it into the future, now as a 'political association', as defined by the new Statute. Ironically, they were deprived of the use of the party's original title precisely as a result of their own labours to popularise their ideology, for the National Council of the Movement decided that the title FE de las JONS belonged to the entire Spanish people and could not, therefore, be appropriated by any one 'association'.

There now began a bitter, intra-*Falange* struggle for recognition and, even before Franco died, the Falangists were jockeying for positions in what was to be the post-Franco era. After Franco's death, on 20 November 1975,[43] it became clearer than ever how far FE had needed Francoism to hold together. In the absence of its father-figure, *Falange* returned to the incoherence and fragmentation which had characterised it in the period prior to the Civil War.

The 1974 Statute of Political Associations was replaced, in June 1976, by a Law which, whilst not recognising the existence of political parties as such, effectively opened the way to their creation. At the same time, the Law implied the dismantling of the Movement.[44] Significantly, the Law of Political Associations was presented to the *Cortes* by the Minister Secretary General of that same Movement, Adolfo Suárez González. It marked his first step out of political obscurity and into the realms of fame and popularity which he was to enjoy for almost five years after his designation as President of the Government shortly afterwards, in July 1976.

By 1976, there were four aspirants to the title of *Falange Española de las JONS*, each claiming to be the only group with the right to bear the name *Falange Española* as a post-Francoist political party. The first claimant was the *Frente Nacional Español* (Spanish National Front), led by Raimundo Fernández Cuesta. In addition, there was *Falange Española* (*auténtica*) (Authentic *Falange Española*), headed by Narciso Perales and Pedro Conde; the *Junta Coordinadora Nacional Sindicalista* (National Syndicalist Coordinating Committee), led by an obscure Madrid Falangist, Eduardo Zulueta;[45] and an untitled group of notoriously violent ultra-Right wingers, headed by the leader of the *Guerrilleros de Cristo Rey* (Warriors of Christ King), Mariano Sánchez Covisa.

Each denied the right of the others to the title, on the grounds of their having betrayed *Falange's* ideals during the Franco regime. Thus, the group led by former Blue Division volunteer, Sánchez Covisa, denounced the claim of the other Falangists since they had 'for forty years . . . been saying that political parties are the cancer of this country'.[46] The application of this group excited the opposition of all three other competitiors, who felt that 'such extremist Right wing groups' would use the title to construct a party with 'the same characteristics as the National Movement'.[47] This was, indeed, a strange objection from men who had participated in the National Movement since its creation, and had devoted all their efforts to maintaining and institutionalising it.

Not surprisingly, given the high proportion of *camisa vieja* Falangists in its ranks and their forty-year connection with the administrative structures charged with assigning the title, the group led by Fernández Cuesta, the *Frente Nacional Español*, was granted the right to change its name to *Falange Española de las JONS* on 1 October 1976, the fortieth anniversary of the designation of the late Francisco Franco as Head of State.

Thus, even after the death of the *Caudillo*, the name of *Falange Española* was inseparably linked to his memory and its partisans still reaped the benefit of their contribution, spread over forty-years, to his political career.

Notes

1. Cf. Equipo 'Mundo', *Los 90 Ministros de Franco* (Barcelona: Dopesa, 1970) pp. 255–56.
2. Raimundo Fernández Cuesta, interview, 15 July 1977.
3. *Texto de las orientaciones que se consideren con valor permanente*, Secretaría General del Movimiento, Madrid, Jan. 1961, quoted in Ros Hombravella, op. cit., p. 319, n. 20.
4. See above, pp. 67, 100.
5. Blanc, J. 'Las hueglas en el movimiento obrero espanol', ın *Horizonte español* (2 vols), vol. II, Ruedo Ibérico, Paris 1966; see also Fernández de Castro, I. & Martínez, J. *España hoy* (Paris: Ruedo Ibérico, 1963) p. 29.

6. Fava, I., Compta, M. & Huertas Clavería, J. M., 'Conflictos laborales que dejaron huella', in *Cuadernos para el diálogo*, Extra no. XXXIII (Feb. 1973) p. 36.
7. The Law, although not passed until 1958, was elaborated primarily on the initiative of José Antonio Girón, Falangist Minister of Labour until 1957. For an analysis of its content and implications, see: Amsden, J. *Collective Bargaining and Class Conflict in Spain* (London: Weidenfield & Nicholson, 1977) pp. 129–62; Oficina Internacional del Trabajo, op. cit., pp. 200–35.
8. Soler, R., loc. cit., p. 5.
9. Ros Hombravella, op. cit., pp. 338–40, 438.
10. Fernández de Castro, I. & Martínez, J. op. cit., p. 34.
11. Ibid., p. 34.
12. The most important of these was *Comisiones Obreras*. Others were the communist *Oposicíon Social Obrera* (*OSO*); *Alianza Sindical*, formed between 1959 and 1960 by socialists, anarchists and members of the Basque *STV*; and two left-wing, Catholic organisations, *Acción Sindical de Trabajadores* (*AST*) and *Unión Sindical Obrera* (*USO*).
13. Fernández de Castro, I. 'Tres años importantes, 1961, 1962, 1963' in *Cuadernos de Ruedo Ibérico*, no. 16, pp. 79–97; Blanc. J. 'Asturias: minas, huelgas y comisiones obreras' in *Cuadernos de Ruedo Ibérico*, no. 1, pp. 70–4.
14. Ley de Consejos de Administración, *BOE*.
15. See Oficina Internacional del Trabajo, op. cit., pp. 148–50; Iglesias Selgas, C., *El Sindicalismo Español*, pp. 49–50, 90, 125–30.
16. Franco's speech to the *Cortes*, in *Arriba*, 23 Nov. 1966.
17. Ibid.
18. Ibid.
19. Ibid.
20. Franco's speech in Barcelona, 28 Jan. 1942 (*Arriba*, 29/1/42).
21. Leading article, *Arriba*, 16 Nov. 1966.
22. Fraga Iribarne, M. in *Arriba*, 25 Nov. 1966.
23. Fernández Miranda, Torcuato, in *Arriba*, 29 Nov. 1966.
24. Solís Ruiz, J. in *Arriba*, 17 Nov. 1966.
25. Ibid., 2 Dec. 1966.
26. Ibid., 8 Dec. 1966.
27. Ibid. Rodríguez de Valcarcel was addressing a meeting of National Delegates for Associations in the Institute of Political Studies, Madrid, when he made this statement.
28. Ibid., 10 Dec. 1966.
29. Ibid., 11 Dec. 1966. Fernández Cuesta makes no mention of the Ley Orgánica del Estado in his memoirs.
30. Such as José Antonio Girón in *Arriba*, 17 Dec. 1966, and Jesus Suevos, *Arriba*, 27 Dec. 1966.
31. *Arriba*, 23 and 27 Dec. 1966; *ABC*, 21 Dec. 1966. The Falangist daily had already joined editorial battle with its rival, *Madrid*, on the same grounds: see *Madrid*, 1 Dec. 1966 and *Arriba*, 2 Dec. 1966.
32. Speech broadcast on radio and television on 10 Dec. 1966, and reproduced by the national Press on 11. Dec. 1966.

33. In the text approved on 10 Jan. 1967, Point 4 of the 1938 edition, which had stated that the CNS would be staffed by Falangist militants, was suppressed. *Fuero del Trabajo*, 3rd edn, Ministerio de Trabajo (Madrid, 1975); Oficina Internacional del Trabajo, op. cit., pp. 167–8.
34. On the 'Matesa' scandal, see e.g.: Carr, R. and Fusi, J. P., *España, de la dictadura a las democracia* (Barcelona: Planeta, 1979) p. 247; Alvarez Puga, E. *Matesa. Más allá del escándalo* (Barcelona: Dopesa, 1974) *passim*; Diario 16, *La historia del franquismo*, 2 vols, Madrid 1984–85, vol. 2, ch. 46.
35. Falangist and National Councillor Jesus Suevos, in *Tiempo Nuevo*, no. 98 (Madrid, 30 July 1969).
36. Manuel Blanco Tobío in *Arriba*, 7 Nov. 1969.
37. For the biography of Adolfo Suárez González, see, e.g.: *Documentos '80*, no. 1, 'Adolfo Suárez, todos los cargos del Presidente' (Barcelona, Feb. 1979); Morán, G., *Adolfo Suárez, historia de una ambición* (Barcelona: Planeta, 1979).
38. For the biography of Rodolfo Martín Villa, see e.g.: *¿Quién es quién en la política española?* Documentación española contemporánea, S.L., no. 4 (Madrid, 1977) p. 293; *Cuadernos para el Diálogo*, no. 228 (10 Sept. 1977) pp. 15–19; Durán Mazuque, M. *Martín Villa*, LUR (Madrid, 1979).
39. *Arriba* (3 Nov. 1969).
40. Cf. *Revista Internacional del Trabajo*, vol. 85, no. 3, OIT, Geneva, Mar. 1972. The Syndical Organisation had, in reality, already been dismantled in Dec. 1976. Although in many respects it lived on, as the *Administración Institucional de Servicios Socioprofesionales (AISS)*, created by Royal Decree in 1976.
41. For the development of the clandestine and tolerated opposition during the Franco regime, see Preston, P., 'La oposición antifranquista' and the bibliographical references therein, in Preston P., *España en crisis*, pp. 217–63; Heine, H., *La oposición politica al Franquismo* (Barcelona: Editorial Crítica, 1983).
42. Leader of the extreme Right-wing group *Fuerza Nueva*.
43. This was also the date of the death of the *Falange's* founder, José Antonio Primo de Rivera, in 1936. There is room for speculation as to the veracity of the date given as that of Franco's death: many Falangists saw the 'coincidence' as the ultimate Francoist 'usurpation' of their iconography.
44. The huge reproduction of the Falangist yoke-and-arrows symbol was finally removed from the façade of the General Secretariat of the Movement in Madrid, on 10 May 1977, barely a month before the first democratic general elections since 1936.
45. For the creation of *Falange Española (auténtica)* and the *Junta Coordinadora*, see below, p. 169.
46. Alberto Royuela, in *El País* (18 Sept. 1976)
47. Márquez Horrillo, D. in *El País* (18 Sept. 1976)

Part III
Falange Idealised

7 1939–59

Whilst the *Falange* as a whole undoubtedly supported the nationalist cause in July 1936 and became, thereafter, an integral part of the Franco regime, it cannot be considered – even within the conglomerate Party formed in April 1937 – as a monolithic bloc. It is necessary to differentiate between two types of Falangists. On the one hand, there were those who lent themselves wholeheartedly and uprotestingly to collaboration with the regime, and whose contribution to its establishment and development has been examined in preceding chapters. On the other, there were those also participated in the regime, but with a view to making their collaboration the means to 'steering' it from within along strictly Falangist lines, for they considered themselves the direct heirs of Primo de Rivera. As such, they believed, it was their duty to keep the flame of 'pure' falangism alive.

Although the purists never entirely gave up hope of being able to influence the course of the regime's development by legitimate means, it was clear that they would have numerous obstacles to contend with, not the least of which was the opposition of some of their own Falangist comrades. The influence of other political currents within FET y de las JONS also conditioned the Falangist radicals' chances of success, as did the changing international situation, especially after 1945. Finally, Franco's ultimate power and the lack of mass support from within and outside Falangist circles meant that, like the 'unshakably faithful' comrades, the *Falange* purists were unlikely to have any existence other than that permitted by, and within the confines of, the Franco regime.

The separation, for purposes of analysis, of an 'opposition' *Falange*, should not, however, be taken to imply that the 'opposition' Falangists had nothing to do with the 'regime' Falangists. They shared common social, political and historical origins, they espoused the same ideology, their responsibility for the outcome of the Civil War was the same, and there was no difference of class interests between them. Moreover, both were prepared, albeit with different motives, to participate in the establishment and running of the Franco regime. Nevertheless, the history of *Falange Española* in the Franco regime would be incomplete without an examination of the 'non-conformist' sector of the party.

Whilst, as we have noted earlier,[1] the opposition offered by *Falange* to the creation of a 'single party' in April 1937 was minimal, it was shortly after this that the first signs were given that *Falange* might not be as unconditionally behind Franco as it appeared to be. Between 1937 and 1938, an 'Old Shirt' Falangist who was highly esteemed by his comrades for his humanitarian qualities, Patricio González de Canales, attempted to form a group entitled *Falange Autónoma* (Autonomous *Falange*).[2] The group went no further than the latent discontent, or discomfort, of a few isolated individuals, as was only to be expected with the war still going on, and with the imprisoned Hedilla as an example to would-be rebels. Nevertheless, González de Canales remained one of the most persistent conspirators of the period, participating in numerous attempts to form clandestine, radical Falangist groups throughout the duration of the regime.

At the same time, though apparently without any connection with *Falange Autónoma*, a clandestine organisation which called itself *Falange Española Auténtica* (FEA) (Authentic Spanish *Falange*) circulated leaflets in which it protested against the Unification of political parties, and urged 'true' Falangists to re-establish the pre-1937 *Falange*. When discussing this episode, however, the word 'organisation', with reference to the source of the leaflets, must be used with care, for it is not certain that these were the work of an organised group, nor that they were produced by Falangists. Those who believed that the leaflets were not of Falangist origin were of the opinion that they formed part of a plan to destabilise the political situation in the Nationalist zone, and that this plan was devised and run from the Republican zone by the Socialist leader, Indalecio Prieto.[3] Certainly, Prieto had talked with *Falange* leader Raimundo Fernández Cuesta in Valencia prior to the latter's release from imprisonment. On that occasion, Prieto gave Fernández Cuesta the personal papers left in Alicante prison by José Antonio Primo de Rivera and, according to Ramón Serrano Suñer, encouraged Fernández Cuesta to join the FEA on his return to the Nationalist zone.[4] Prieto's own account of his connections with Primo de Rivera and Fernández Cuesta, however, give no indication that such was his intention although it is possible that, realising an important political advantage had been lost by the execution of Primo de Rivera, he believed the error could be repaired by returning Fernández Cuesta to the Nationalist camp. Fernández Cuesta himself, wary and laconic about this, as about most matters on which he was questioned by this writer, would not divulge the content of his conversation with Indalecio Prieto, and stated that the FEA was no more than 'a few isolated Falangists who did not agree with the Unification'.[5]

Other Falangists, however, did believe in the existence of the FEA and that the author of the leaflets was Vicente Cadenas Vicent. Cadenas was head of *Falange's* Press and Propaganda office in San Sebastian in 1937, and had fled to Italy, via France, at the time of the Unification, in order to avoid being implicated in the trials held against Hedilla and his supporters.[6] Cadenas himself denies responsibility for either the organisation or the pamphlets.[7] Yet it is worthy of note that the two Falangists most frequently associated with the FEA, Fernández Cuesta and Cadenas, were living in the same house close to the time of the Unification, for Fernández Cuesta stayed for some time in Cadenas' house in France following the former's departure from Valencia, *en route* for nationalist Spain.[8]

None of these people was involved, however, when the FEA reappeared as a motive for mutual mistrust and suspicion among Franco's followers, in 1939. In that year, three Falangists, Narciso Perales, Eduardo Ezquer y Gabaldón, and Tito Meléndez, were arrested on the charge of forming the organisational triumvirate of the FEA, with the intention of conspiring to assassinate or overthrow Franco.[9] Perales states that he had nothing to do with the group, although it is difficult to accept his assertion that he did not even know Meléndez, since the latter had been one of Hedilla's close collaborators prior to April 1937.

As far as Eduardo Ezquer was concerned, this was one more in a long series of accusations. He was well known in Falangist circles for his activities at the head of the *Falange* in the province of Badajoz in the party's foundational years. He had a penchant for parading well-disciplined detachments of uniformed Falangists round the province and proudly states, with reference to the period immediately prior to the Civil War, that he and his 'boys' had already 'managed, with noble behaviour ('de una manera hidalga'), in open and gentlemanly struggle, to reduce the Marxist groups which predominated in the province'.[10] As a result of his 'gentlemanly' habits, he was expelled from the province by the Civil Governor of Badajoz at the end of 1935. Shortly after the 1937 Unification, he was arrested and accused of 'rebellion against the *Generalísimo* and collaboration with the reds', and spent the next few months in the prisons of Cádiz, Puerto de Santa María, Gerona and Burgos.[11] As in the case of Manuel Hedilla, it would have been politically prejudicial to execute Ezquer, but his disobedience could be punished and his resistence worn down by imprisonment and police surveillence.

At about the time when the FEA arrests were made, in November 1939, a clandestine *Junta Política* was formed in Madrid. It was the most determined of the attempts to organise an opposition group in the first years of the Franco regime, and the longest lived. Nine members composed the *Junta*: Emilio Rodríguez Tarduchy, President;[12] Patricio González de Canales, Secretary; Ricardo Sanz, representative for Asturias; Daniel Buhigas, Galicia; Ventura López Coterilla, Sevilla; Luis de Caralt, Cataluña; José Pérez de Cabo, Levante;[13] Gregorio Ortega, Canary Isles; and Antonio Cazañas, Morocco. The man responsible for making contact with other Falangists was González de Canales who, as a National Inspector of the Movement, could combine his official trips around the country with visits to possible and effective collaborators, without arousing suspicion. In Castilla, for example, he contacted two Falangists of long standing: José Antonio Girón and Luis González Vicén. Girón was already involved in a 'rival' opposition group, led by General Juan Yagüe, and would commit himself no further than Yagüe was prepared to go. Yagüe, when approached, refused to join the *Junta*. González Vicén wanted no part in any conspiracy, as was hardly surprising in one who not only had a promising Movement career ahead of him, but was also a member of the *Falange* intelligence service.[14]

After two years of making contacts and internal discussions about the necessity to effect the national syndicalist revolution, the *Junta* met in the Spring of 1941 to discuss a plan to assassinate Franco. A similar plan to assassinate Serrano Suñer had previously been considered and rejected, for those who believed that Serrano could be of more use to *Falange* alive than dead were able to prevail over those who held the opposite view. This new and more ambitious plan was also finally rejected for fear that the disappearance of Franco might be the occasion for the invasion of Spain by a Germany anxious to have Spain as an active ally in its war effort. In view of the impossibility of being an effective force, and in view of the lack of support either from other clandestine nuclei or from the mass of Falangists in general, the *Junta* then went into voluntary liquidation.[15]

The relationship between these tenacious renegades and the regime was undoubtedly uncomfortable, but hardly dangerous and even strangely opportunistic. Constantly dogged by police and the agents of the Intelligence Service, frequently under arrest, the likes of González de Canales, Ezquer, and Perales nevertheless persisted in their clandestine meetings and even used their periods of confinement for further conspiring. Ezquer, for example, whilst confined to Gerona after his arrest in 1939, managed in 1940 to organise a group known as the *Ofensiva de Recobro Nacional Sindicalista*, (ORNS) (Offensive for

National Syndicalist Recovery). ORNS established small nuclei in several provinces and even attempted to blow up a power station in Valencia in 1940 before the police intervened and Ezquer was again incarcerated.[16]

At the same time, when at liberty to do so, many of these Falangists earned their living from positions provided by the regime. Franco and his collaborators – particularly, perhaps, the Falangists of 'unshakable loyalty' – might be irritated by the presence of 'opposition' within their own ranks, but took drastic action against it on very few occasions (Hedilla, Juan Domínguez, José Pérez de Cabo). The majority of the party was firmly behind the *Caudillo*, as were the capitalist classes which supported and benefited from the maintenance of the status quo. Consequently, no threat of any significance was posed by a minority whose ability to attract a following was negligible, and whose desire actually to overthrow the regime had not been demonstrated by either word or deed.

Whilst in Gerona in 1939, Ezquer had maintained intermittent contact with Narciso Perales, then stationed as Army Medical Officer in Guadalajara. Their discussions around the organisation of a 'real *Falange*' did not, however, go beyond private conversations until 1944, when a group of Falangists (including Ezquer, Rodríguez Tarduchy and Perales[17]) began to meet regularly at Ezquer's house in Madrid, to talk and to prepare leaflets. Approaches were made to the 'Falangist General', Yagüe, but he had not been in a position to engage in conspiratorial activities since his earlier involvements had been discovered in 1940 and he had been promoted to a position in the Army which at once ensured his loyalty and made him easy to keep under surveillance. By 1944, General Yagüe was among those who regularly expressed their 'unshakable fidelity' to Franco. The tentative attempts of the group were suspended in view of the poor response they aroused in the mass of Falangists who, like Yagüe, were not pepared to commit themselves to projects whose possibilities of success were minimal.

The clandestine[18] existence of *Falange* purists was not an end, however. In 1945, the *Alianza Sindicalista* (Syndicalist Alliance) was formed by a group of Falangists and Anarchists of the *CNT*, in an attempt to revive and formalise relations which dated, intermittently, from the early 1930s.[19] Among about thirty others, the Falangists who participated were Narciso Perales, who wrote the Alliance's initial manifesto, Patricio González de Canales, Lamberto de los Santos,[20] and one of Ezquer's collaborators, a Prison Officer by the name of Pantoja, who apparently was in contact with the imprisoned Anarchist leader, Cipriano Mera, and acted as his representative in the Alliance[21] After a single meeting, the group was reported to the police and, officially, no more meetings could be held. Nevertheless, the Falangists continued to meet, without anarchist participation, into the early 1950s, and managed to establish small groups in some provinces. For a time, Dionisio Ridruejo collaborated in their efforts to promote national syndicalism through extra-official channles.[22]

The attempt to create the 'Syndical Alliance' was born from the awareness that, contrary to what official propaganda might state, the Franco regime did not protect the interests of the lower-middle and working classes and that, consequently, those classes constituted a potential mass following for a group whose ambitions had, equally, been less than totally satisified by the Franco regime. Clearly, support for a group which advocated 'national syndicalist revolution' was not going to come from the capitalist oligarchy which, in 1936, had encharged the military with precisely the suppression of what it saw as the threat of revolution. Nor could it be expected from those members of the party who had been coopted by the regime. Hence the attempt to appeal to the working classes and hence the use of a trade union, rather than an immediately political, strategy. In addition, it was hoped that the renewal of contact with the CNT would smooth the way to gaining the confidence of the working classes. However, this was not the moment for trade union activities on the margins of the official organisation, and repression was inevitable.

Even if it had not been liquidated from above, it is highly doubtful whether the *Alianza Sindicalista* would ever have made any headway among its putative clientèle. On the one hand, in spite of the Civil War and the subsequent repression, loyalties to the old Left wing organisations were still strong. On the other, for all they might appear with names which did not mention *Falange* specifically, people knew the origins of the men involved and could not dissociate them from their Movement correligionaries, then engaged in bringing the working masses to 'order' from official positions. In any case, even though the 'Alliance' Falangists claimed they were not the same as the 'collaborationist' Falangists, they could not deny that they had taken sides against the traditional working class organisations during the Civil War. Even with the anarchist 'seal of approval', that was too bitter a pill to swallow.

It was significant that the *Alianza Sindicalista* was founded at the end of the Second World War, when it was clear that fascist ideologies in Europe had, for the moment at least, been defeated. The Falangist opposition felt either that Franco could be replaced without 'someone worse' (Hitler, for example) taking his place, or that they would have more room for manoeuvre if Franco were obliged by the external situation to leave, or to be politically more flexible. Thus, whilst one end of the Falangist spectrum prepared to 'resist to the end', but hung a portrait of Prince Juan Carlos in its meeting room, the other prepared, not to resist, but to attack, and sought to reach agreement with the anarchists.

The political short-sightedness of both extremes prevented them from seeing two important factors. Firstly, that the Allied Powers were unwilling to alter the status quo in Spain. Secondly, that the autarchic economic policy adopted by the regime from 1939 onwards had not yet, in 1945, led to the latter's debilitation but, rather, to its consolidation, through the enriching of the capitalist classes whose economic and political support were essential to it.

The international blockade imposed by the Allies justified the kind of survival economic policies and practices which, together with black market dealings and the manipulation of State economic controls, facilitated the accumulation of capital in the hands of those classes which had felt their position and interests threatened by the policies of the Second Republic. The support they consequently pledged to the regime strengthened it and assured its continuance, thereby providing, in turn, the grounds for the continuation of the anti-Francoist blockade.

This situation changed with the onset of the 'Cold War' in the mid 1940s and the adoption of communism, rather than fascism, as the enemy of world democracy. Hence the reluctance of the Western Powers to take steps which might provoke the fall of 'strong government' in Spain and a return to Republicanism or, what would, of course, be worse, to a communist regime.[23] Those Falangist groups not totally identified with the Franco regime failed to understand this real international situation and even, in their most optimistic moments, shared the hopes of the Alphonsine Monarchists and the Left-wing opposition that external intervention would be the cue for the removal of Franco as Head of State.[24]

By the end of the 1940s, the activity of the Falangist opposition had been reduced to a minimum, in a national and international context completely unfavourable to it. In the decade of the 1950s, a series of internal and external developments reduced it practically to nothing. By 1948, the 'alternative' *Falange* had 'entered a period of paralysis',[25] from which it was not to begin to recover until the end of the decade.

Perhaps with the wisdom of hindsight, Falangist apologists attribute the conversion of the Falangist opposition into 'a latent, rather than a *de facto*, force',[26] to a mixture of the repression carried out by the forces of law and order and a notable improvement in the standard of living of the middle and working classes. Not only was it still impossible to attempt any kind of proselytism on anything grander than an individual and personal scale, but also people were beginning to think that, thanks to Franco, life was getting better. The end of autarchy and the re-insertion of Spain into the international capitalist system, culminating in the Hispano-American Agreements signed in 1953, opened the way to the development of a fully-fledged consumer society, in which people were more concerned with emerging from a subsistence-level existence than with political criticism.

In truth, however, and the radical Falangists must surely have known it, this was only part of the explanation. The problem was not that people were not interested in politics. Of course they were. The first strikes in the history of the regime were staged in 1947 and prohibited Left-wing parties increased their actvities and following considerably in the 1950s – so much so that the end of the decade witnessed a particularly ferocious purge against them.[27] The fundamental problem was the lack of credibility of the Falangist 'opposition'. A secondary problem was the incapacity of essentially middle-class people, of university education and environment, to make contact in the working class circles where they were attempting to gain support:

> Although we (members of the Falangist opposition in 1955–56) were of lower middle class origin, our status as University students immersed us in a University world and that was the world we knew best and in which we moved with greatest facility. It was difficult for us to enter the working class world, firstly because of the logical rejection – which was not ideological, but class-based – on the part of the workers themselves. They said, "This is a *señorito*". Secondly, it was an unknown world for us, in which we could not work effectively.[28]

As a consequence of this failure to make any progress in the 'unknown world' of the working class, and in an anxious effort to recruit a new following not identified with the Franco regime, it was in University circles that the 'opposition' *Falange* carried out most of its activity and registered most of its success, limited though it was, in the decade of the 1950s. Thus, Falangist students played an active part in the attempt to revitalise Spanish Universities and were closely involved in the agitation which, with increasing frequency and intensity, shook the campuses in those years. With the Falangist opposition seeming to be rejuvenated by university groups espousing the national syndicalist ideology, militants of long standing like Perales and Gonzáles de Canales felt optimistic again. In fact, their initial enthusiasm was short-lived, for the 'new opposition' quickly became disillusioned when it realised that effective opposition, that is, opposition which would propose, and might achieve, the replacement of the Franco regime by a totally different system, simply was not possible with FET y de las JONS as the starting point. 'It was', says an ex-Falangist, 'as if we had come up against a wall which it was impossible to jump over from the standpoint of the *Falange*.'[29]

The revolutionary impulses of the Falangist students were invariably repressed by pro-Francoist sectors of the Movement or stymied by Party leaders, as was demonstrated on such occasions as the visit, in 1954, of HM Queen Elizabeth II to Gibraltar. In protest against this visit, the SEU organised a demonstration outside the British Embassy in Madrid. The demonstration was perfectly in line with the regime's 'Gibraltar is Spanish' policy, and the fact that 'the Ministry of the Interior had encouraged the students' protest'.[30] Yet it was broken up by the police and the Spanish Foreign Minister sent apologies to the British Ambassador.[31] The students, confused and irritated by this contradictory situation, staged a second demonstration, this time in front of the *Dirección General de Seguridad*. It was also dispersed by force. Behind the scenes, too, there were unplanned repercussions. A group of people who had official posts in the Movement youth organisation and the SEU, and who were 'trying to take seriously the idea of the *Falange*', protested against what they considered to be the 'indecent attitude of the Ministry of the Interior towards the students', and were consequently dismissed from their posts.[32]

Perhaps the most disappointing aspect of the Falangist response to the students' protest was that it was frequently the older members of the self-styled 'non-regime' groups which vetoed, or failed to support, the initiatives of the younger members.[33] As a result of the lack of support from their own comrades, and of growing awareness of the contradiction between 'opposition' and '*Falange*', many Falangist students withdrew from Falangist groups and either joined clandestine Left-wing parties or remained on the margins of political activity. As in the case of the *Falange's* connection with the anarchists, there is a curious ambiguity in the attitude of opposition Falangists towards these erstwhile comrades. On the one hand, they are inordinately proud that the *Falange* was 'the quarry which provided many militants for socialist parties',[34] and, on the other, resolutely opposed to the ideology of those parties.

The *Sindicato Español Universitario* (SEU) had held the official monopoly of student representation since the 1940s, when the Vice-secretary General of the Party, Pedro Gamero del Castillo, prepared the legislation which institutionalised this situation. As Falangist David Jato had predicted at the time of that legislation, the Students' Union had atrophied under the dead weight of a bureaucratic structure which had reduced the student role to a minimum and its efficacy to vanishing point.[35] By 1954, and as a result of the resumption of relations with the Western democratic world, a certain cultural 'defrosting' was beginning to accompany the improvements of a socio-economic nature in Spanish life. The war was not forgotten, but post-war generations were reaching adult age, and their parents, under-standably, preferred to look forward to consumer comforts enjoyed in 'Franco's peace', rather than backwards to times of war and privation. They were assisted by a regime which now needed, on the one hand, to stimulate a population capable not only of producing but also of purchasing and, on the other, to erase and de-politicise the collective memory of the war.

In the accompanying atmosphere of relative openness, cultural and political life began to return to the hitherto dead body of the Spanish Universities. A small group of people began to work towards the development of a democratic student organisation,

> taking advantage of the birth of an opposition cultural move-ment. . . . Books by Gabriel Celaya and Blas de Otero were being published; it was the time of "Bienvenido, Mr. Marshall"; and the cinema clubs offered films which had been prohibited until then.[36]

In 1954, as series of cultural seminars, entitled 'Encuentros entre la poesía y la Universidad' ('Encounters between Poetry and the University'), were organised in the premises of the SEU in Madrid, in which contemporary poets were invited to present their work and then to discuss it with the students. The discussions, says one of the principal organisers of the seminars, were always highly politicised and, though ingenuous, consequently alarmed the Establishment.[37]

This attempt to break the acritical monotony of Spanish university and cultural life was enthusiastically received by all who participated and, the following year, it was decided to broaden the scope of the attempt, with a 'Congress of Young University Writers'. The idea had the approval and active collaboration of the Rector of Madrid University, Pedro Laín Entralgo, and was jointly organised by students of democratic political inclination and members of a "progressive" sector of the SEU. The Minister of Education, Joaquin Ruiz Jiménez, and Laín Entralgo believed that a process of reform from within was possible and proposed to further that end from their official positions. The opposition of the Minister of the Interior, Blas Pérez, of the Party Vice-secretary, Romojaro, and of the most reactionary sectors of the *Falange*, proved stronger, however, than the enthusiasm and idealism of the democrats. The Congress, planned for November 1955, was prohibited.

In spite of the antipathy they clearly aroused, the intellectuals engaged in the effort to democratise and open up the University to a diversity of political and cultural influences and ideas, began to think about the organisation of a congress of students at national level. The manifesto announcing the National Congress of Students was drawn up in secret and read for the first time in *Tiempo Nuevo*, a cultural circle created under the auspices of the General Secretariat of the Movement and which had come to be the venue of students and intellectuals dissatisfied with the regime.[38] The document was then circulated in the Universities and thousands of signatures were collected in support of its call for an end to the monopoly of the SEU as the students' representative. Some days later, the Faculty of Law, considered to be the nerve-centre of anti-SEU operations, was invaded by a band of Falangists belonging to the extreme Right-wing organisation, *Guardia de Franco*, who set about the students with sticks and clubs. The premises of the SEU were attacked in reprisal.

Against this background of unrest and violence, the antagonism between SEUists and reformers came to a head in February 1956, in the clash which almost caused the death of Falangist Miguel Alvarez and which provoked the Cabinet reshuffle which removed Ruiz Jiménez from the Ministry of Education and Fernández Cuesta and Romojaro from the Party Secretariat.[39]

For the 'opposition' *Falange*, the events of the period between 1954 and 1956, throughout which the syndicalist sector remained noticeably passive, certainly showed that there were greater possibilities of mass support and effective mobilisation in the Universities than elsewhere. They also showed, however, that anything less than total opposition would be too weak to withstand both the repression exercised by the regime and the scepticism of those whose support the dissatisfied Falangists sought. February 1956 called the bluff of the half-measures that certain members of the *Frente de Juventudes* and the SEU had adopted in the somewhat naïve hope of securing the approval of both the regime and its opponents:

> Obviously, in those years, we were convinced that, because of the atmosphere of Spanish society, it was not possible to introduce Pablo Inglesias, to rescue Besteiro, or to say that there were positive elements in Marxism. Obviously, no one puts his finger into a red-hot crucible; but it was necessary to be cooling it down. So we began with what appeared to be the easiest aspect: cultural values. In the magazines we published, such as *Juventud*, *La Hora*, or *Alcalá*, we tried to rescue those values. Until the visit of Queen Elizabeth to Gibraltar, the students were totally in favour of the régime and they had confidence in us. A student congress was held, which we had organised . . . Franco attended the closing session in the University, and the students applauded and acclaimed him tremendously. Then came the contradiction of official encouragement to protest against the visit to Gibraltar, and finding themselves up against the police when they arrived at the British Embassy. That turned the students against us. From then onwards, all that had been gained was lost.[40]

On the basis of the victory registered over the forces of reform, the regime *Falange* prepared to reassert its presence and authority through the project for the institutionalisation of the regime and the Movement, which began to be discussed in the National Council in that same year, 1956. Although that 'victory' was illusory, the main part of Falangist effort was concentrated on its consolidation, and the rebel Falangists could not hope for anything other than hostility from their politically more ambitious comrades. This was especially true in the latter years of the decade, when apparently less authoritarian sectors of the Movement were also anxious to consolidate and improve their positions.

With the entry into the Government, in February 1957, of a group closely associated with the *Opus Dei*, and generally considered to be apolitical (ie. not identified with any particular party) 'technocrats',[41] opposition began to arise within the *Falange* at points which appeared to have little to do with the *Falange* of the FEA or the *Alianza Sindicalista*. Thus, for example, in the ranks of the extreme Right-wing *Guardia de Franco*, clandestine nuclei began to be formed in 1958, with the professed objective of reviving the ideological line followed by the JONS of Ramiro Ledesma and Manuel Hedilla. This was a strange attitude indeed to be adopted by a group which, two years ealier, had devoted itself to the physical repression of those who questioned the system ruled by the man responsible for the trial and imprisonment of Hedilla. A year later, in 1959, the leader of the *Guardia de Franco*, Luis González Vicén, was elected President of another new opposition current, the *Círculos Doctrinales 'José Antonio'* ('José Antonio' Doctrinal Circles).

When, in the sixties, these nascent opposition currents grew to form distinct and separate groups, it was not because their basic beliefs and interests made them incompatible, but because questions of emphasis and personal animosity made unity impossible. The situation in 1934–35, with the dual protagonism of Ledesma Ramos and Primo de Rivera, each with his own following, must have been very similar. In 1935, however, the historic role of the *Falange* was yet to be fulfilled and internal power struggles therefore had some meaning with respect to possible future developments. By 1960, *Falange's* instrumental usefulness had reached, and passed, its maximum and internal developments were consequently of considerably less significance than twenty-five years earlier.

The Falangist groups which began to arise in the wake of the approval, in 1958, of the Fundamental Principles of the Movement, had two main objectives. Firstly, they aimed to show that although the institutional framework and the historical context at the end of the 1950s were very different to those extant at the time of *Falange's* creation in 1933, Falangism was, nevertheless, applicable to the contemporary situation. Secondly, they wished to demonstrate that the 'real' *Falange*, represented by themselves, had been betrayed by the 'false' *Falange*, represented by those who had collaborated with the regime. The fact that many 'real' Falangists had once been collaborators was explained as the 'evolution' of their position, though the question of how this was compatible with their professed unaltered and uninterrupted fidelity to the 'true' doctrine was never raised. Such groups proliferated in the 1960s, particularly after 1964, with the initiation of a period of relative liberalisation, captained by Manuel Fraga Iribarne, from the Ministry of Information and Tourism.

Nevertheless, the Falangist 'opposition' remained opposition within the system it had participated in establishing, never clarifying the question of whether it was the game or only the rules it wanted to change. For a Falangist to shout 'Franco, you are a traitor!' when the lights went out at the high point in a religious ceremony in the basilica of El Escorial, attended by all the Movement, Government, military and Church dignitaries, undoubtedly required a good deal of courage.[42] It was, however, the courage of the child who sticks out his tongue when the parental back is turned. The rebellious offspring was duly chastised, but the familar links remained. It was a gut-reaction which had little to do with critical analysis of the regime and its foundations, including the *Falange* itself. It had even less to do with deciding that either, or both, must be removed by force if they could not be persuaded to bow out gracefully of their own accord. For all the rumoured plots to kill Franco which have been attributed to the *Falange*,[43] not one was ever put into practice. Indeed, it was not until 1973 that a Left-wing group carried out the key assassination of Admiral Carrero Blanco which finally opened the way to political change that went further than simply rearranging the same elements in a different pattern. Finally, the Falangist opposition was an opposition which always came within the category of the 'tolerated opposition'.

This is not to deny that it suffered its share of persecution. It could hardly have expected to be credible at all if it had not and, as in the 1930s, it used such persecution to support the argument that it was not the ally of the regime. However, as some former Falangists now admit, they consciously took advantage of the degree of tolerance extended to the Falangist opposition to form their groups, particularly in the Universities.[44] In many cases, parental affiliations or connections with other, non-university Falangist organisations were sufficient to liberate young Falangists caught participating in opposition activities from anything worse than a severe reprimand in police headquarters. In other cases, a beating was administered as the punishment for 'playing at little reds'.[45] The propagandistic utility of such treatment increased as the possibility of Franco's demise grew, in so far as it could be used as part of the strategy employed by the *Falange* to maintain that it had nothing to do with the regime.

In 1960, a group of Falangists decided to revive a discussion group which had orginally been founded by José Primo de Rivera in the 1930s, the 'Happy Whale' ('*la Ballena Alegre*'). It met, as it had done thirty years earlier, in the basement of the Café 'Lyón', in Madrid. As well as the name and the venue, the essentially Falangist initiative and character of the group was maintained. Nevertheless, it was the policy of the '*Ballena*' group that anyone could attend and participate, irrespective of ideology or political affiliation. The '*Ballena*' discussion group, which was 'not an organised activity, just a weekly meeting',[46] represented an attempt at Falangist reconstruction after the paralysis of the preceding decade. The main protagonists of the effort were already veteran members of the Falangist opposition, such as Narciso Perales, Ceferino Maestu, and Patricio González de Canales. In addition, they were now joined by a number of younger Falangists from the organisational and administrative levels of the *Frente de Juventudes*. For about a year, the group met to discuss different aspects of the problem of revitalising the *Falange*. Its meetings were brought to an abrupt halt, however, on orders from the Ministry of the Interior after a fight broke out, apparently provoked deliberately by ultra Right-winger Mariano Sánchez Covisa, during one of the meetings. The police intervened and the group was subsequently banned.[47]

There were two further attempts to find an outlet for the 'alternative' *Falange*, which arose in part from the options discussed and the contacts made in the *'Ballena Alegre'*. Firstly, the magazine *Sindicalismo* in its first version, edited by Maestu and Perales.[48] Secondly, a series of meetings held with workers in the industrial district of Villaverde (Madrid), also organised principally by Maestu and Perales. At the first of these meetings, recalls Perales, there were seven people, of whom five were policemen. At the last – for they were prohibited after a short time – there were some 350 workers.[49] The magazine *Sindicalismo* was first published, in theory, on a monthly basis but, in practice, when the censor had left enough text to make up one issue, in 1964. 'Logically', says Maestu,

> it had to have a Falangist focus, otherwise it would have been absolutely impossible. But there were lots of other things in it that weren't strictly Falangist but reflected rather, a time at which a group of us were moving towards critical positions and ideological concepts of a different type.[50]

Maestu was, in effect, already a member of a non-Falangist trade union organisation, the *Unión de Trabajadores Sindicalistas* (Syndicalist Workers' Union) and was soon afterwards involved with the clandestine *Comisiones Obreras* (Workers' Commisions). *Sindicalismo* eventually suffered the same fate as most previous attempts at Falangist opposition:

> Fraga, who was then Minister of Information and Tourism, finally prohibited its publication indefinitely. He called me personally and

told me that he would no longer authorise the publication of the magazine because he was tired of it causing him problems in Cabinet meetings, especially with Camilo Alonso Vega, who was then Minister of the Interior.[51]

At a time when the working class opposition spearheaded by clandestine Left-wing groups was becoming more frequent and organised, the group around Perales and Maestu was trying to take advantage of a general tendency towards the politicisation of labour conflicts, to promote their particular brand of trade unionism. According to their tenets, the class struggle would be done away with via the dismantling of the capitalist economic system and the integration of all members of society into an organically-arranged system of production and participation.[52] Whilst they maintained that the *Falange* had never been in power, it was not clear from their discourse how power was to be achieved in the future as the necessary pre-condition for the revolutionary measures they proposed, such as the expropriation of the large landowners or the nationalisation of the banks. Equally unclear was how the nationalist element in the Falangist ideology could be compatible with the irreversible insertion of Spain into an international system, in which Spain's position was that of Euro-American colony. Finally, the Falangist argument that Man is first and foremost a product of his spiritual, not his material, state and environment, was difficult to accept for classes which had a traditional belief in the opposite and a life-experience which seemed to corroborate that belief. In short, it was as difficult in the 1960s as it had been in the 1940s to find support among classes who were not convinced that a Falangist by any other name was not still a Falangist and, as such, represented classes and interests diametrically opposed to their own.

Notes

1. See above, pp. 44–5.
2. Romero Cuesta, A., *Objetivo: matar a Franco* (Madrid: Ediciones 99, Madrid 1976), p. 69; Falangist Javier Morillas, interviewed in Madrid, 22 Jan. 1977. Cf. Ridruejo, D., in *Cuadernos para el diálogo* (Madrid, Apr. 1966).
3. Cf. Southworth, H., *Antifalange*, p. 216. Falangists and others show a certain obsession with linking Primo de Rivera and Prieto; see for

example: Gibello, A., *Apuntes para una biografía polémica*, pp. 208–12, 335–8; Rojas, C., *Prieto y José Antonio*. *Socialismo y Falange ante la tragedia civil* (Barcelona: Editorial Dirosa, 1977) *passim*; Zugazagoitia, J., *Guerra y vicisitudes de los españoles* (Barcelona: Editorial Crítica, 1977) pp. 23, 103, 176, 264. In personal conversation with this writer, Ernesto Giménez Caballero expressed the opinion that the ideal leader for the *Falange* was not Primo de Rivera, nor Hedilla, but Indalecio Prieto (interview, Madrid, 11 July 1978).

4. Serrano Suñer, R., *Entre Hendaya y Gibraltar*, p. 75, and *Memorias*, p. 178. On the contact maintained between Fernández Cuesta and Republican Ministers, see also Zugazagoitia, op. cit., pp. 254, 411.

5. Raimundo Fernández Cuesta, interview, 15 July 1977. His account of his contact with Prieto is considerably more detailed in *Testimonio*, p. 107–12. Cf. Prieto, I. *Palabras al viento* (Mexico: Ediciones Minerva, 1942) pp. 234–6.

6. Juan Aparicio López, interview, 24 June 1977; Ridruejo, D., *Casi unas memorias*, p. 99.

7. Vicente Cadenas Vincent, interview in Madrid, 25 Jan. 1978.

8. Ibid., and Fernández Cuesta, interview, 15 July 1977.

9. Narciso Perales, interview, 31 Dec. 1976; Alcazar de Velasco, A., interview, 15 Feb. 1977, and *Los 7 días de Salamanca*, pp. 173, 181.

10. For Ezquer's activities at the head of the Extremadura *Falange*, see: Ximénez de Sandoval, F. op. cit., pp. 185, 366; *Arriba* (18 Apr. 1935; 2 May 1935); *FE* (19 Apr. 1934); *Actualidad Española* (8 May 1969); Crozier, B. *Franco* (London, 1967).

11. Eduardo Ezquer y Gabaldón, interview in Madrid, 28 Feb. 1977. The accusation of 'collaboration with the reds' seems highly unlikely in view of Ezquer's persecution of the Socialists before the war.

12. Former member of General Primo de Rivera's *Unión Patriótica* and of the *Unión Militar Española*, Rodríguez Tarduchy was a member of *Falange* from November 1933 onwards. He was a frequent contributor to *Arriba* in the 1940s, on military and political affairs. His articles never contained any reference to Franco.

13. Author of the first book of Falangist doctrine, *¡Arriba España!*, published in Aug. 1935. Pérez de Cabo was tried by Court Martial and shot in 1942 (see above, note 41, p. 92).

14. Romero Cuesta, A., op. cit., p. 77, taken from the personal notes of Gonzáles de Canales; Narciso Perales, interview, 31 Dec. 1976.

15. Ibid.

16. Eduardo Ezquer y Gabaldón, in *Actualidad Española* (8 May 1969) and interview with the present writer, 28 Feb. 1977. I am grateful to novelist and historian Luis Romero for the information regarding the Valencia power station.

17. Ezquer, E. interview, 28 Feb. 1977, Perales, N. interview, 31 Dec. 1976.

18. Raimundo Fernández Cuesta maintains that 'clandestine' was hardly an applicable term, since the General Secretariat of the Movement and the Police were fully aware of the existence of the Falangist 'opposition' (interview, 15 July 1977).

19. For the relation between Falangism and anarchism see, eg.: Ramiro

Ledesma Ramos in *La Conquista del Estado* (2, 23, 30 May 1931) and *JONS* (May and Oct. 1933); *Arriba* (2 May 1935, and 23 January 1936; Abad de Santillań, D., *Memorias, 1897–1936* (Barcelona: Planeta, 1977) p. 217; Velarde Fuertes, J., Prologue to Lopez, J., *Una misión sin importancia* (Madrid: Editorial Nacional, 1972) p. 38; Jiménez Campo, J. op. cit., pp. 241–55.

20. De los Santos was one of those tried in Apr. 1937 for his opposition to the Decreee of Unification.

21. Perales, N., interview 31 Dec. 1976, Cipriano Mera makes no mention of this *Alianza Sindicalista* in his memoirs, *Guerra, exilio y carcel de un anarcosindicalista* (Paris: Ruedo Ibérico, 1976).

22. Perales, N., interview, 31 Dec. 1976.

23. The Tripartite Note issued by France, Great Britain and the United States in Mar. 1946 made it abundantly clear that the Allies did not intend to intervene in the internal affairs of Spain.

24. David Jato, interview, 1 June 1977. Cf. Preston P. in Preston, P. (ed.), *España en crisis*, p. 234; Fernández de Castro, I. & Martínez, J., *España hoy*, pp. 7–11; 'Juan Hermanos' in *Tiempo de Historia*, no. 92–3 (July–Aug. 1982).

25. Narciso Perales, interview, 7 Jan. 1977.

26. Ibid.

27. Cf. Ramirez, L., *Nuestros primeros 25 años* (Paris: Ruedo Ibérico, 1964) pp. 165–214; Preston, P. in *España en crisis*, pp. 236–42; Fernández de Castro, I. & Martínez, J. op. cit., pp. 22–41; Welles, B., *Spain: the Gentle Anarchy* (London: Pall Mall Press, 1965) pp. 185–220).

28. Former *Frente de Juventudes* leader and Syndical Organisation official, Antonio Castro Villacañas, interviewed in Madrid, 23, 24 Nov. 1977.

29. Former Falangist Angel de Lucas, in personal conversation in Madrid, 24 Dec. 1975.

30. Castro Villacañas, A., interview, 23 Nov. 1977.

31. Ibid., David Jato Miranda, interview, 3 June 1977.

32. Ibid.

33. Former Falangist Eduardo Zaldivar, interviewed in Madrid, 21 Dec. 1977. Former Falangist José Luis Rubio, interview, 23 Mar. 1979, summed up the young militants' disappointment: 'We realised that there could be no reform without liberty, and that liberty was impossible in a totalitarian system'.

34. Antonio Castro Villacañas, interview, 23 Nov. 1977.

35. David Jato, interview, 7 July 1977.

36. Múgica Herzog, E. in *El País*, 3 Oct 1976. Múgica, then an active member of the clandestine Spanish communist party, was an important figure in the student movement of the 1950s. See also, Mesa, R. op. cit., pp. 29–53.

37. Ridruejo, D., in the report he compiled for the National Council of the Movement in 1956.

38. *El Español*, 24 Feb. 1956; the information given there is corroborated by one of the authors of the manifesto Ramón Tamames, in *El País*, 3 Oct. 1976. See also, Lizcano, P. *Generación del '56. La universidad contra Franco* (Barcelona: Grijalbo, 1981) pp. 132–53.

39. See above, pp. 107–8.

40. Castro Villacañas, A., interview, 24 Nov. 1977. *Alcalá, La Hora* and *Juventud*, financed from State funds, undoubtedly represented an important attempt to promote a new image for the *Falange* among young intellectuals. The traditional Falangist element was still, nevertheless, very strong.
41. Falangists interviewed frequently expressed views which indicated their belief that the *Opus Dei* was one of the most important factors which prevented *Falange* from realising its national syndicalist revolution. In fact, the *Opus* was not *Falange's* enemy, but its rival for the support of the same social classes and for positions of political power; cf. Vidal Beneyto, J. '¿Falange contra Opus Dei?' in *Indice*, no. 214 (1966).
42. This occurred in 1955. In 1960, the leader of the SEU militias was the protagonist of a similar incident in the Valle de las Caídos. As Franco approached across the esplanade in front of the basilica, the SEU leader ordered the Falangist escort of which he was in charge to about-turn. As punishment for this act of defiance, he was deported to Spanish Guinea.
43. See Romero Cuesta, A., op. cit., pp. 65–118. Alcazar de Velasco also claims to have offered his services as the assassin of Franco (though he does not say to whom), in *El País* (20 June 1977); in an unpublished edition of his *Los 7 días de Salamanca*, photocopies from which were given to this writer by D. Eduardo Ezquer, Alcazar de Velasco writes that he made the proposal to kill Franco at a meeting of Falangists, shortly before the Unification in Apr. 1937, but the proposal was not accepted. Cf. also J. L. Rubio, interview, 23 Mar. 1979; Conde Soladana, P. in *Interviú*, no. 18 (Madrid, 16–22 Sept. 1976).
44. Demetrio Castro Alfín and Eduardo Zaldivar, interview, 21 Dec. 1977; Eugenio Pordomingo, interview, 2 Jan. 1979; Antonio Castro Villacañas, interview, 24 Nov. 1977.
45. Castro, D. and Zaldivar, E., interview, 2 Mar. 1978.
46. Castro Villacañas, A., interview, 23 Nov. 1977.
47. Ceferino Maestu, interview, 14 Dec. 1977; Perales, N., interview, 31 Dec. 1976.
48. *Sindicalismo* was banned in 1965 and did not reappear until 1974.
49. Narciso Perales, interview, 31 Dec. 1976.
50. Ceferino Maestu, interview, 14 Dec. 1977.
51. Ibid.
52. They did not explain how it was that the capitalist system still needed to be dismantled after twenty-five years of a trade union organisation which, manned by Falangists, was based on the concepts they were now proposing as something new.

8 1960–76

The efforts of the 'alternative' *Falange* were not, however, directed exclusively towards the working classes, nor concerned primarily with syndicalism. At the end of 1959, a series of meetings took place in the Madrid premises of the 'Medina Circle' of the Party's *Sección Femenina*. The purpose was the creation of the 'José Antonio' Doctrinal Circles, to keep alive the doctrine of José Antonio Primo de Rivera, *Falange's* founder. In reality, the Circles constituted an operation of 'preaching to the converted'. The participants in the initial meetings were, for the most part, Falangists of long standing, with the addition of some of the younger members of the regime hierarchy: Pilar and Miguel Primo de Rivera; Julián Pemartín; Jesus Fueyo (first Director of the Institute of Political Studies); Patricio González de Canales; Lula de Lara, Carmen Isasi, Maruja Cuervo and Viki Eiroa, four stalwarts of the *Sección Femenina*; Miguel Primo de Rivera y Urquijo, the nephew of *Falange's* founder and member of one of Spain's most powerful banking families; Antonio Castro Villacañas; and Diego Márquez Horrillo.[1] As we have noted earlier, some of these people had already been associated in previous years with ill-fated attempts to create an 'alternative' *Falange*, but many former 'opposition' Falangists were reluctant to become involved with this new group because 'politically, it was very confused'.[2] As in the 1930s, the *Falange's* essential contradiction in wanting to be at once an elitist and a popular movement had crystalised in the form of two factions, one selective and limited in its appeal, the other attempting to take root wherever it could, particularly among the working classes.

The concern of the *Círculos Doctrinales 'José Antonio'* was 'to save for posterity the revolutionary essence of national-syndicalist thought, personified especially in José Antonio'. For some members, a further prime objective was to 'differentiate the *Falange* from the Movement'. With this double aim, the founders of the Circles took as their starting point the determination to ensure that

> in their doctrinal propositions, (the Circles) should be so orthodoxly Falangist that incorporation into them would be impossible for those who, originating in the Spanish Right, had militated first in the primitive *Falange* and then in the National Movement as pseudo-Falangists.[3]

This, in fact, should have excluded automatically a good many of the aforementioned founder members, except, of course, that no definition of pseudo Falangism' was given, and it could be tacitly assumed that those who qualified for exclusion on the first count were saved by their innocence on the second.

In their anxiety to differentiate themselves from the Movement and other sectors of the Right, the Circles were similar to the groups formed by Perales and Maestu. They differed, however, in two aspects. To begin with, the Circles were concerned with political doctrine, whereas Perales and his collaborators were concerned with trade union practice. Secondly, Perales was aiming outside the *Falange* in his search for support, whereas the founders of the Circles hoped to 'recover and unite the real Falangists, then dispersed throughout the organisations of the Movement, or withdrawn from active politics'.[4] Once again, the contradictory nature of the professed ideals and the reality of the human composition of the Circles is apparent.

At the beginning of 1960, Circles had been formed in Madrid, Barcelona, Sevilla and Jerez de la Frontera. By the end of 1961, some twenty Circles had ben formed in various other provinces. In Madrid, the President, veteran Falangist Julián Pemartín, was obliged by ill health to cede his place to Luis González Vicén. The following year, the Madrid Circle began to programme a series of lectures which aroused the suspicions of the authorities from whom permission had to be sought to hold any kind of public meeting, and the programme was suspended. The participants in the discussions were to have been Falangist economist and writer, Juan Velarde Fuertes; Jesus Fueyo; Adolfo Muñoz Alonso, late Director of the Institute of Syndical Studies and author of numerous works on life and doctrine of José Antonio Primo de Rivera; González Vicén; Ceferino Maestu; González de Canales; and Manuel Cantarero del Castillo, journalist and one-time exponent *par excellence* of the notion of Falangist socialism.[5] With the exception of Maestu, all of them had at least one official post in the regime to his name.

The Circles' newspaper, *Es así*, was published for the first time in January 1963. Thereafter, it appeared in March, July and November of the same year and in May 1964, its final appearance before it was banned. It was in the pages of *Es así* that the Circles expounded their interpretation of national syndicalist doctrine, with the mixture of conceptual confusion and resentful demagogy characteristic of the group.

The first edition was typical. In it, the President, Luis González

Vicén, explained the nature and beliefs of the *Círculos Doctrinales*, defining them in negative, rather than in positive terms: 'neither fascism, nor a sect, nor an exclusivist group'. He claimed that the members believed in trade unionism as the means to supercede capitalism, although he did not consider the point that the two are not necessarily incompatible and, indeed, can even be mutually beneficial.[6] Finally, he expressed the group's belief in the organisation of the State on the basis of a bi-cameral parliamentary system – hardly the ideal of the totally anti-parliamentarian Primo de Rivera, but quite in keeping with the *Cortes* and National Council of the Movement of the Franco regime.[7]

In the same edition, in an article entitled 'Class-based Schism', an indirect attack was made on the Government, through a direct attack on the General Directorate of Internal Commerce. The article was occasioned by the holding of elections in the Chambers of Commerce, Industry and Shipping. Characteristic of the way in which the organisations of the employer classes were allowed to retain their autonomous existence after the Civil War, whilst the workers' organisations were totally suppressed, the Chambers of Commerce were not integrated into the official Syndical Organisation. The elections were seen as a unilateral action which might have far-reaching consequences, and might set a precedent for similar action by the workers. This was the crux of the matter. The anonymous author of the article was worried by the possibility of a situation which would be tantamount to admission of the failure of the official Syndical Organisation, and saw the elections as 'the first crack, wide, deep and irreversible, which has been opened publicly in the politico-syndical structure of the nation'.[8]

The thought of the people behind *Es así* was certainly critical and outspoken. It was clear, however, that rather than wanting to see the regime razed to the ground, they were simply scandalised by the decadence into which parts of it had, in their opinion, been allowed to fall. What they wanted was a thorough purge to restore, or to provide for the first time in some areas, the purity and orthodoxy of the ideology on which the regime was nominally founded.

The National President of the Circles, Luis González Vicén, until 1964 a member of the National Council of FET y de las JONS, resigned from his post in mid-1965. According to his successor, Diego Márquez Horrillo, Vicén resigned because he could no longer tolerate being 'harrassed and pursued from the upper echelons of power',[9] on account of a letter which the Circles had sent to the Minister Secretary

General of the Movement, José Solís, in 1963. In the letter, the Circles had expressed support for the public denunciation, made by a group of intellectuals, of police brutality against workers. This represented a remarkable change of heart in a man who had once been a member of a Francoist secret service and leader of the *Guardia de Franco*, well known for its use of strong-arm tactics in defence of the regime. On resigning, González Vicén wrote to the governing body of the Circles a letter in which the same sense of aggrieved honour as had permeated the pages of *Es así* was perceptible. Referring to the suppression of the paper, he wrote:

We must accept that we have received a rebuff from the régime . . . with respect to our political conduct or the expression of our ideas about the future of the régime and about the situation of our Fatherland. I knew that such ideas were not going to be well received, coming, as they did, in the middle of the replete national siesta after the great meal. I knew that régimes of personal command have no other way to power than that of adulation, but I know too that certain values still hold sway in the world: dignity, self-pride and one's duty to one's country.[10]

With supreme cynicism, González Vicén included the entire Spanish populace in the 'great meal' and the 'national siesta', writing as though he and his co-religionaries had had nothing to do with it. The truth was, firstly, that the first twenty years of Francoism had been a period of peace and plenty only for a select minority and, secondly, that the majority of Falangists, including Dr. González Vicén, had also participated in the 'feast'.[11] González Vicén's letter made only the vaguest disapproving allusion to 'regimes of personal command' in general, but did not openly attack the Franco regime in particular. Playing safe in the final analysis, the Circles were attempting to create for themselves an image of martyred rejection at the hands of the regime. Their line was sufficiently ambiguous to permit either dignified acceptance, should the regime offer to readmit them on their terms, or identification with non-regime groups, should the Franco regime be succeeded, as seemed a real and even imminent possibility, by a different socio-political system.

By October 1965, with the departure of González Vicén, the death of Miguel Primo de Rivera, lack of funds and a decline in membership, the Circles had entered a period of stagnation. The election of Márquez Horrillo as President, however, brought a change of tactics.

The basic belief in 'national syndicalist solutions for the problems of Spain' remained unchanged, but now Juvenile, Labour and University sections were created; a programme of lectures, discussion groups and public meetings was arranged; and a total of seventy Circles had been opened throughout Spain by 1966.[12] Although the Circles were anxious not to be identified with the regime, it is possible that this sudden burst of activity was financed, or at least subsidised, by the Movement Secretariat.[13]

The campaign to differentiate the *Falange* of the Doctrinal Circles from that of the *Movimiento Nacional* was increased in the latter half of the decade, and a new element was added to the list of the Circles' claims: the necessity for the unity of all Falangist groups. The Circles were reacting to, but not necessarily against, the direction in which the regime was leading the process of its own institutionalisation. The latter half of the 1960s saw the promulgation of a series of Laws and Decrees which clearly indicated that the *Falange* could by no means expect to hold a privileged position. Such was the significance for the *Falange* of the Organic Law of the State (10 January 1967), the Organic Law of the Movement and its National Council (28 June 1967),[14] the Basic Law of the Juridical Regime of the Movement, and the Law Providing for the Succession of the Head of State (23 July 1969), whereby Franco designated Prince Juan Carlos de Borbón y Borbón as his successor. In response to an article about the *Falange* published in *Cuadernos para el diálogo*, the Madrid Circle issued an open letter, in which it explained the historical process of the 'confusion' between *Falange* and Movement.[15] In May 1969, Circles published a critique of the first draft of the Law of the Juridical Regime of the Movement, and seminars were held by the University section to analyse a recent Government White Paper on education. Lectures were organised explaining different aspects of national syndicalism. Finally, in an interview given in February 1969, Márquez Horrillo stated that the most important task for the Circles was 'to achieve the unity of all Falangist groups, and we are going to devote all our efforts to that task'.[16]

The public declaration made by the Circles in 1969, with respect to the Basic Law of the Juridical Regime of the Movement, showed that, in its opportunistic pragmatism, the 'alternative' *Falange* was little different to its 'official' comrades. By 1969, political plurality was a reality to the extent that the Party Secretary, Solís, had drawn up a Statute of Political Associations. The Circles, like the 'official' *Falange*, supported the regime's steps towards liberalisation, limited though these were, not because they believed in political plurality, but because they were powerless to oppose the regime. Moreover, it was not in their interest to do so. In the same way that the syndicalist sector of the Falangist 'opposition' attempted to capitalise on the efforts of contemporary Left-wing trade union movements, the Circles took advantage of the degree of tolerance by then afforded to the moderate opposition, such as the group entitled '*Tácito*'. The demands made by the Circles in their 1969 declaration could have been subscribed to by any contemporary opposition group: immediate regulation of the free association of Spaniards; total freedom of ideas and tendencies, and full autonomy of associations; incorporation of all Spaniards into 'the common political task'; and the negation of the faculty attributed to certain administrative officials, of temporarily suspending any given association. The Falangists of the Doctrinal Circles were differentiated from the other groups, however, by origins which, as they were aware, were going to be something of a stigma. The declaration ended:

> The Presidents of the *Círculos "José Antonio"*, in their condition of Falangists, and precisely for that reason, ask that the aforementioned possibilities and rights be granted to all Spaniards without exception. They reject any position of privilege for themselves, as well as any limitation which may be imposed on them, based on misunderstood loyalties or disciplines.[17]

Since they did not wish to risk the political isolation which had almost killed *Falange* off in 1936, however, they neither denied nor reneged on those 'loyalties' and 'disciplines'.

As if to assist them in their efforts to promote a non-regime image for themselves, the police impeded, but did not prevent, the commemorative masses arranged by the Madrid Doctrinal Circle for 29 October and 20 November 1969 in the basilica of the Valle de los Caídos, Primo de Rivera's burial place.[18] Nine days after the latter event, the *Círculos* announced their intention of forming the association *Falange Española de las JONS*,[19] thereby marking the start of the tussle for the title which monopolised the activity of all Falangist groups in the first half of the 1970s.

Whilst the 'José Antonio' Doctrinal Circles were denouncing the plight of the working classes in letters to the Secretary General of the Movement in 1963, the Perales sector of the 'alternative' *Falange* was making fresh efforts to gain a foothold in traditionally Left-wing territory, this time under the title of the Workers' National Front

(*Frente Nacional de Trabajadores* – FNT). At the same time, a student branch of the FNT was formed. This was the Syndicalist Students' Front (*Frente de Estudiantes Sindicalistas* – FES), led by Perales' son, Jorge Perales Rodríguez, José Real, the actor Juan Diego (who later became a member of the Spanish communist party) and Sigfredo Hillers de Luque.[20] Both organisations were small, clandestine and intent upon emphasising the novelty and validity of national syndicalist solutions for contemporary problems. They competed with the Circles, which they considered 'a peripheral group'[21] for the title of *Falange Española* and the exclusive right to use the Falangist iconography.

As the decade advanced, internal conflicts arose and intensified between FNT and FES, particularly between Ceferino Maestu and Sigfredo Hillers, over organisational questions. According to Perales, Hillers suffered a narrowness of mind which only admitted ultra-authoritarian interpretations of national syndicalist doctrine. Hillers would have been ideal, he says, for organising an army barracks, but not for running a political group.[22] As a result of these internal discrepancies, FNT separated from FES in 1965 and adopted the title of Revolutionary Syndicalist Front (*Frente Sindicalista Revolucionario* – FSR). The intention of the FSR was to create a revolutionary trade union organisation orientated towards workers not already associated with the *Falange* and, in particular once again, towards the anarchists. In a determined and transparent effort to play down the Falangist content of the group and to play up its out-going nature, the FSR adopted for its flag the red and black traditional to Spanish anarchism and, as its symbol, a black spiral, to represent the renovation from within and towards the exterior, which FSR aspired to effect.[23]

In 1966, the FSR, provisionally headed by veteran 'opposition' Falangist Narciso Perales Herrero, held an assembly in Madrid, as a result of which a Central Committee was elected. It was composed of eight members, of whom Perales was the first Vice President, and Manuel Hedilla Larrey the President. Excused the death penalty in 1937 and sentenced instead to life imprisonment, Hedilla had begun his sentence in the prison of Las Palmas, in the Canary Islands. In 1941, he requested the reduction of his sentence to that of twenty years imprisonment. The request was granted at the beginning of 1942 and, in addition, the sentence was converted from imprisonment to confinement in Palma de Mallorca. He was finally released in 1946 and returned to Madrid, where he held an administrative post in a national airline for a short time.[24] Politically, he did not openly adopt any particular position, nor did he appear to be interested in doing so, for he despised the proliferation of Falangist grouplets, yet would never have considered espousing any other ideology. Moreover, he was not in a position to engage in political activities which might arouse Franco's distrust, for he was subject to police surveillance and to the pressure of 'alternating offers and threats'.[25] Thus, when in 1965 Hedilla accepted the invitation to participate in the *Frente Sindicalista Revolucionario* it represented an unexpected return to active politics, even if he had never actually renounced his Falangism. The leaders of the FSR probably thought they had effected an intra-*Falange* '*coup*', having at once gained a victim of Francoism as their figurehead and having stolen a march on the sector of the 'opposition' led by González Vicén, which had begun in 1958 to claim the cause of Hedilla as its own. Furthermore, by incorporating into their group a direct hierarchical descendent of José Antonio Primo de Rivera, the FSR was preparing a strong claim to the title of FE de las JONS.

After the FES–FNT split in 1965, the *FES*, led by Hillers de Luque, continued to operate in university circles, but the extreme authoritarianism of the organisation in general, and of Hillers in particular, caused the progressive undermining of its membership in favour of other Falangist groups. The most orthodox of FES's members were formed into an élite corps, with the separate title of Falangist Youth (*Juventud Falangista*), which, after the style of the upper stratum of the *Opus Dei*, constituted a semi-secret sect, with vows, special rituals and iron discipline.[26]

In 1966, the FSR was declared illegal. This did not, however, dampen the ardour of its members, who, besides toying with the completely absurd idea of attempting a *coup d'état*, engaged themselves in the more realistic task of organisation and propaganda on the factory shop-floor. To support their propaganda with action, militants participated in a number of the strikes which took place in that year, particularly in the engineering sector of Madrid.[27] By that time, the initially relatively clear picture of 'alternative' Falangist groups had become temporarily somewhat confused.

In 1964, and on the initiative of the General Secretariat of the Movement, the 'Manuel Mateo' Social Centre was set up in Madrid. Its objectives were the education, instruction and cultural recreation of trade union militants. Its inspiration was the national syndicalist ideology, although, like the '*Ballena Alegre*' group, the "Manuel Mateo" Centre was open to anyone who wished to take part in the meetings held there, or use its facilities, such as the reading room.[28]

Unlike the FSR, there was no doubt as to the Falangist nature of the 'Manuel Mateo' Centre. Its newspaper, *Orden Nuevo* (*New Order*), was liberally scattered with quotations from Primo de Rivera and references to the Falangist and JONSist doctrine and history. Narciso Perales participated in the meetings organised by the Centre, as did Ceferino Maestu,[29] and Falangist comrades Zaragoza,[30] Hernando,[31] and Rebull.[32]

Maestu was then in contact with members of the clandestine Spanish communist party and, apparently on his initiative, Marcelino Camacho, Julián Ariza and other PCE militants began to use the premises of the 'Manuel Mateo' Centre for their meetings, with the consent of Syndical Organisation official José Hernando Sánchez.[33] This coincided with the beginnings of the Workers' Commissions movement in Madrid, of which Camacho and Ariza subsequently became the most outstanding leaders. Perales withdrew his collaboration at this point, on the grounds that Camacho and his political correligionaries were 'diverting the political line of the Centre'. In particular, Perales disagreed with the conversion of a *Comité de Jurados y Enlaces* (Committee of Workers' Representatives), which he had helped to establish, into a section of Workers' Commissions.[34] In theory, there should have been no contradiction in the co-existence of *Comisiones Obreras* and the 'Manuel Mateo' Falangists, since both professed to be open to all political creeds and concerned primarily with labour matters. In practice, of course, since the political thought behind the one was opposed to that behind the other, it was inevitable that the two should ultimately prove incompatible.

The Minister Secretary General of the Movement, José Solís Ruiz, knew of the meetings in the 'Manuel Mateo' Centre and allowed them to continue until he received notification 'from above' that they were dangerous and must be stopped. The Centre was consequently closed in 1966. The clandestine meetings, usually chaired by Camacho, were for a time transferred to the headquarters of the *Círculos Doctrinales 'José Antonio'*, in Madrid.[35] These activities were also interrupted, however, when, at the end of an abortive attempt to demonstrate in the area of the New Ministries in Madrid, Ariza, Camacho and Maestu were arrested, in June 1966.[36] On the day before it was due to be held, the trial was 'prepared' by the Public Prosecutor and the defence lawyer, Manuel Cantarero del Castillo, in the premises of the Woodworkers' Union (*Sindicato de la Madera*), of which Cantarero was then President.[37]

By 1968, a certain tension had arisen within the FSR, on account of a lack of consensus with respect to the political line proposed by the President, Manuel Hedilla. Whilst the Vice President, Perales, was in Latin America in that year, Hedilla founded the *Frente Nacional de Alianza Libre* (FNAL) (National Front of Free Alliance). He was accompanied in the venture by a small group of military men and the extreme Right-wingers Blas Piñar, García Reboul and Pérez Viñeta. The FNAL was less radical than the FSR in its national syndicalist militancy; indeed, Hedilla had always been opposed to the inclusion of the word 'revolutionary' in the latter's title.[38] In reality, the FNAL aspired to being a legal platform, or screen, for the FSR, with the object of re-grouping dispersed Falangists.[39] Shortly afterwards, in 1970, Hedilla died, with the FNAL still amounting to very little as an independent group. Hedilla had said that Perales was the only man capable of being National Chief of *Falange* and, says a Falangist militant, 'everyone recognised him as such in fact'.[40] Perales did not, however, assume the leadership of FSR/FNAL but, by mutual agreement, ceded the position to Patricio González de Canales. After the death of Hedilla, the ultra Right-wing members of FNAL left the group and support tended to be given, rather, to FSR, which continued to operate independently, under the *de facto* leadership of Perales.[41]

Whilst the main activity of the 'alternative' *Falange* in the 1960s centred around the 'José Antonio' Doctrinal Circles, the FNT, the FES and the FSR, a number of other small nuclei were formed. Financed solely from the subscriptions paid by their members, and without having any kind of organisational infrastructure, they were small, disconnected and short-lived. Such groups as the *Unión de Trabajadores Sindicalistas* (Union of Syndicalist Workers), *Acción Sindicalista Revolucionaria* (Revolutionary Syndicalist Action), *Frente Sindicalista Unificado* (United Syndicalist Front), or *Frente de Trabajores Nacional Sindicalistas* (National Syndicalist Workers' Front) were reminiscent, in their size and penury, of the *Frente Español* or the *Movimiento Español Sindicalista* (MES), of the early 1930s. Indeed, an attempt was even made to revive the *Central Obrera Nacional Sindicalista* (CONS), founded by Ramiro Ledesma Ramos in 1934. In 1968, however, the national and international situation was completely different to what it had been thirty four years earlier. Not only was Spain no longer the impoverished agrarian country it had been in the thirties, but also it was no longer possible for a faltering *Falange* to look to Fascist Italy, to Nazi Germany, or to anti-republican forces at home for moral amd material support.

In the decade of the 1970s, the action of all political groups, including the Falangists, was conditioned by the pressure for, and apparent imminence of, political as well as social and economic change. In addition, for the 'alternative' *Falange*, the seventies saw the clarification of the confusion which had accumulated in the latter half of the preceding decade. By 1975, the numerous small groups which had sprung up ten years previously had gradually been reduced to two main blocs which survived, 'immune to discouragement',[42] into the post-Franco era.

The *Frente Sindicalista Revolucionario* (FSR), reinforced by former members of the *Frente Nacional de Alianza Libre* (FNAL), began the decade with the objective of spearheading fresh attempts to rescue Falangism from oprobrium and of making itself felt 'in the scattered ranks ("diáspora") of the Falange, through activity consequent with the goal of recovering the content of the movement'.[43] The two groups continued to operate on parallel lines, but their fields of operation were different. The *FNAL* was an intra-Falangist group which aimed at reconstructing a united *Falange* from within the movement's own ranks, recovering former and marginated Falangists. The FSR, on the other hand, in spite of the difficulties of the task, continued to orientate its appeal outside the *Falange* itself, particularly in the factories and other work-places.

In 1974, using the traditional Falangist tactic of concluding intra-group alliances in order simply to subsist, the FNAL was reinforced by the incorporation of two of the syndicalist fractions created in the late 1960s, and two student groups.[44] The FSR, for its part, began to disintegrate at about the same time. Perales splintered off to form yet another group in 1975 and, in the same year, a second group of FSR members announced the creation of the *Partido Sindicalista Auto-gestionario* (PSA) (Autonomous Syndicalist Party). One of its leaders explains the creation of the PSA and its separation from the FSR as a response to the excessively Falangist line imposed on the latter by Perales, with a consequent under-emphasis of the syndicalist aspects of the organisation.[45] Moreover, it was considered that, having failed to make any headway as a union organisation, it was necessary to adopt a more overtly political role in order to be effective.

The creation of the PSA was in clear, deliberate and openly admitted imitation of the *Partico Sindicalista* founded by the anarchist Angel Pestaña in 1934, also in the belief that the political interests of the working classes could not adequately be represented and defended by a trade unionism which lacked a separate party structure. This new attempt, like that of the anarchists, was a failure. In the case of the PSA, the failure was due to three entirely foreseeable reasons. In the first place, the non-Falangist members of the working classes distrusted groups which they knew to be of Falangist origin. Secondly, the majority of politically conscious workers were already members of, or in sympathy with, Left-wing organisations. Thirdly, Falangist workers already had a political organisation: FE de las JONS, in either its 'official' or its 'alternative' version. There was no room for a party which offered nothing new and held out few hopes of success. The atmosphere of optimism which accompanied the death of Franco in November of that year (1975), plus the advent of legalised political opposition, democracy, 'Europeanisation', and a relatively bouyant economic situation did not provide the necessary combination of economic gloom, working class agitation and middle-class fear which had provided the national syndicalists with a potentially favourable breeding ground in the second half of the 1930s.

The development of the other main current of the 'alternative' *Falange*, the 'José Antonio' Doctrinal Circles, in the decade of the 1970s was little more brilliant than that of their syndicalist counterparts, FSR and FNAL.

Following the decision to found FE de las JONS as a political association, announced in 1969, the Doctrinal Circles had begun in 1970 to set up a series of 'promotional committees' (*juntas promotoras*). The first was created by the Barcelona Circle and the example was followed, in the course of the year, by numerous other provincial Circles. At the same time, 'in view of the possible regulation of political associations', and thinking of 'the recovery of the name *Falange Española de las JONS* for the whole of the Spanish people',[46] the campaign to demonstrate that *Falange* and régime were two different entities continued. When, in 1970, the Secretary General of the Movement, Torcuato Fernández Miranda, suspended the annual commemoration of the foundation of *Falange*, the Circles celebrated the anniversary in their respective meeting rooms, with defiant speeches affirming their position of 'radical intransigence' and 'rational and sincere criticism of our own history and of the socio-political reality which surrounds us'. They denounced, too, the 'social conquests which are presented to us as solutions . . .' because 'there are no social conquests, only partialities, the work of a paternalistic capitalism, which is every day less a national capitalism'. These meetings and speeches were accompanied by a letter of protest in similar vein to the National Council of the Movement, a meeting of which had been the official subsitute for the customary gathering in the 'Teatro de la Comedia' in Madrid.[47]

That same year, 1970, the *Juntas Promotoras* and the Circles called for a national demonstration to be staged in Alicante on 22 November, to commemorate the 34th anniversary of the death of *Falange's* founder on the site of his execution. The gathering was not authorised by the police, allegedly as a result of pressure from Fernández Miranda.[48] Police and Civil Guards were called out to prevent the entry into Alicante of the large contingents of Falangists who, nevertheless, began to arrive on 21 November 1970. In spite of the preventive measures, some four thousand Falangists managed to enter Alicante.[49] Their leaders tried to secure authorisation for the demonstration but, in view of the discovery – which filled them with 'perplexity and anxiety' – that 'the order of unhesitating repression came from the Head of State himself and that the President of the Madrid *Círculo 'José Antonio'*, Diego Márquez Horrillo, would be tried by a Council of War if serious disturbances occurred in Alicante', the Falangists limited themselves to ordering a mass to be said for Primo de Rivera on the morning of 22 November in an Alicante chuch.[50] Outside the church, the anti-riot squads were waiting, and took action, 'though without excessive force'.[51] The incidents ('fortunately not very serious') culminated with the arrest of a few young members of FES and the *Círculos Doctrinales*, on account of their having distributed publicly the text of the speech which was to have been delivered at the suspended mass meeting.[52] The national President of the *Círculos Doctrinales* drew the conclusion that,

> the repercussions of the aborted Alicante meeting were translated, basically, into respect, even on the part of the Administration, for the serene behaviour of the Falangists in such critical moments, and affiliations *en masse* from old and new Falangists to the groups which tried to achieve unity in Alicante.[53]

This opinion was not unanimous. Rank and file militants of the organisation, particularly the younger members, were disappointed by the submission of their leaders to the orders of the Ministry of the Interior and the General Secretariat of the Movement, precisely when those same leaders were encouraging militants to disobey Party hierarchs. They found it difficult, too, to relate such submission to the claims made that the 'opposition' *Falange* had nothing to do with the *Movimiento Nacional*. It was in Alicante in 1970 that a process of disillusionment and separation began for many young *Falange* militants, in the same way that the events in the University in 1956 had been the turning point for the preceding generation of 'opposition'

Falangists.[54] In effect, in spite of the revolutionary tone of the speeches, lectures and publications, there were indications in the same that, in the Circles' scheme of things, the old relationship of obedience-command was to be maintained between people and parties:

> The Spanish people cannot be content with a slow process of opening-up, because it will not resign itself to being considered a political minor. However much they may insist on monopolising the political areas, the pressure groups cannot prevent popular participation from being a fact, although its role is to follow the flag of realism so that the democratising operation, an absolutely legitimate demand, may be carried out without violence.[55]

Throughout the 1970s, the Circles and their 'Promotional Committees' continued, within limits, to criticise the status quo and to defy the prohibitions imposed on the celebration of commemorative events. Nevertheless, these always took place, prohibitions notwithstanding. It is noticeable, too, that the meetings and lectures of the Circles were frequently held in such respectable and official places as the premises of the Savings Banks or the Municipal Institute of Education in Madrid, with the attendance of mayors, councillors and other worthy representatives of the Establishment.

By 1971–72, however, the idea of resuscitating FE de las JONS as such was an essential part of the programme of all Falangist groups and the competition for the title was becoming keener. The factionalism and jockeying for positions of pre-eminence which had occurred in 1936 and 1937 were present again in the 1970s, even though by then, the goal – power – was in relative rather than in absolute terms. Thus, in December 1971, a group made up by FES, the *Círculos 'Ruiz de Alda'* and the *Asociación Juvenil 'Octubre'*, and led by Sigfredo Hillers, accused the *Círculos Doctrinales 'José Antonio'* of trying to monopolise the title FE de las JONS. The national Secretary of the Circles replied, denying the accusation and accusing the Hillers group, in turn, of persistently torpedoing the Circles' efforts to achieve Falangist unity.[56]

In June 1973, the Circles held their 'IV National Event' in Toledo. It ended in uproar during the address given by the guest speaker, Manuel Valdés Larrañaga, then Vicesecretary General of the Movement. The reason was not only the obvious contradiction between anti-Movement rhetoric and the invited participation of a top Movement official, but also the rumour that the Circles were being financed by the General Secretariat of the Movement.[57] As a result of the scandal, the Secretary General, Fernández Miranda, closed all the Circles in the country and prohibited their activities for three months. As when FE de las JONS was subject to similar closures in the 1930s, this was, nevertheless, useful anti-Movement propaganda for the Circles.

The Circles were re-opened in early 1974 and in 1975 requested information from the National Council of the Movement as to the legitimacy of the use of the title FE de las JONS by a political association formed in accordance with the Statute of Political Associations approved in December 1974. They were given the same negative answer as had been given to the 'regime' Falangist pretenders to the title: the name was part of the patrimony of all Spaniards and could not be assigned to any one group. Not content with this verdict, the Circles issued a public invitation to all Falangist groups to collaborate in the formation of an association bearing the prohibited title and, in April 1975, the Circles presented the necessary papers to the National Council of the Movement for approval. Their application was again rejected, in June 1975. The piqued response of the Assembly of Presidents of Circles and Promotional Committees came in September 1975: 'not to constitute, sponsor, nor support any political association which did not bear the title of FE de las JONS'. This, said the National President, 'showed clearly their rejection of the National Movement's associationism'.[58] Their 'rejection' did not, however, prevent them from making a third attempt in 1976, 'in accordance with the requisites of the Law of Political Associations'.[59]

The call to unity issued in 1975 by the Circles was as unsuccessful as their attempts to appropriate *Falange's* original title. The *Círculos Doctrinales 'José Antonio'* and the Falangist sector led by former Party Secretary Raimundo Fernández Cuesta were at daggers drawn, precisely over the question of the title, whilst the FSR and FES groups continued their separate courses unheeding. Only the FNAL responded. In January 1976, and on the initiative of Patricio González de Canales, a meeting was held between representatives of FNAL and *Círculos Doctrinales 'José Antonio'*. It was decided to form a political party with the title FE de las JONS, with seven members from each of the constituent groups composing a *Junta Nacional*, the governing body at national level. In February of that year, González de Canales died, and the union of the two groups collapsed in May 1976, as a result of disagreements over political strategy and discipline.[60]

Thus, by 1976, the first year of the post-Franco era, the Falangist 'opposition' was grouped into two main blocs, expressed in two national congresses.

In May 1976, the so-called *Hedillistas* (former members of FSR, FNAL and CONS) held a meeting in Madrid which marked the public constitution of *Falange Española auténtica* (FEa). The group had been created in embryonic form by Narciso Perales, when he left the *FSR* in 1975. He did not, however, assume its national leadership at this first Congress. The President elected was a young engineering worker from Valladolid, Pedro Conde Soladana.[61]

In June 1976, the *Círculos Doctrinales 'José Antonio'* formed a Liaison Committee (*Junta Coordinadora*) with a number of other small Falangist groups, to organise the 'First National Syndicalist Congress' in Madrid.[62] This three day event, held in the Congress and Exhibition Centre of the Ministry of Information and Tourism,[63] was a curious mixture of pretentious organisational efficiency and real political confusion. Entitled 'Towards Unity', the Congress in fact merely served to point up the *dis*unity existing between the different groups. The continual harping on unity of the speakers could not disguise the tension between the *Junta Coordinadora* and other Falangist blocs, nor the conflict latent within the *Junta* itself. The final event of the Congress, a gathering in front of the house where José Antonio Primo de Rivera was born, ended in a clash with members of *Falange Española auténtica*, the most prominent and aggressive of whom was Miguel Hedilla Rojas, youngest son of the second National Chief of *Falange*, Manuel Hedilla Larrey.[64]

In the same month of June 1976, the Falangists grouped together under the leadership of Raimundo Fernández Cuesta, with the collective title of *Frente Nacional Español*, published an open letter in which they justified their claim to the title FE de las JONS, and invited all Falangist groups to unite. The *Frente Nacional Español* based its claim to the title essentially, though not exclusively, on the "Old Shirt" composition of its membership:

> Our application is legitimated by the signature of surviving comrades of the first party card-holders of *Falange Española de las JONS*, of National Councillors nominated by the JONS or appointed by José Antonio, and those whom Manuel Hedilla designated during his leadership, as well as by the signatures of thousands of Falangists of all generations currently affiliated to the *Frente Nacional Español*.[65]

The contradiction between the *Falange's* original anti-party attitudes and the decision to form what was a political party in all but constitutional status and parliamentary functions, was equally rationalised and justified, with arguments reminiscent of the belligerence offered forty years earlier to the Second Republic:

> Since, under the legality in force and projected . . . the entry into the political arena of certain forces constitutes a danger and a worry for the men, classes and lands of Spain, our common proposal must be to oppose to that threat of rupture, not a negative attitude of mere resistence, but a positive and creative attitude, demonstrating that the *Falange* . . . can give the Spanish people satisfaction for its aspirations of justice and freedom, ouside international capitalism and Marxism, and outside party Liberalism.[66]

The letter expressed the belief that all Falangist groups must unite and that such unity '(did) not seem difficult, since what separates us at present is accidental. Between us there are no differences of ideological content. It is precisely our ideological identity which must unite us'.[67] As in 1934 and 1937, however, personal differences, coupled with individual anxieties for protagonism, proved stronger than common 'ideological identity'.

Pedro Conde Soladana, leader of the *Hedillista* sector of the 'alternative' *Falange*, reacted to Fernández Cuesta's proposals in the following terms:

> We believe that the only name for which Don Raimundo Fernández Cuesta can change the present one of *Frente Nacional Español*, is FET y de las JONS, which he has served faithfully for forty years; but not for FE de las JONS, which he has ignored and trampled on during that same period of time.[68]

The response of the *Junta Coordinadora* was equally negative. The *Junta's* Secretary, Eduardo Zulueta, issued a *communiqué* announcing the *Junta's* intention to 'present an application similar to that of FNE, laying claim to the name of FE de las JONS' and lamenting that the concession of the title 'must necessarily be an administrative decision, and, therefore, alien to the Falangists themselves'.[69]

In spite of this announcement, and in spite of fifteen years of propaganda denouncing those considered 'collaborationists', such as Raimundo Fernández Cuesta, Miguel Primo de Rivera, or Manuel Valdés Larrañaga, in July 1976, the representatives of the *Junta*

Coordinadora and FES signed an agreement, entitled the 'Pact for Unity', with the *Frente Nacional Español*. Under the terms of the pact, the decision of the Ministry of the Interior as to the concession of the title would be considered final and binding. A constituent period would then be opened, in which 'the ideological scheme, the programme and the statutes of the party would be worked out by everyone, without a previously established hierarchy and without privileges for anyone'.[70]

Once the title *Falange Española de las JONS* had been officially assigned to the FNE, in October 1976, the *Círculos Docrinales 'José Antonio'*, considering that the Fernández Cuesta sector had not completed its side of the 'Pact for Unity', themselves adopted the status of political party, without altering their original title. The FES, for its part, also became a political party, with the name of *Falange Española independiente*. The third of the aspirants to the old title, *Falange Española auténtica*, like the *Círculos Doctrinales*, retained its original name and, as such, registered officially as a political party, in accordance with the provisions of the 1976 Law of Political Associations.

Thus, in spite of *Falange*'s original anti-party, anti-parliamentarian doctrine, the defence of whose purity formed the backbone of the Falangist 'opposition's' *raison d'être*, all sectors of that opposition had adopted party status by the end of 1976. Once more, *Falange* had sacrificed ideological concepts to the demands of political pragmatism.

Notes

1. Perales, N., interview, 7 Jan. 1977; Castro Villacañas, A., interview, 23 Nov. 1977.
2. Perales, N., interview, 7 Jan. 1977; he states that he signed as a founder member but never attended any of the meetings.
3. Márquez Horrillo, D., *Círculos 'José Antonio'* (Bilbao: Albia Política, 1977) pp. 14–15.
4. Ibid.; Pordomingo, E., interview, 2 Jan. 1979.
5. See, Cantarero del Castillo, M., *Falange y socialismo* (Barcelona: Dopesa, 1973).
6. As the experience of the Catholic and 'yellow' unions of the late 19th and early 20th centuries in Spain had demonstrated.
7. *Es así* (Madrid, Jan. 1963).
8. Ibid.
9. Márquez Horrillo, D., op. cit., p. 19.

10. González Vicén, L., in Márquez Horrillo, D., op. cit., p. 20.
11. González Vicén, for example, as well as being a member of the National Council of FET y de las JONS, was head of the Casualty Department at one of Madrid's largest State hospitals, where he also ran a private practice.
12. Márquez Horrillo, D., op. cit., p. 21.
13. This was suggested to the present writer by a former Falangist. Although the rumour was confirmed by former Vicesecretary General of the Movement, Manuel Valdés Larrañaga (interview, 22 Nov. 1977), with respect to 1973, it is not known when such financing began. The poor typographical quality of the Circles' publications such as *Unidad y Autogestión*, *Eje*, *Acción* or *Aula Azul*, was in marked contrast to the well-printed pages of *Alcalá*, *La Hora*, or *24*, produced by the SEU with official funds from the Movement Secretariat.
14. Amongst other things, the Organic Law of the Movement regulated the possible formation of political associations, thereby implying that the political monopoly of FET y de las JONS was coming to an end.
15. 'Contemplación analítica del Estatuto Orgánico del Movimiento', in *Cuadernos para el diálogo*, no. 68, Nov. 1968. The Circles' reply appeared in the *Boletín de los Círculos José Antonio* (Madrid, Dec. 1968).
16. 'Círculos José Antonio: hacia la unidad de los Falangistas' in *Nuevo Diario* (Madrid, 19 Feb. 1969).
17. *Boletín de los Círculos 'José Antonio'* (Madrid, June 1969) *Diario SP* (Madrid, 29 May 1969).
18. Eduardo Zaldivar, interview, 21 Dec. 1977; E. Pordomingo, interview, 2 Jan. 1979; 'Legitimidad de una fecha. Legitimidad de una idea', the text of a speech made by Márquez Horrillo on 29 Oct. 1969 and reproduced in the *Boletín del Círculo 'José Antonio'* (Madrid, Dec. 1969).
19. *Informaciones* (Madrid, 29 Nov. 1969).
20. Born in 1934, Hillers de Luque was, like many members of his generation, a member of the *Frente de Juventudes* from an early age. He was a member of the *Guardia de Franco* in 1953, head of a *Falange* centurion in 1955, and a teacher in the Youth Front *Escuela de Mandos* in 1959. Hillers has published two books, *Estilo y ética falangistas* (1974) and *España: una revolución pendiente* (Madrid: Ediciones FES, 1975).
21. Falangist youth leader, Javier Morillas, interview, 22 Feb. 1977.
22. Narciso Perales, interview, 7 Jan. 1977.
23. Perales states (4 Jan. 1977) that the FSR was formed in secret between 1961 and 1962, and that 1965 was the date of its definitive establishment.
24. Hedilla Rojas, M. I., interview, 24 Feb. 1977; Alcazar de Velasco, A., interview, 15 Feb. 1977; Llorens Borras, J. A. (ed.), op. cit., pp. 557–619.
25. Hedilla Rojas, M. I., interview, 24 Feb. 1977. Dionisio Ridruejo describes Hedilla's attitude in his account of a visit to Hedilla in 1944, in *Casi unas memorias*, p. 264.
26. Demetrio Castro Alfín, interview, 2 Mar. 1978. Since the University was an important field of recruitment for both FES and *Opus Dei*, and both were aiming at middle class youth, it is perhaps not merely coincidental that FES should adopt a style and methods similar to those of its rival.
27. Narciso Perales states (interview, 4 Jan. 1977) that FSR militants

participated in the strike at the 'Saint Gobain' factory, whilst José Luis Rubio recalls (interview, 29 Mar. 1979) their taking part in the strikes staged in the 'Standard Electric' works. Such activity is barely reflected, however, in the FSR's periodicals. Certainly, these differed from the majority of Falangist publications in that they reported and analysed current events in labour circles, rather than devote space to treatises on doctrinal questions, but they were reporting on events in other countries more often than on those in Spain. Documentary evidence of FSR's participation in the working class mobilisation of the mid-1960s is limited to a series of leaflets addressed to the 'Comrades of Standard Electric'.

28. Manuel Mateo, founder member, in 1934, of the *Central Obrera Nacional Sindicalista*, had been a member of the communist party before joining the primitive *Falange*.

29. Maestu now states that he did not participate as a Falangist, since he was by then 'estranged' from *Falange*.

30. Head of the workers' section of the official trade union organisation, in the Banking sector.

31. Collaborator of the Press Director in the Ministry of Labour, Falangist Antonio Gibello.

32. Member of FSR, which did not, however, participate as a group.

33. Maestu, C., interview, 14 Dec. 1977. Cf. Ariza, J., *CC.OO.*, Avance/ Mañana (Madrid, 1976) pp. 18–19; Iglesias Selgas, C., *El sindicalismo español*, pp. 54–5.

34. Narciso Perales, interview, 7 Jan. 1977; Javier Morillas, interview, 22 Feb. 1977. Cf. Ariza, J., op. cit., p. 15: 'in Madrid and Barcelona, participation (in the 1963 syndical elections) was high, which explains the fact that the first Workers' Commission to appear in the capital was called the *Comisión de Enlaces y Jurados de Empresa*'. The *enlaces* and *jurados* were the only representatives elected directly by the workers in the Spanish official trade union system.

35. Eduardo Zaldivar, interview, 2 Mar. 1978. Zaldivar, then a member of the Circles, was entrusted by Márquez Horrillo with the job of opening their premises every Sunday morning for a period of six or seven weeks, to admit Camacho and others. See also Ariza, J., op. cit., p. 19.

36. Zaldivar, E (2 Mar. 1978). Ariza, J., op. cit., p. 20, states that on that occasion, 181 people were arrested, of whom 19 were sent for trial. The four leaders, whom Ariza names as Camacho, Maestu, Hernando (Secretary of the 'Manuel Mateo' Centre) and Martinez-Conde, were held in prison for twelve days before being given provisional liberty.

37. This information was provided by a member of the 'José Antonio' Doctrinal Circles who wishes to remain anonymous. It has not been possible, however, to confirm this information in any other source.

38. José Luis Rubio, interview, 23 Mar. 1979; Javier Morillas, interview, 22 Feb. 1977.

39. Narciso Perales, interview, 7 Jan. 1977.

40. Javier Morillas, 22 Feb. 1977; M. I. Hedilla Rojas, interview, 24 Feb. 1977.

41. Ibid.

42. 'Inasequibles al desaliento'. According to José Antonio Primo de Rivera,

this was an essential quality of all true Falangists.

43. Narciso Perales, interview, 4 Jan. 1977.

44. The syndicalist groups were *Acción Sindicalista Revolucionaria* and the *Frente Sindicalista Unificado*; the student groups were the *Juntas de Oposición Falangistas* and the *Frente de Estudiantes Nacional Sindicalistas*. Like most of the 'alternative' Falangist groups other than the main currents (FSR, FNAL, FES and *Círculos Doctrinales*) these groups were composed mainly of young, lower middle class people, without any political formation or experience and without any formal structure or regular finance for their activities.

45. José Luis Rubio Cordón, interview, 23 Mar. 1979. Rubio adds that he disagreed with Perales' refusal to enter into any kind of cooperation with Left-wing opposition groups such as the CNT, *Comisiones Obreras*, or the *Plataforma de Convergencia Democrática*, thereby wasting the 'opposition' *Falange*'s last opportunity to be an effective political force.

46. Márquez Horrillo, D., op. cit., p. 26.

47. Speech made by Márquez Horrillo on 29 Oct. 1970 and reproduced in the *Boletín de los Círculos 'José Antonio'*, Madrid, Dec. 1970. See also, *Arriba*, 29 and 30 Oct. 1970.

48. Márquez Horrillo, D., op. cit., p. 30.

49. Ibid., p. 31; Castro, D. and Zaldivar, E., interview, 21 Dec. 1977.

50. Ibid.

51. Ibid.

52. The *Frente de Estudiantes Sindicalistas* (FES) had been supporting the *Círculos Doctrinales* since its split with the *Frente Nacional de Trabajadores* in 1965.

53. Márquez Horrillo, D., op. cit., p. 33. The Movement Press made no reference to these events, reporting only the official commemoration.

54. Demetrio Castro Alfín, interview, 23 Feb. 1979; Eugenio Pordomingo, interview, 2 Jan. 1979.

55. Márquez Horrillo, D., op. cit., p. 34.

56. Ibid., p. 36.

57. See above, note 13. It was also rumoured that Fernández Miranda had been appointed Secretary General of the Movement with the express task of 'getting rid of *Falange*' ('de cargarse la Falange').

58. Márquez Horrillo, D., op. cit., p. 45; *Pueblo* (Madrid, 8 and 9 Apr. 1975).

59. Ibid., p. 48; *Informaciones* (Madrid, 5 Jan. 1976).

60. Márquez Horrillo, D., op. cit., p. 45; Narciso Perales, interview, 21 Jan. 1977.

61. *El País* (23 May 1976); *Ya* (28 May 1976); *Rojo y Negro* (*Boletín informativo de los Círculos '4 de marzo' y la Asociación Juvenil 'Amanecer'*), no. 0, June 1976. Conde Soladana projected a strongly anti-Movement and populist image. He was dismissed from the FASA–Renault car works and briefly imprisoned in 1974 for his participation in labour disputes and strike action in Valladolid.

62. The other Falangist groups participating were the Association of Former Members of the SEU, Association of Former Members of the *Frente de Juventudes*, *Asociación Juvenil 'Amanecer'*, *Círculos '4 de marzo'*, *Agrupación Juvenil 'Bandera Roja y Negra'*, Young Falangists, and the

Civil War volunteers organisation, *Antíguas Banderas de Falange*.

63. It has not been possible to ascertain, either from the organisers or from the appropriate Department of the Ministry of Information and Tourism, who financed this Congress. It seems highly unlikely, however, that the funds came solely from the subscriptions of participants. The hire of the Congress Centre alone would have amounted to several thousands of pesetas.

64. Personal observation at the *I Congreso Nacionalsindicalista, FE de las JONS* (Madrid, 26–9 June 1976). See *El País* (26, 27, 28, 29 and 30 June 1976); *Arriba* (29 and 30 June 1976); *El Alcazar* (26 June 1976); *Cambio 16*, no. 239 (5 July 1976).

65. *Arriba, Pueblo, ABC* (18 June 1976).

66. Ibid.

67. Ibid.

68. *El País* (18 June 1976).

69. *ABC* (18 June 1976).

70. Márquez Horrillo, D., op. cit., p. 48; *Informaciones* (9 July 1976) (see also the editions of 7 August 1976 and 16 Sep. 1976); *El País, Arriba* (18 July 1976).

Conclusion: After Franco . . .

In spite of the common origins and ideology of its component sectors, *Falange* entered the post-Franco era in total disunity. On the one hand, the officially denominated FE de las JONS, under the leadership of veteran Falangist Raimundo Fernández Cuesta, grouped together those whose identification with the Franco regime was unashamed and even exultant, as they showed at the gathering organised in Madrid to commemorate the first anniversary of Franco's death, on 20 November 1976.[1] On the other hand, the various 'opposition' Falangist groups attempted to provide a minimal organisational structure for those who did not wish 'to be against (the National Movement), but within it, yet maintaining their own leaders'.[2]

In the Autumn of 1976, yet another call to unity had been made by the sector led by Fernández Cuesta, on the occasion of the first congress of the recently legalised FE de las JONS, on 29 October 1976. Even before the meeting began, it was clear that ideas of unity were merely wishful thinking. On 28 October 1976, groups of *Hedillista* Falangists toured the streets of Madrid to dissuade comrades of the Fernández Cuesta faction from sticking up posters announcing the congress, and anti-Fernández Cuesta placards appeared on the top of the Puerta de Alcalá, where they had been placed by supporters of *Falange Española auténtica*.[3] The congress was attended by many familiar figures from the *Movimiento Nacional*, such as Pilar Primo de Rivera and her nephew, Miguel, Blas Piñar López, Dionisio Sanz, José Utrera Molina and Gonzalo Fernández de la Mora. Also present were groups of militants representing former members of the SEU, the *Círculos Doctrinales 'José Antonio'*, the 'Ruiz de Alda' Circles, and the FES. It ended up in uproar. The FES leader, Sigfredo Hillers de Luque, suggested in the course of his speech that the Franco regime should now be 'profoundly criticised'. The regime Falangists leapt instantly to the defence of the *Caudillo's* memory and of their own personal and political history. After an exchange of blows and insults between the various factions, most of the 'comrades' left the hall, leaving the Chairman, Fernández Cuesta, entirely incapable of controlling *mêlée*, to address a much-diminished audience.[4]

This congress marked a change in the regime *Falange's* tactics. From attempting to erase or deny collaboration with Francoism, as they had

176

done since November 1975, fidelity to 'the values of 18 July 1936' now became the basis of the appeal of the Fernández Cuesta faction. Even after the *Generalísimo's* death, Franco and Francoism were, for them, the principle element in the political survival of *Falange*. Thus, on the occasion of the first anniversary of Franco's death, Fernández Cuesta wrote at length of the identity between Franco and José Antonio Primo de Rivera:

Franco and José Antonio, two exceptional figures in our history, are united not only in their thought and work and their desire to serve. They are also united in the content of their testament, two examples of Catholic faith and dedication to Spain, and in the day and hour of their death, and even in the place where their bodies rest for ever from the battle for Spain and for the Spanish people. I am sure – because I knew them both and I knew their far-sightedness and patriotism – of the complete understanding between José Antonio and Franco, in order that their exceptional qualities should render the best service to the cause of Spain.[5]

In the same way, *Falange* and regime were identified with one another:

Without the war and the Victory, the *Falange* would not have achieved so rapidly the implantation and difusion it did achieve. Without the *Falange* and its sacrifices, the war would have been a grand and heroic military operation leading to the prevention of the triumph of Communism, to the re-establishment of material order, and to making possible co-existence between Spaniards. But it would have lacked the popular and ideological content which the *Falange* gave it, and the State would have been merely authoritarian, without the ambition of incorporating the totality of Spanish life which has guided its activity.[6]

The wheel had come full circle, however, and the situation which, in 1976, made possible the formal re-creation of *Falange Española de las JONS* merely returned it to the political ineffectiveness from which 'the war and the Victory' had rescued it forty years earlier. The performance of Fernández Cuesta's party in the general elections held in June 1977 demonstrated that, after forty years of Francoism, the majority of the Spanish people did not wish to be represented by a party which based its appeal primarily on its identification with the previous régime. The extreme Right as a whole polled less than 1% of all the votes cast, and FE de las JONS in particular a mere 0.21%.[7] The Falangist 'opposition' fared little better. The Doctrinal Circles presented candidates in 11 provinces, FE *auténtica* in 22, and FE *independiente* in 1. Between them, they polled 40 359 votes,[8] which indicated that the efforts of the preceding 40 years to dissociate the *Falange* from the Franco régime had failed to carry conviction for all but a tiny minority of Spaniards. Not a single candidate from either of the Falangists currents was elected to the *Cortes* on 15 June 1977.

The 'opposition' *Falange* which survived the electoral débacle subsequently underwent a certain process of realignment. Whilst FEa and FEi broke irreparably with their correligionaries, the *Círculos Doctrinales 'José Antonio'* allied themselves with the régime *Falange* and the extreme Right of the political spectrum. Only those who chose the latter course thereby resolved the grand contradiction of the Falangist 'opposition', between trying to attract a new clientèle whilst maintaining all the old watch-words, symbols, discourse and values. In joining forces with the *Falange* of Fernández Cuesta and Blas Piñar, the *Círculos* showed that they had understood that it was not possible to dissociate Falangism from Francoism, since both were part of the response given by the Spanish upper and middle classes to the circumstances of the Second Spanish Republic, both grew out of those circumstances, and each needed the other to continue thereafter. The remaining opposition Falangists who failed, or refused, to recognise the essential as well as the historical unity between Falangism and Francoism, made little progress in their attempt to find supporters for the former who, at the same time, rejected the latter. Their efforts were necessarily rendered futile by the illogicality of wishing to promote, in abstraction, one essential component of a coherent system, whilst rejecting the system as a whole. Thus, whilst the National Union (*Unión Nacional*, formed by *FE de las JONS*, *Fuerza Nueva* and *Círculos Doctrinales 'José Antonio'*) managed to elect one candidate to the *Cortes* in the general elections of March 1979, the 'opposition' *Falange* (FEa and FEi) marginally increased their share of the total vote, but still failed to achieve Parliamentary representation.[9]

By then, a minimal party structure was virtually all that remained of *Falange*. After the death of its patron, the sprawling State administrative apparatus which had been its domain was dismantled with remarkable ease and rapidity. In spite of the efforts of both Franco and the *Falange* to leave the future of post-Franco Spain 'tied up, and well tied up', the two had undergone a simultaneous process of decay and had been overtaken by the pace of economic development and the pressure from increasingly open, voluble and numerous democratic opposition movements.[10]

Without Franco, *Falange* survived little more than four years; without an independent Party apparatus to sustain them, the formal structures of the Franco regime were done away with in barely eighteen months. Between March 1976 and June 1977, in a two-fold transitional operation, the institutions embodying the Franco regime were removed, and those designed to give substance to the democratic monarchy of Juan Carlos I were moved into place. Thus, the Law of Political Associations, announced in March 1976 and approved by the *Cortes* in June of that year, at once opened the way to the legislation of all political currents and implied the end of the political monopoly officially exercised thereto by FET y de las JONS. The legislation of free trade unions in May 1977 was accompanied by the dismantling of the Syndical Organisation, from December 1976 onwards, and the distribution of its staff throughout the rest of the State bureaucracy. Similarly, the Law of Political Reform, approved by popular referendum in December 1976, and the subsequent legalisation of political parties in February 1977, meant the abolition of the existing *Cortes*; the establishment of parliamentary democracy based on the election of representatives by universal suffrage; and the dissolution of the General Secretariat of the Movement, with its National Council and its Delegations and Departments at national, provincial and local levels.[11] This process was carried out between March and May 1977.

Little protest against these measures came from any of the Falangist sectors. On the contrary, they had taken stock of the post-Franco situation and had realised that the days of the yoke and arrows were over. Consequently, they were all more concerned with modifying their legal status, in a hasty attempt at least to salvage the name of *Falange*, than with attempting to oppose what was already a *fait accompli*.

José Antonio Primo de Rivera had stated in 1933 that his ideology, as well as being a school of thought, was also a way of being.[12] The parlous state to which *Falange* had returned by 1979 belied the fact that, for almost forty years, that apparently innocuous notion had been imposed as a reality on contemporary Spain, to the virtual exclusion of all other possible ways of thinking and being. *Falange* was able to achieve this, moreover, without having exclusive access to either political or economic power, which it shared with other forces present in the regime and which lay, ultimately, in the hands of General

Franco. The secret of *Falange's* success lay in the role assigned to it by the régime.

In the first place, *Falange* had provided the oligarchy which emerged from the Civil War with a body of doctrine suitable for laying the ideological foundations of the post-war New State. The quasi-revolutionary content of the Falangist credo combined the protection of the interests of those who had fomented and won the Civil War with elements of novelty and modernity which disguised the reactionary character of the regime. In the second place, *Falange* served as the controlling apparatus for the great mass of people whose interests had not benefitted from the war. Small time victors and losers of all descriptions had to be kept under political surveillance whilst, at the same time, they must be organised and exploited economically. In addition, they were persuaded that such control and exploitation was the best for everyone and even indispensable, given the 'naturally undisciplined character of *homo hispanicus*.

Both the 'official' and 'opposition' *Falanges* fulfilled the role assigned to the Party in the post-war division of labour. The former, not only with the unconditional support it gave to whatever decisions the *Caudillo* might take, but also through the thousands of Party members who staffed the administrative structures of the regime. No other contemporary political group could boast as many people working in, and for, it. Even at the end of 1976, when the organisms which had composed FET y de las JONS were on the verge of disappearance, the staff of the General Secretariat throughout Spain was still estimated at over one million people, of whom some 11 000 were situated in Madrid.[13] Moreover, no other group enjoyed *Falange's* economic privileges: when Franco died, in 1975, the annual income of FET y de las JONS from State sources was estimated at 9 000 million pesetas.[14]

The 'opposition' *Falange* made its contribution to the maintenance of the regime in those areas which, it was felt, were most open to the 'danger' of Left-wing influences: the working classes and the Universities. The 'opposition' *Falange* was not working consciously to hand these areas over to Francoism, but what its militants did not appear to understand was that any attempt to undermine the implantation of democratic opposition to Franco in those areas was automatically beneficial to the regime.

Finally, both 'left' and 'right' of the Falangist spectrum accepted and propagated the ideology and values which the Franco regime recognised and proclaimed as its own.

Whether the *Falange* would have been revived by those who organised the attempted military *coup* of 23 February 1981, or the *coup* evidently planned for 27 October 1982, clearly belongs to the realms of speculation. It is worthy of note, however, that the Decree which the October 1982 rebels planned to issue based the decision to depose the King on his alleged 'infidelity' to the 'Fundamental Principles of the Movement' and expressed the determination of the military *Junta* which would have replaced the Monarch to impose 'strict observance' of those Principles in the future.[15]

The Council of War held against those responsible for the 1981 *coup* did not reveal any implication on the part of *Falange*, except for the individual involvement of former Syndical Organisation official, Juan García Carrés. Nevertheless, the course of action followed by the Falangists in 1981 and 1982 suggests that they may have hoped that a military *deus ex machina* would again save them, as in 1936, from extinction. After the failure of the attempted risings, and after the electoral victory of the Spanish Socialist Party in October 1982, the only remaining Falangist forces of any consideration, FE de las JONS and *Fuerza Nueva*, virtually went into voluntary liquidation. The leader of *Fuerza Nueva*, Blas Piñar López, announced the dissolution of his party on 20 November 1983,[16] whilst Raimundo Fernández Cuesta announced his resignation as head of FE de las JONS in February 1983.

In the transitional period which followed General Franco's death, it had become increasingly clear that the majority of Spaniards actively wanted to live in the kind of liberal democratic regime which was, and always had been, anathema to the Falangists. In spite of the obstacles encountered along the way, by 1983, democracy had, in effect, been reestablished and even partially consolidated in Spain.[17] The Falangists, remnants of an outworn era, could not ignore that reality. Some resigned themselves to a residual existence on the fringes of national politics.[18] Others withdrew to winter quarters, to await new opportunities. As even they admitted, however, Spain seemed unlikely to provide them in the near future.[19]

Notes

1. Personal observation, and *El Alcazar* (15, 20 Nov. 1976); *Diario 16* (6–11 Nov. 1976); *Ya* (21 Nov. 1976); *El País* (17, 20 Nov. 1976). Participant groups included: *FE de las JONS, Hermandad Nacional de Alféreces*

Provisionales, Fuerza Nueva, Guerrilleros de Cristo Rey, Confederación Nacional de Ex-Combatientes, Guardia de Franco, and *Fundación Francisco Franco.* Leading figures present included Franco's daughter and son-in-law (the 'Duke and Duchess of Franco'), their son, Francisco Franco junior, José Antonio Girón, Blas Piñar, Raimundo Fernández Cuesta, and former Party Secretary, José Utrera Molina.

2. FE *independiente* militant, Joaquín Barquero, in a letter to the newspaper *SP* (29 May 1969).
3. *Informaciones* (29 Oct. 1976).
4. Personal observation and *Informaciones* (29 Oct. 1976); *El País* (30, 31 Oct., 5 Nov. 1976); *ABC* (31 Oct., 7 Nov. 1976); *Cambio 16* (8 Nov. 1976).
5. *El Alcazar* (20 Nov. 1976).
6. Ibid.
7. Linz, J.J. in *Rivista italiana de scienza politica*, no. 3, 1978. The vote polled by *Unión de Centro Democrático* (UCD), however, whose leader was a former Secretary General of the Movement, Adolfo Suárez, showed that a considerable portion of the populace was willing to be represented by the derivatives of that regime. UCD obtained almost 35% of the votes cast, giving its candidates 167 seats out of a total of 350.
8. *El País* (10 May 1977); Linz, J. J., loc. cit.; *Informaciones* (18 June 1977).
9. Whereas the minority groups including FEa had obtained 0.43% of the total vote in June 1977, their share increased to 1.28% in March 1979. The extreme Right also increased its share from 0.6% to 2.2%. *Unión Nacional* alone accounted for 2.1% of the latter figure; Rodríguez Aramberri, J., in Claudín, F. (ed.) *¿Crisis de los partidos políticos?*, Dédalo (Madrid, 1980) p. 130. See also, *Informaciones, El País* (Madrid, 3 Mar. 1979).
10. For the role of the democratic opposition in the transition to democracy, see, e.g.: Preston, P., 'La oposición anti-franquista' in Preston, P. (ed.), *España en crisis*, pp. 254–63; Claudín, F. 'Le nouveau mouvement ouvrier' in *Les Temps Modernes*, no. 357 (Paris, 1976); Equipo de Estudio, *Al filo de la crisis* (Madrid: Punto Crítico, 1975). *Prueba de fuerza entre el reformismo y la ruptura* (Madrid: Elías Querejeta, 1976) and *Lucha por el poder* (Madrid: Elías Querejeta, 1976); Carr, R. & Fusi, J.P., op. cit., pp. 269–309; Debray, R. & Gallo, M., *Mañana España; conversaciones con Santiago Carrillo* (Madrid: Akal, 1971); Oneto, J., *Arias entre dos crisis* (Madrid: Editorial Cambio 16, 1975); and the interviews with Enrique Múgica (PSOE), Joaquín Almunia (PSOE), Julián Ariza (CC.OO.), Jerónimo Saavedra (UGT), and Jordi Solé Tura (PSUC) in Ellwood, S.M., *Spain in Franco's Shadow*, an unpublished collection of interviews with contemporary political figures, compiled in Spain between Jan. 1980 and Jan. 1981.
11. Paradoxically, the General Secretariat of the Movement was the Ministry encharged with organising the referendum of the Law which decreed that same Ministry's disappearance.
12. Primo de Rivera, J.A., foundational speech, 29 Oct. 1933. Cf. Fernández Cuesta, R. speech made on 29 Oct. 1953: 'Falangism, more than a concrete programme . . . is an attitude and a way of understanding life.'
13. *Blanco y Negro*, no. 3384 (Madrid, 9–15 Mar. 1977).

14. Gallego, S., 'El Movimiento que viene y va' in *Cuadernos para el diálogo* (12 Feb. 1977).
15. *Tiempo*, no. 23 (Madrid, 18–25 Oct. 1982).
16. The total vote polled in the Oct. 1982 elections by the coalition of which *Fuerza Nueva* was part ('*Unión Nacional*') was 100 899, in comparison to the 362 413 votes obtained in Mar. 1979 (*El País*, Madrid, 21 Nov. 1982).
17. For an analyses of the transitional process, see Preston, P., *The Triumph of Democracy in Spain* (London: Methuen, 1968) *passim* esp. pp. 160–227.
18. Under the leadership of former *Círculos Doctrinales* president, Diego Márquez Horrillo, FE de las JONS presented a handful of candidates in the June 1986 General Elections. None was elected.
19. *Fuerza Nueva* reappeared as a political party on 26 Oct. 1986 with the title *Frente Nacional* (National Front). Presented by its leader, Blas Piñar, as 'an alternative to the present system', its immediate objective was announced, not as participation in Spanish elections, but as the achievement of representation in the European Parliament.

Bibliography

The bibliography has been divided into two sections, which detail, respectively, primary and secondary sources. The first of these has been divided again into six sub-sections, which include published and unpublished documents from official, Party and personal sources contemporaneous with the events examined in the text of the present study. The second section of the bibliography has been divided into two sub-sections, which cover non-contemporary materials used in the course of the research.

1 PRIMARY SOURCES

1.1 Reports, Circulars, Conference Papers and Minutes of Political Parties and Trade Union Organisations

Agrupación de Antíguos Miembros del Frente de Juventudes, *Proyecto de esquema ideológico actualizado*, proposal presented to the Second National Assembly of Former Members of the *Frente de Juventudes* (Madrid, May 1966).

Cadenas Vicent, V., *Actas del último Consejo Nacional de FET y de las JONS (Salamanca, 18–19 Apr. 1937) y algunas noticias referentes a la Jefatura Nacional de Prensa y Propaganda*, private edn (Madrid, 1975).

Círculo Doctrinal 'José Antonio', *Conclusiones aprobadas en la reunión nacional de Círculos Doctrinales 'José Antonio'* (Madrid, 31 Jan. 1966).

Círculos Doctrinales 'José Antonio', *Declaración que formula la Junta de Presidentes de los Círculos Doctrinales 'José Antonio' de España, reunida en Madrid en octubre de 1969*.

Comunión Tradicionalista, *El crimen de la Falange en Begoña* (17 Aug. 1942).

I Congreso Nacional de FET y de las JONS (Minutes of the 1st National Congress of FET y de las JONS) (Madrid: Prensa Gráfica, Oct. 1953).

I Congreso Nacional de la Juventud Falangista, papers presented and conclusions of the 1st National Congress of Falangist Youth (Madrid, 1971).

Esteban, J. M. and Pedregal, A., *El problema agrario en España*, paper presented at the 1972 Provincial Syndical Forum by the representatives of Extremadura in Barcelona.

Junta Nacional de Círculos Doctrinales 'José Antonio', *Declaración que formula la Junta Nacional de Círculos 'José Antonio', reunida en Madrid, el día 15 de mayo de 1966*.

Junta Nacional de Círculos Doctrinales 'José Antonio', *Declaración que formula la Junta Nacional de Círculos 'José Antonio', ante los problemas políticos planteados en la actualidad en España* (Castelldefels (Barcelona), Apr. 1972).

Junta Superior de Mandos Sindicales, *Llamamiento de la Organización Sindical Española: posición ideológica del sindicalismo español* (Madrid: Central Nacional Sindical, 1960).

184

Llamada a la juventud española, manifesto issued at the 2nd meeting of the Congress of Falangist Youth (1973).

Junta Promotora (Madrid), *II Concentración Nacional*, papers presented at the second national gathering of the Promotional Committees of FE de las JONS (28 Nov. 1971).

Juntas Promotoras and Círculos Doctrinales 'José Antonio', *Carta circular a todos los camaradas* (circular letter to all members with respect to Juan Carlos de Borbón) (21 Nov. 1972).

Lamata Mejía, P., *Ejemplo y experiencia del sindicalismo español*, report of the Secretary General of the *Organización Sindical Española* to the Syndical Congress at its meeting in Madrid, 5 Mar. 1962 (Madrid, 1962).

Seminario de Estudios del Círculo Doctrinal 'José Antonio', Madrid, *Consideraciones en torno al 'Libro Blanco' de la Educación en España* (Madrid, Apr.–May 1969).

Seminario de Política Sindical del Círculo Doctrinal 'José Antonio', Madrid, *Sindicalismo: problemas en torno al perfeccionamiento de las estructuras sindicales* (Madrid, 1967).

Ridruejo, D., *Informe al Consejo Nacional de FET y de las JONS sobre los sucesos universitarios de 1956* (Madrid, Apr. 1956).

Solís Ruiz, J., *El II Pleno del Congreso Sindical*, report to the second plenary session of the Syndical Congress, 10 Mar. 1962) (Madrid: Servicio Nacional de Información y Publicaciones Sindicales, 1962).

1.2 Ministerial Publications

Boletín Oficial del Estado (BOE): various editions between 1937 and 1970; specific references are given in appropriate footnotes.

Centro de Estudios Sindicales, *La Organización Sindical Española* (Madrid, 1957).

Delegación Nacional de Prensa, Propaganda y Radio del Movimiento *Sindicalismo, empresa y trabajo*, Ediciones del Movimiento (Madrid, 1965).

Fuero del Trabajo, Estado Nacionalsindicalista, 1938 (1st edn); Ministerio de Trabajo, Madrid, 1975 (3rd edn).

Fundamentos del Nuevo Estado (Madrid: Ediciones de la Vicesecretaría de Educación Popular, 1943).

Notas sobre la Falange como Partido Unico (Madrid: Editora Nacional, 1939 (?)).

Santos Reiriz, J., *Cubre tu pecho de azul (lecturas para la juventud española)* (Madrid: Delegación Nacional del Frente de Juventudes, 1950).

Servicio Español del Profesorado *La revolución nacional desde la Universidad* (Madrid: Delegación de Educación Nacional, 1939).

1.3 Newspapers and Periodicals

1.3.1 National Press

Extensive use was made of the following national dailies:

ABC, Madrid

Alcazar, el, Madrid

Arriba, Madrid

Informaciones, Madrid
País, el, Madrid
Pueblo, Madrid
Ya, Madrid
Shorter series or single editions of the following newspapers and periodicals:
Acción Española (Madrid, 1933).
Actualidad Española (Madrid, 1969).
Adelanto, el (Salamanca, 1937).
Blanco y Negro (Madrid, 1977, 1982).
Cambio 16 (Madrid, various years, esp. 1976–82).
Cuadernos para el diálogo (Madrid, 1966–77).
Destino (Madrid, 1974).
Diario SP (Madrid, 1969).
Documentos '80 (Barcelona, 1979).
Español, el (Madrid, 1956).
Historia 16 (Madrid).
Historia Internacional (Madrid).
Historia y Vida (Madrid, 1975).
Indice (Madrid, 1966–74).
Interviú (Madrid, 1976).
Madrid (Madrid).
Nuevo Diario (Madrid, 1969–70).
Observer, The (London, 1947).
Personas (Madrid, 1981–82).
Posible (Madrid, 1976).
Tiempo (Madrid, 1982).
Tiempo de Historia (Madrid, 1980–82).

1.3.2 Falangist Press
The entire collection of the following Party publications was consulted:
Arriba, weekly (Madrid, 1935–36).
Arriba España (Pamplona, 1937–55).
Es así (Madrid, 1963–64).
FE (Madrid, 1933–34).
Haz (Madrid, 1935–36).
No importa (Madrid, 1936).
Shorter series or single numbers of the following internal publications were
also used:
Acción (*Boletín de la Sección Juvenil del Círculo 'José Antonio' de Santa Cruz
de Tenerife*) (Santa Cruz de Tenerife, 1972).
Alcalá (Madrid, 1952–55).
Arriba (segunda época), Juventud Falangista (Madrid, 1971).
Aula azul (Barcelona: Sección universitaria de *FE de las JONS*, 1968–69).
Autogestión, Acción Revolucionaria Sindicalista (Barcelona, 1975).
Boletín del Círculo Cultural Hispánico (Barcelona, 1973).
Boletín del Círculo 'José Antonio' de Madrid (Madrid, 1968–70)
Boletín del Círculo Doctrinal 'José Antonio' de Zaragoza (s/d).
Boletín de la Hermandad de la División Azul (Madrid, 1942).
CONS (*Organo difusor de las Centrales Obreras Nacional Sindicalistas,*

organización de trabajadores del Frente Falangista Revolucionario) (1975 ?).
Eje, Juventud Falangista (Barcelona, 1974).
Escorial (Madrid, 1941).
Estamos, Sección de Juventudes, Círculo 'José Antonio' (Madrid, 1965).
F.N.S. (Boletín del Frente Nacional-Sindicalista) (1969 ?).
Fotos (1937).
Hoja de Campaña de la División Española de Voluntarios (División Azul), 1941–45.
Hojas informativas de la Junta Promotora Provincal de FE de las JONS de Madrid (Madrid, 1970).
Hora, la (Madrid, 1954).
Juventud Falangista: documentos de trabajo, Servicio Nacional de Formación e Información, Juventud Falangista (Madrid, 1974).
Juventudes de FE de las JONS: hojas e doctrina nacionalsindicalista (Barcelona, 1973–74).
Juventud (Madrid, 1952).
Lucha (boletín de divulgación joseantoniana) (Melilla, 1973–74).
No importa (boletín mensual de difusión nacionalsindicalista) (Barcelona, 1968 ?).
No importa (órgano nacional de las Juntas Promotoras de FE de las JONS) (Barcelona, 1971).
Participación, Juventud Falangista (Madrid (?), 1973.)
Persona (boletín de las Juntas Universitarias de FE de las JONS) (Sevilla, 1973).
Plataforma quincenal de expresión falangista, Madrid, 1972.
Resurgir (Madrid: Juventud Falangista, 1968).
Revista 24 (Madrid, 1950).
Rojo y Negro (boletín de la sección de Acción Social del Círculo 'José Antonio' de Barcelona) (Barcelona, 1971).
Rojo y Negro (boletín informativo de los Círculos '4 de marzo' y la Asociación Juvenil 'Amanecer') (Madrid, 1976).
Sí (boletín del Frente Universitario Nacional Sindicalista, FUNS) (Valencia, 1972).
Tercera vía, Círculos 'José Antonio' de Andalucía (1973).
Tiempo Nuevo (Madrid, 1969).
Unidad y Autogestión (Madrid: Falanges Universitarios, 1972).
Vertical (boletín del Círculo 'José Antonio' de Sevilla) (Sevilla, 1970).

1.4 Anthologies, Documents and Speeches

Acto de afirmación sindicalista, speeches made at the gathering organised by the Association of Former Members of the *Frente de Juventudes* and the *Círculos Doctrinales 'José Antonio'* (Madrid, 23 May, 1963).
Adsuara, E., *Palabras ante la tumba de Ramiro Ledesma Ramos* (28 Oct. 1970).
Arrese Magra, J. L., *Dos discursos del Ministro Secretario, camarada Arrese (Valencia, 21 July, 1941; Reus, 22 Oct. 1942)* (Madrid: Ediciones de la Vicesecretaría de Educación Popular, 1942).
Hacia una meta institucional (Madrid: Ediciones del Movimiento, 1957).

188 *Bibliography*

Cantarero del Castillo, M., *Conversaciones sobre presente y futuro de los Falangistas, celebradas en Madrid el día 28 de enero de 1974, en el club 'Don Hilarión'*.

Conquista del Estado, la, anthology of articles selected by Juan Aparicio (Barcelona (?): Ediciones FE, 1939).

Escobar y Kirkpatrick, I., *Testimonio sobre una gran traición*, type-written, undated (1978?).

Escrito dirigido por los Círculos Doctrinales 'José Antonio' al Gobierno, collective letter from the Madrid 'José Antonio' Doctrinal Circle to the Government, 1966.

Fernández Cuesta, R., *Continuidad falangista al servicio de España* (Madrid: Ediciones del Movimiento, 1955).

El 18 de julio (lecture given at the University of Zaragoza in 1961, to inaugurate a course devoted to the history of the 'War of national liberation') (Madrid: Doncel, 1962).

El Movimiento político español (lectures, speeches and writings, 1951–52) (Madrid: Ediciones Prensa del Movimiento, 1952).

Notas sobre política económica española (collection of articles on economic topics published in *Arriba* in 1953–54), Delegación Nacional de Provincias de FET y de las JONS (Madrid, 1954)

Franco Bahamonde, F., *Nosotros somos una solución* (speech delivered by Franco at the closure of the 1st Syndical Congress, 4 Mar. 1961) (Madrid: Servicio Nacional de Información y Publicaciones Sindicales, 1961).

Nuestra revolución (speech delivered by Franco at the closure of the 2nd Syndical Congress, 10 Mar. 1962) (Madrid: Servicio Nacional de Información y Publicaciones Sindicales, 1962).

El sindicalismo, fuerza decisiva del futuro (speech delivered at the plennary session of the national Council of *FET y de las JONS*, 9 Mar. 1963) (Madrid: Servicio Nacional de Información y Publicaciones Sindicales, 1963).

Frente Nacional Español, *Las asociaciones políticas en las Cortes*, collection of articles and speeches regarding the proposed Law of Political Associations (Madrid, June 1976).

Giménez Caballero, E., *Sindicalismo y socialismo en España* (collection of articles on syndicalism and Socialism) (Madrid: Ediciones y Publicaciones Populares, Organización Sindical Española, 1972).

Giménez Torres, F., *El futuro del sindicalismo español* (lecture given by the secretary General of the Syndical Organisation in Sabadell (Barcelona), 19 Jan. 1961) (Madrid: Servicio Nacional de Información y Publicaciones Sindicales, 1961).

Girón de Velasco, J. A., *Palabras de Girón* (speeches, 1950), Universidad Laboral, Juntas Rectoras de los Montepíos Interprovinciales de Cataluña (Barcelona, 1950).

Quince años de pólitica social dirigida por Franco (opening address, 1st Iberoamerican Congress on Social Security, 22 May 1951) (Madrid: Ediciones OID, 1951.

La libertad del Hombre, meta de la revolución social española (lecture given in Sevilla, 3 Nov. 1951) (Madrid: Doncel, 1951).

Gómez de Aranda, L. *Sindicalismo y desarrollo económico* (lecture given by the Technical Under-Secretary of the General Secretariat of the Movement,

on the 25th anniversary of the promulgation of the *Fuero del Trabajo*)
(Madrid: Servicio Nacional de Información y Publicaciones Sindicales,
1963).

González   Vicén, L., *Valor actual de la Falange*, speech delivered in
Pontevedra, Jan. 1964.

Jato Miranda, D., *XXXV aniversario de la muerte de José Antonio Primo de
Rivera (lección política pronunciada por el camarada David Jato, 20/XI/
1971*), Editorial 'la Nueva España', Jefatura Provincial del Movimiento
(Oviedo, 1971).

JONS, anthology of articles selected by Juan Aparicio, (Madrid: Editora
Nacional, 1943).

Márquez Horrillo, D., *Legitimidad de una fecha. Legitimidad de una idea*,
speech made before the *Círculo Doctrinal 'José Antonio'* of Madrid, 29 Oct.
1970.

Primo de Rivera, J. A., *Obras completas* (Madrid: Ediciones de la Vicesecretaría de FET y de las JONS, 1945).

Obras completas (chronological edn) (Madrid: Publicaciones Españolas,
1952).

Breve antología de José Antonio (Madrid: Ediciones Umbral, 1971).

Redondo Ortega, O. *Textos políticos* (Madrid: Doncel, 1975).

Ruiz de Alda Miqueleiz, J., *Obre completa* (Prologue by R. Fernández
Cuesta, Biography by P. Ruiz de Alda) (Barcelona: Ediciones FE, 1939).

Sánchez Mazas, R., *Fundación, Hermandad y Destino* (anthology of articles
from *FE* and *Arriba*) (Madrid: Ediciones del Movimiento, 1957).

Serrano Suñer, R., *Siete discursos* (Bilbao: Ediciones FE, 1940).

Sindicato Español Universitario, *Con la misma esperanza*, (Madrid:
Ediciones SEU, 1963).

Solís Ruiz, J., *El sindicalismo nacional en la vanguardia del empeño por una
España nueva* (address given by the Minister Secretary General of the
Movement and National Delegate for Syndicates at the closure of the 1st
Syndical Congress, 4 Mar. 1961) (Madrid: Servicio Nacional de Información
y Publicaciones Sindicales, 1961).

La Organización Sindical en vanguardia (closing address, Syndical Economic Council, Córdoba, 12 Dec. 1962) (Madrid: Servicio Nacional de
Información y Publicaciones Sindicales, 1961).

Acción asistencial del sindicalismo español (Cortes speech, 20 Dec. 1965),
Tiempo Nuevo (Organización Sindical Española), Madrid, 1966.

Veyrat, M. and Navas-Migueloa, J. L., *Falange, hoy* (interviews with selected
Falangists), G. del Toro, Madrid, 1973.

1.5 Memoirs and Theoretical Works by Protagonists

Abad de Santillán, D., *Memorias, 1897–1936* (Barcelona: Planeta, 1977).

Alcazar de Velasco, A., *La Gran Fuga* (Barcelona: Editorial Planeta, 1977).

Los 7 días de Salamanca (Madrid: G. del Toro, 1976).

Idem., uncensored, unpublished edn, Madrid, 1976.

Alvarez Puga, E. *Diccionario de la Falange* (Barcelona: Dopesa, 1977).

Ansaldo, J. A., *¿Para qué . . . (de Alfonso XIII a Juan III)* (Buenos Aires: Editorial Vasca Ekin, 1951).

Areilza, J. M., and Castiella, F., *Reivindicaciones de España* (Madrid: Instituto de Estudios Políticos, 1941).

Arrese Magra, J. L., *El Estado totalitario en el Pensamiento de José Antonio*, Ediciones de la Vicesecretaría de Educación Popular, Madrid, 1945.

Capitalismo, Cristianismo, Comunismo (Madrid: Ediciones Radar, 1947).

La revolución social del Nacional Sindicalismo (Madrid: Ediciones del Movimiento, 1959).

Una etapa constituyente (Barcelona: Editorial Planeta, 1982).

Beneyto Pérez, J., *El Nuevo Estado español. El régimen nacional sindicalista ante la tradición y los sistemas totalitarios*, Biblioteca Nueva, Cadiz-Madrid, 1939.

Brocá, S. *Falange y filosofía* (Salou: Editorial Universitaria Europea, 1976).

Cantarero del Castillo, M., *Falange y socialismo* (Barcelona: Dopesa, 1973).

Conde Soladana, P., *FE de las JONS (auténtica)* (Bilbao: Ediciones Albia, 1977).

Eguiagaray, F., *Actualidad de José Antonio en las corrientes del pensamiento universal*, Madrid, 1961.

Escofet, F., *De una derrota a una victoria: 6 de octubre 1934–19 de julio de 1936* (Barcelona: Argos Vergara, 1984).

Espâna, J. B., *Nueva aurora (exégesis de la doctrina sobre la que resurge la verdadera España)* (Avila: Senén Martín, 1937(?)).

Fernández Cuesta, R., *Testimonio, recuerdos y reflexiones* (Madrid: Ediciones Dyrsa, 1985).

García Serrano, R., *La gran esperanza* (Barcelona: Planeta, 1983).

Gil Robles y Quiñones, J. M., *La Monarquía por la que yo luché* (Madrid: Taurus, 1976).

Giménez Caballero, E., *Memorias de un dictador* (Barcelona: Planeta, 1979).

Hillers de Luque, S., *Estilo y ética falangistas*, Madrid, 1974.

España: una revolución pendiente (Madrid: Ediciones FES, 1975).

Iglesias Selgas, C., *El sindicalismo español* (Madrid: Doncel, 1974).

Iniesta Cano, C., *Memorias y recuerdos* (Barcelona: Planeta, 1984).

Jato Miranda, D., *La rebelión de los estudiantes*, private edn, Madrid, 1975 (1st published 1953).

Jerez-Riesco, J. L., *La Falange, partido fascista* (Barcelona: Ediciones Bau, 1977).

Laín Entralgo, P., *Descargo de conciencia (1930–1960)* (Barcelona: Barral Editores, 1976).

'Lanzas' (pseudonym of Ledesma Ramos), R., *¿Fascismo en España?*, 2nd edn (Barcelona: Ariel, 1968).

Ledesma Ramos, R., *Discurso a las juventudes de España* (Madrid: Ediciones FE, 1939).

El sello de la muerte (Madrid: Editorial Reus, 1924).

Legaz Lecambra, L. and Gómez Aragón, B., *4 Estudios sobre Sindicalismo vertical*, Zaragoza, 1939.

Lizarza Iribaren, A., *Memorias de la conspiración, 1931–1936. Cómo se preparó en Navarra la Cruzada* (Pamplona: Editorial Gómez, 1954).

Llorens Borrás, J. A., (ed.), *Manuel Hedilla, testimonio* (Barcelona: Ediciones Acervo, 1972).

Martín Sanz, D., *El problema triguero y el Nacional-Sindicalismo* (Valladolid: Afrodisio Aguado, 1937).

Martínez Val, J. M., *¿Por qué no fué posible la Falange?* (Barcelona: Dopesa, 1975).

Moreno Hernández, M., *El nacionalsindicalismo de Ramiro Ledesma Ramos* (Madrid: Delegación Nacional de Organizaciones del Movimiento, 1963).

Mota, J., *Hacia un socialismo europeo: ¿Falange o comunismo?* (Barcelona: Ediciones Bau, 1974).

Pemartín, J. *¿Qué es lo nuevo?*, Espasa-Calpe, 3rd edn, Madrid, 1940.

Teoría de la Falange, 3rd edn (Madrid: Ediciones de la Sección Femenina, 1948).

Prieto, I. *Palabras al viento* (Mexico: Ediciones Minerva, 1942).

Primo de Rivera, P., *Recuerdos de una vida* (Madrid: Ediciones Dyrsa, 1983).

Ridruejo, D., *Escrito en España* (Buenos Aires: Losada, 1962).

Casi unas Memorias (Barcelona: Planeta, 1976).

Los cuadernos de Rusia (Barcelona: Planeta, 1978).

Royuela, A., *Diccionario de la ultra-derecha* (Barcelona: Dopesa, 1977).

Serrano Suñer, R., *Entre Hendaya y Gibraltar* (Madrid: Ediciones y Publicaciones Españolas, 1942).

Memorias (Barcelona: Planeta, 1977).

Sanz Orio, F., *Los Sindicatos españoles, una creación para el mundo* (Madrid: Servicio de Información y Publicaciones Sindicales, 1948).

Solís Ruiz, J., *Nuestro sindicalismo* (Madrid: Servicio Nacional de Información y Publicaciones Sindicales, 1955).

Solís Ruiz, J. *et al.*, *José Antonio: actualidad de su doctrina* (Madrid: Delegación Nacional de Organizaciones del Movimiento, 1961).

Sainz Rodríguez, P., *Testimonio y Recuerdos* (Barcelona: Planeta, 1978).

1.6 Contemporary Accounts

Aguado, E., *Ramiro Ledesma, fundador de las JONS* (Madrid: Ediciones de la Vicesecretaría de Educación Popular de FET y de las JONS, 1941).

Albiñana, J. M., *Prisionero de la República*, Madrid, 1931.

Alcazar de Velasco, A., *Serrano Suñer en la Falange* (Madrid: Ediciones Patria, 1941).

Alcocer, J. L., *Radiografía de un fraude (Notas para una historia del Frente de Juventudes)* (Barcelona: Planeta, 1978).

Ariza, J., *CC.OO.* (Madrid: Avance/Mañana, 1976).

Barba, B., *Dos años al frente del Gobierno Civil de Barcelona*, Madrid, 1948.

Borrás, T., *Ramiro Ledesma Ramos* (Madrid: Editora Nacional, 1971).

Bravo Martínez, F., *Historia de la Falange Española de las JONS* (Madrid: Ediciones FE, 1940).

José Antonio ante la justicia roja (Madrid: Ediciones de la Vicesecretaría de Educación Popular, 1941).

José Antonio, el hombre, el Jefe, el camarada, Ediciones Españolas, 1939.

Dávila y de Celis, S., *De la Organización Juvenil al Frente de Juventudes* (Madrid: Editora Nacional, 1941).

José Antonio, Salamanca . . . y otras cosas (Madrid: Afrodisio Aguado, 1967).

Dávila, S. and Pemartín, J., *Hacia una historia de la Falange: primera contribución de Sevilla*, Jerez de la Frontera, 1938.

Doussinague, J. M., *España tenía razón*, Madrid, 1950.

Esteban Infantes, E., *La División Azul* (Madrid: Editorial AHR, 1956).

Foxá, A. de, *Madrid de Corte a cheka* (Madrid: Editorial Prensa Española, 1976).

García Serrano, R., *Eugenio, o la proclamación de la primavera,* Ediciones Jerarquía (Bilbao: Delegación Nacional de Prensa y Propaganda de FET y de las JONS, 1938).

García Venero, M., *La historia de la Unificación. Falange y Requeté en 1937* (Madrid: Distribuciones Madrileñas, 1970).

Falange en la Guerra de España. La Unificación y Hedilla (Paris: Ruedo Ibérico, 1967).

Giménez Caballero, E., *Genio de España*, 7th edn (Madrid: Doncel, 1971).

Los secretos de la Falange (Barcelona: Editorial Yunque, 1939).

Hamilton, T. J., *Appeasement's Child* (London: Gollancz, 1943).

Lopez, J., *Una misión sin importancia* (Madrid: Editorial Nacional, 1972).

López Rodó, L., *La larga marcha hacia la monarquía* (Barcelona: Noguer, 1977).

Márquez Horrillo, D., *Círculos José Antonio* (Bilbao: Albia Política, 1977).

Martínez de Bedoya, J. *Siete años de lucha*, Valladolid, 1939.

Mera, C., *Guerra, exilio y carcel de un Anarcosindicalista* (Paris: Ruedo Ibérico, 1976).

Montes Agudo, G., *Julio, el de la serena confianza* (Madrid: Vieja Guardia, 1939).

Pepe Sainz, una vida en la Falange, Ediciones Pal.las de Horta, 1939(?).

Relatos ejemplares, Afrodisio Aguado, Madrid, 1948.

Travesuras que escuecen, Vieja Guardia, Aguiliar, Madrid, 1939.

Mora, M. F. de la, *Las sangrientas cinco rosas*, private edn, 1972.

Mora Figueroa, J. de, *Datos para la historia de la Falange gaditana*, Jerez de la Frontera, 1974.

Pestaña, A., *Terrorismo en Barcelona (Memorias inéditas)* (Barcelona: Planeta, 1979).

Serrano Suñer, R., *Semblanza de José Antonio joven* (Barcelona: Pareja y Borrás, 1958).

Silvia, A., *Cara al sol – lecturas patrióticas* (Gerona/Madrid: Dalmau Carles Pla, 1940).

Ximénez de Sandoval, F., *José Antonio, biografía apasionada*, private edn, Madrid, 1972.

Camisa azul (retrato de un falangista), Valladolid, 1939.

Zayas, A. de, *Historia de la Vieja Guardia de Baleares*, Madrid, 1955.

Zugazagoitia, J., *Guerra y vicisitudes de los españoles* (Barcelona: Editorial Crítica, 1977).

2 SECONDARY SOURCES

2.1 Non-Contemporary Monographs and General Works

Alvarez Puga, E., *Matesa, más allá del escándalo* (Barcelona: Dopesa, 1974).

Amsden, J., *Collective bargaining and class conflict in Spain* (London: Weidenfeld & Nicholson, 1972).

Aparicio, M. A., *El sindicalismo vertical y la formación del Estado franquista* (Barcelona: Eunibar S.A., 1980).

Arrarás, J., *Historia de la Segunda República Española* (Madrid: Editora Nacional, 1968).

Azpiazu, J. (S.J.), *El Estado corporativo*, 5th edn (Madrid: Compañía Bibliográfica Española, 1952).

Bellod, J. J., *José Antonio y el sindicalismo nacional* (Madrid: Ediciones Jornal, Servicio de Relaciones Exteriores Sindicales, s/d. (1954?).

Benet, J. *et. al.*, *Dionisio Ridruejo: de la Falange a la oposición* (Madrid: Taurus, 1976).

Blinkhorn, R. M., *Carlism and crisis in Spain, 1931–1939* (Cambridge University Press, 1975).

(ed)., *Spain in Conflict* (London: Sage Publications, 1986).

Brenan, G., *The Face of Spain* (Buenos Aires: Losada, 1952).

Calamai, M., *La lotta di classe sotto il Franchismo* (Bari: De Donato Editore, 1971).

Cardona, G., *El poder militar en la España contemporánea hasta la guerra civil* (Madrid: Siglo XXI, 1984).

Carr, R. and Fusi, J. P., *España, de la dictadura a la democracia* (Barcelona: Planeta, 1979).

Casas de la Vega, R., *Las milicias nacionales*, 2 vols (Madrid: Editora Nacional, 1977).

Las milicias nacionales en la guerra de España (Madrid: Editora Nacional, 1974).

Chase, A., *Falange, the Axis' Secret Army in the Americas* (New York: G. P. Putnam, 1943).

Chueca Rodriguez, R. L., *El fascismo en los comienzos del régimen de Franco. Un estudio sobre FET-JONS* (Madrid: Centro de Investigaciones Sociológicas, 1983).

Cierva, R. de la, *Historia de la Guerra Civil Española: Antecedentes, Monarquía y República, 1898–1936* (Madrid: Editorial San Martín, 1969).

Historia ilustrada de la Guerra Civil española (Barcelona: Ediciones Danae, 1970).

La historia se confiesa (Barcelona: Planeta, 1976).

Clemente, J. C., *Historia del Carlismo contemporáneo, 1935–1972* (Barcelona: Grijalbo, 1977).

Coverdale, J. F., *Italian Intervention in the Spanish Civil War* (Princeton University Press, 1975).

Crozier, B., *Franco* (London, 1967).

Ellwood, S. M., *Spain in Franco's Shadow*, unpublished MS (Madrid, 1981).

Equipo de Estudio *Al filo de la crisis*, Punto Crítico, Madrid, 1975.

Prueba de fuerza entre el reformismo y la ruptura (Madrid: Elías Querejeta, 1976).

194 *Bibliography*

Lucha por el poder, Elías Querejeta (Madrid, 1976).
Equipo 'Mundo', *Los 90 minisros de Franco* (Barcelona: Dopesa, 1970).
Fernández de Castro and Martínez, J., *España, hoy* (Paris: Ruedo Ibérico, 1963).
Ferri, Ll. et. al., *Las huelgas contra Franco* (Barcelona: Planeta, 1978).
Foard, D. W., *Ernesto Giménez Caballero (o la revolución del poeta)* (Madrid: Instituto de Estudios Políticos, 1975).
Fontana, J. (ed.), *España bajo el franquismo* (Barcelona: Critica, 1986).
Fuentes Irurózqui, M., *El pensamiento económico de José Antonio Primo de Rivera* (Madrid, 1966).
Fusi, J. P., *Franco* (Madrid: Ediciones 'El País', 1985).
Gallego Méndez, M. T., *Mujer, Falange y franquismo* (Madrid: Taurus, 1983).
Galkin, A., *Fascismo, Nazismo, Falangismo* (Buenos Aires: Editorial Cartago, 1975).
Gallo, M., *Spain under Franco* (London: Allen & Unwin, 1973).
García Lahiguera, F., *Ramón Serrano Suñer: un documento para la historia* (Barcelona: Argos Vergara, 1983).
Gibello, A., *José Antonio. Apuntes para una biografía polémica* (Madrid: Doncel, 1974).
Gibson, I., *En busca de José Antonio* (Barcelona: Planeta, 1980).
Heine, H., *La oposición política al Franquismo* (Barcelona, 1983).
Historia de la Cruzada Española, 8 vols (Madrid: Ediciones Españolas, 1940–44).
Historia del franquismo, 2 vols, Diario 16 (Madrid, 1984–85).
La Guerra Civil Española, 24 vols, Historia 16 (Madrid, 1986–87).
Hovey, H. A., *U.S. Military Assistance* (NY: Praeger, 1965).
Izquierdo, M. P., *De la huelga general a las elecciones generales* (Madrid: De la Torre, 1977).
Jackson, G., *The Spanish Republic and the Civil War, 1931–1939* (Princeton University Press, 1965).
La República española y la Guerra Civil, 1931–1939 (Barcelona: Crítica, 1976).
Jellinek, F., *La Guerra Civil en España* (Madrid: Ediciones Jucar, 1977).
Jerez Mir, M., *Elites políticas y centros de extracción en España, 1938–1957* (Madrid: Centro de Investigaciones Sociológicas, 1982).
Jiménez Campo, J., *El fascismo en la crisis de la II República* (Madrid: Centro de Investigaciones Sociológicas, 1979).
Kitchen, M., *Fascism* (London: Macmillan, 1976).
Lizcano, P., *La generación del '56 (La Universidad contra Franco)* (Barcelona: Grijalbo, 1981).
Ludevid, M., *40 años de sindicato vertical* (Barcelona: Editorial Laia, 1976).
Mainer, J. C., *Falange y literatura* (Barcelona: Editorial Labor, 1971).
Mancisidor, J. M., *Frente a frente* (Madrid: Editorial Almena, 1975).
Mandel, E., *El Fascismo* (Madrid: Akal, 1976).
Martín, R., *La contrarrevolución falangista* (Paris: Ruedo Ibérico, 1971).
Matthews, H. L., *The Yoke and the Arrows* (London: Heineman, 1958).
Mayor Martínez, L., *Ideologías dominantes en el sindicato vertical* (Madrid: Editorial Zero, 1972).

Mesa, R. *et al.*, *Jaraneros y alborotadores* (*Documentos sobre los sucesos estudiantiles de febrero 1956 en la Universidad Complutense de Madrid*) (Madrid, 1982).

Miguel, A. de, *Sociología del Franquismo* (Barcelona: Euros, 1975).

La herencia del franquismo (Madrid: Editorial Cambio 16, 1976).

Morán, G., *Adolfo Suárez, historia de una ambición* (Barcelona: Planeta, 1979).

Morodo, R., *Acción Española: orígenes ideológicas del franquismo* (Madrid: Ediciones Tucar, 1980).

Mussolini, B., *El Estado corporativo* (Salamanca: USI, s/d).

Nolte, E., *Three faces of Fascism* (NY: Mentor Books, 1969).

Oficina Internacional del Trabajo, *La situación laboral y sindical en España* (Geneva, 1969).

Oneto, J., *Arias entre dos crisis, 1973–1975* (Madrid: Editorial Cambio 16, 1975).

Pavón Pereyra, E., *De la vida de José Antonio* (Madrid: Ediciones FC, 1947 (?)).

Payne, S. G., *Falange – a History of Spanish Fascism* (Stanford University Press, 1961).

(ed.), *Política y sociedad en la España del siglo XX* (Madrid: Akal, 1978)

Preston, P., *The Coming of the Spanish Civil War* (London: Methuen, 1983).

Las derechas españolas en el siglo xx: autoritarismo, fascismo y golpismo (Madrid: Editorial Sistema, 1986).

La destrucción de la democracia en España (Madrid: Ediciones Turner, 1978).

The Triumph of Democracy in Spain (London: Methuen, 1986).

(ed.) *España en crisis* (Madrid: Fondo de Cultura Económica, 1978).

(ed.) *Revolution and War in Spain, 1931–1939* (London: Methuen, 1984).

¿Quién es quién en la política española? 4 vols (Madrid: Documentación Española Contemporánea, S.L., 1977).

Ramiréz, M., *España, 1939–1975: régimen político e ideología* (Barcelona: Guadarrama, 1978).

Redondo Gómez, J., *La evolución del sindicalismo español* (Madrid: Servicio Nacional de Información y Publicaciones Sindicales, 1956).

Ramírez, L., *Nuestros primeros 25 años* (Paris: Ruedo Ibérico, 1964).

Río Cisneros, A. del, *José Antonio y la revolución nacional* (Madrid: Ediciones del Movimiento, 1964).

Momentos políticos (Madrid: Ediciones del Movimiento, 1953).

José Antonio y España (Madrid: Publicaciones del Servicio Español de Magisterio y Ediciones Prensa del Movimiento, 1952).

El ideal de José Antonio y el Movimiento (Madrid: Ediciones del Movimiento, 1973).

Río Cisneros, A. del and Pavón Pereyra, E., *José Antonio, abogado* (Madrid: Ediciones del Movimiento, 1963).

Rojas, C., *Prieto y José Antonio. Socialismo y Falange ante la tragedia civil* (Barcelona: Editorial Dirosa, 1977).

Romero Cuesta, A., *Objetivo: matar a Franco* (Madrid: Ediciones 99, 1976).

Ros Hombravella, J. *et al.*, *Capitalismo español: de la autarquía a la estabilización, 1939–1959* (Madrid: Edicusa, 1978).

Rubio Muñoz Bocanegra, F. (ed.), *Pensamientos políticos de José Antonio* (Madrid: Delegación Nacional de Sindicatos, 1954).
Rudel, C., *Phalange, histoire du fascisme en Espagne* (Paris, 1972).
Sánchez Diana, J. M., *Ramiro Ledesma Ramos. Biografía política* (Madrid: Editora Nacional, 1975).
Saña, H., *El franquismo sin mitos. Conversaciones con Serrano Suñer* (Barcelona: Grijalbo, 1982).
Saz, I. and Tussell, J., *Fascistas en España* (Madrid: CSIC, 1981).
Sferazza, M. and Tandy L., *Giménez Caballero y la 'Gaceta Literaria,* (Madrid: Ediciones Turner, 1977).
Shubert, A., *Hacia la revolución* (Barcelona: Crítica, 1984).
Southworth, H. R., *Antifalange: estudio crítico de 'La Falange en la Guerra de España', de M. García Venero* (Paris: Ruedo Ibérico, 1967).
El mito de la cruzada de Franco (Paris: Ruedo Ibérico, 1963).
Suárez Cortina, M., *El fascismo en Asturias (1931–1937)* (Silverio Cañada Editor, 1981).
Suárez Fernández, L., *Francisco Franco y su tiempo*, 8 vols (Madrid: Ediciones Azor, 1985).
Tamames, R., *Estructura económica de España* (Madrid, 1964).
Thomas, H., *The Spanish Civil War* (Harmondsworth, Middx: Penguin Books, 1965).
Togliatti, P., *Lectures on Fascism* (NY: International Publishers, 1976).
Tuñon de Lara, M. *et al.*, *La Guerra Civil Española 50 años después* (Madrid: Labor, 1984).
Tusell, J., and García Queipo de Llano, G., *Franco y Mussolini* (Barcelona: Planeta, 1985).
Velarde Fuertes, J., *El nacionalsindicalismo 40 años después* (Madrid: Editora Nacional, 1972).
Viñas, A., *La Alemania Nazi y el 18 de julio* (Madrid: Alianza, 1974).
Guerra, dinero, dictadura (Barcelona: Crítica, 1984).
Welles, B., *Spain, the gentle anarchy* (London: Pall Mall Press, 1965).
Woolf, S. J. (ed.), *Fascism in Europe* (London: Methuen, 1981).

2.2 Articles

Abella, A., Cardona, G. and Mateo, F., 'La Sanjurjada' in *Historia 16*, no. 76 (Madrid, Aug. 1982).
Aparicio, M. A., 'Aspectos políticos del sindicalismo español de pos-guerra' in *Sistema*, no. 13 (Madrid, Apr. 1976).
Aróstegui, J., 'Conflicto social e ideología de la violencia, 1917–1936' in *España, 1898–1936: estructuras y cambio* (Madrid: Edit. Universidad Complutense, 1984).
Blanc, J., 'Las huelgas en el movimiento obrero español' in *Horizonte español*, vol. II (Paris: Ruedo Ibérico, 1966).
'Asturias: minas, huelgas y comisiones obreras' in *Cuadernos de Ruedo Ibérico*, no. 1 (Paris, June–July 1965).
Calvo Serer, R., 'La politique intérieure dans l'Espagne de Franco' in *Ecrits de Paris* (Paris, Sept. 1953).

Claudín, F., 'Le nouveau mouvement ouvrier' in *Les Temps Modernes*, no. 357 (Paris, 1976).

Compta, M. *et. al.*, 'Conflictos laborales que dejaron huella' in *Cuadernos para el Diálogo*, Extra XXXIII (Madrid, Feb. 1973).

Elorza, E., Jimenez, J. and Montero, J. R., 'El nacimiento de la Falange' in *Historia 16*, no. 91 (Nov. 1983).

Fernández de Castro, I., 'Tres años importantes: 1961, 1962, 1963' in *Cuadernos de Ruedo Ibérico*, no. 16 (Paris, 1967).

Fraga Iribarne, M., 'Revolución y restauración' in *Alcalá*, no. 28 (Madrid, Feb. 1953).

García, E., 'La "nueva izquierda" falangista' in *Cuadernos de Ruedo Ibérico*, no. 6 (Paris, Apr.–May 1966).

Gil Pecharromán, J., 'Albiñana, el rey de los ultras' in *Historia 16*, no. 45 (Jan. 1980).

González Calleja, E., 'Los pistoleros azules' in *Historia 16*, no. 98 (June, 1984).

Hedilla Rojas, M. I., 'El exterminio de la Falange obrera' in *Historia Internacional*, nos 11–12 (Feb.–Mar. 1976).

'Juan Hermanos', 'El final de la esperanza' in *Tiempo de Historia*, no. 92–3, (July–Aug. 1982; first published in *Les Temps Modernes*, Paris, 1950).

Linz, J. J., 'From *Falange* to *Movimiento-Organización*' in Huntington & Moore, *Authoritarian Politics in Modern Society*, (NY, 1970).

Maravall, J. M., 'Transición a la democracia: alineamientos políticos y elecciones en España' in *Sistema*, no. 36 (Madrid, May 1980).

Marquina Barrio, M., 'Conspiración contra Franco' in *Historia 16*, no. 72 (Apr. 1982).

'El atentado de Begoña' in *Historia 16*, no. 76 (Madrid, Aug. 1982).

Martínez Alier, J., 'España, verano 1970' in *Cuadernos de Ruedo Ibérico*, no. 25 (Paris, June–July 1970).

Montero Díaz, S., 'La evolución intelectual de Ramiro Ledesma Ramos' in Ledesma Ramos, R., *Escritos filosóficos* (Madrid: Sucesora de Minuesa de los Ríos, 1941).

Preston, P., 'Teoría y práctica del fascismo español' in *Cultura, sociedad y política en el mundo actual*, Nuevos Cuadernos de la Magdalena (Madrid: Universidad Internacional Menéndez Pelayo, 1981).

Rodríguez Aramberri, J., 'Origen y evolución del sistema de partidos en la España democrática: un ensayo de interpretación' in Claudín, F. (ed.), *¿Crisis de los partidos políticos?* (Madrid: Dédalo, 1980).

Saz Campos, I., 'Falange e Italia, Aspectos poco conocidos del fascismo español' in *Estudis d'Historia Contemporánia del Pais Valenciá*, no. 3 (Facultat de Geografia e História, Departament d'História Contemporánia, Universidad de Valencia, 1982).

Soler, R., 'The new Spain' in *New Left Review*, no. 58 (London, Nov.–Dec. 1969).

Southworth, H. R., 'Qu'est ce le fascisme?' in *l'Esprit* (Paris, Mar. 1969).

'Falange, an analysis of Spain's fascist heritage' in Preston, P. (ed.), *Spain in Crisis* (Brighton: Harvester Press, 1976).

Thomas, H., 'The hero in the empty room' in *Journal of Contemporary History*, vol. I, no. 1 (London, 1966).

Introduction to *The Roots of the Right. Selected writings of José Antonio Primo de Rivera* (London: Jonathan Cape, 1972).

'Spain' in Woolf, S. J. (ed.), *European Fascism* (London: Weidenfeld & Nicholson, 1968).

Triguero, J., 'La generación de Fraga y su destino' in *Cuadernos de Ruedo Ibérico*, no. 1 (Paris, June 1965).

Vidal Beneyto, J., '¿Falange contra Opus Dei?' in *Indice*, no. 214 (Madrid, 1966).

Viñas, A., 'Berlín: salvad a José Antonio' in *Historia 16*, nos 1 & 2 (Madrid, May–June 1976).

Index